AFGHAN ALTERNATIVES

AFGHAN ALTERNATIVES

Issues, Options, and Policies

Edited by

Ralph H. Magnus

Transaction Books
New Brunswick (U.S.A.) and Oxford (U.K.)

Library of Congress Catalog Number: 84-28033
ISBN: 0-88738-050-6 (cloth)
Printed in the United States of America

Library of Congress Cataloging in Publication Data

Afghan alternatives.

Papers from the International Conference on Afghan Alternatives, sponsored by the U.S. Information Agency, the National Strategy Information Center, and the Earhart Foundation, held at the Monterey Institute of International Studies in Nov. 1983.

1. Afghanistan—History—Soviet occupation, 1979- —Addresses, essays, lectures. I. Magnus, Ralph H. II. International Conference on Afghan Alternatives (1983 : Monterey Institute of International Studies) III. United States Information Agency. IV. National Strategy Information Center. V. Earhart Foundation.
DS371.2.A337 1985 958′.1044 84-28033
ISBN 0-88738-050-6

Dedicated
to the Memory of
Frank N. Trager
1905-1984

Distinguished scholar, generous colleague, and friend of freedom and human dignity for Afghanistan and the Afghan people.

Contents

1

Introduction

Ralph H. Magnus

This volume originated from the International Conference on Afghan Alternatives, sponsored by the U.S. Information Agency, the National Strategy Information Center, and the Earhart Foundation, held at the Monterey Institute of International Studies in November 1983. The concept of the conference was to bring together a relatively small but diverse group from a number of nationalities and backgrounds to discuss at some length and depth the issues raised by the tragic conflict that has continued between the overwhelming majority of the Afghan people and the Soviet invaders since December 1979.

Although the major sponsorship of the conference was provided by the U.S. Information Agency, the participants were chosen and the deliberations were structured (to the extent that this wide-ranging collection of individuals could be structured) solely by the decisions of the conference coordinator and cochairmen in order to achieve the broadest possible representation of viewpoints on the major issues. As conference coordinator, I would like to express my personal and professional appreciation to the officials of the U.S. Information Agency and the Department of State, in particular to Phyllis Oakley, Ray Peppers, Walter P. White, and Bill Stetson, for their valuable advice and support. Additionally, Harmon E. Kirby, regional director for Pakistan, Afghanistan, and Bangladesh in the State Department, not only provided a prepared statement setting forth U.S. policy, but joined in our discussions as an active and valuable participant.

The conference could not have been held without the dedicated support of William G. Craig, president of the Monterey Institute of International Studies, and his staff, especially the academic dean, Glynn Wood, and the director of the language laboratory, Bunelle Hall. Linden E. Chubin, a graduate of the Monterey Institute, served as assistant to the conference coordinator, and was invaluable in the preparations for and operation of the conference. Student volunteers from the Monterey Institute, as well as from the Naval Postgraduate School, provided many valuable hours of service. The manuscript was prepared with the efficient and dedicated work of Irene Dixon and Cecil V. Potter of Pacific Grove, California. Finally, I must thank Professor Sherman E. Blandin, chairman of the Department of National Security Affairs at the Naval Postgraduate School, for his understanding and support in this project, as well as other projects dealing with Afghanistan.

Although our participants have widely varying views as to the practicality and necessity of accommodation to Soviet interests and views in the achievement of a solution to the Afghan conflict, they all shared the fundamental belief that the Soviet Union's actions in Afghanistan have constituted a dangerous and illegitimate use of force, even terror, against a hitherto independent and nonaligned state. Thus, while the changing of the current views of the Soviet government is probably the most important single element necessary for a solution to the conflict, the organizers felt that there was little to be added to the free exchange of ideas by having Soviet representatives present (presuming they would have come in any case). The Soviet's defense of their activities in Afghanistan is well known, and has been repeated at many meetings of the United Nations and other international gatherings. This position has been rejected repeatedly by overwhelming margins by the international community in the UN General Assembly, as well as by the Organization of the Islamic Conference, the Commonwealth of Nations, and the Nonaligned Movement.

The suggestion made to the contributors of discussion papers was to make their contributions as wide-ranging, provocative, and suggestive of future alternatives as possible, rather than formally academic or historical in style. You will judge for yourselves, but we believe that these presentations which form the themes for the chapters in this volume succeed admirably in their task of providing stimulation for lively thought and discussion, and even for some heated controversy among the participants; we trust they will do the same for the readers. The reader may note that one of the characteristics of the discussions, along with the informal exchanges that continued among the participants outside of the conference sessions, was that not all of the discussions are strictly relevant to the formal topic of the presentation—issues are raised at one session and commented upon later; questions are reargued and rephrased. In short, the varying interests, expertise, and concerns of the participants caused them to ignore the artificial and formal structures of the discussions. In our opinion, this informality only contributes to the interest of the discussions. As editor, I have made every effort to retain the informality and spontaneity of the exchange of views as they emerged in the course of the discussions.

For the preparation of this volume, both the contributors of discussion papers and the participants were given the opportunity of expanding, correcting, or rephrasing their contributions. As most of the participants took advantage of this opportunity, the reader may find some references to later events, as well as changes in the discussion papers reflective of suggestions and comments made during the conference. Thus, the original papers and verbatim transcript of the discussions have been edited by both the participants and the editor. Anyone who has had the experience of examining a verbatim transcript of his/her own remarks can readily appreciate the necessity of this process. Still, neither the discussion papers nor the discussions have been changed fundamentally from their original sense in the process of making them more understandable.

As the current situation in Afghanistan began with the actions of the Soviet Union, Jiri Valenta begins his examination with the Soviet decision to invade. This, he believes, was a complex process on which we have as yet little hard information. It was shaped by domestic, regional, and global forces, but most important of all was the unfavorable situation at the time inside Afghanistan. Since then, continued Afghan resistance has demonstrated a number of Soviet weaknesses. In general, it has been an unpopular war and has had negative impacts on both domestic and foreign politics for the Soviets.

Valenta suggests that Soviet options involve a continuation of the present limited, protracted commitment, hoping for a long-term military solution; a large-scale military escalation for a quick victory; or a "Finlandization" style of negotiated withdrawal with security guarantees, but without the continuation of a Leninist regime in Kabul. The West, he believes, must not accept Soviet domination of Afghanistan, both for reasons related to the security of the region and for the dangerous impression such an action would make on the minds of Soviet decision makers regarding the utility of the use of force in obtaining their expansionist goals. Thus, we must pursue a two-track policy of extending aid, including military aid, to the Afghan freedom fighters while offering negotiations. Without the actions of the Afghan *mujahidin,* the Soviets would have no incentive to negotiate. Both Robert G. Neumann and Harmon E. Kirby stress the incremental, bureaucratic nature of most decision making in foreign policy and their belief that this was probably the case with the Soviet decision to invade. Marian K. Leighton points out that it is often difficult to discern any difference in the Soviets' view of offensive and defensive motivations, but in any case they apparently find the current cost of their actions tolerable. Gregory M. Kortanek emphasizes the important point that the reaction of the United States to Soviet actions in Afghanistan, particularly the establishment of the U.S. Central Command, has created a new situation which now affects Soviet options in the region.

Louis Dupree and Noor A. Husain examine the long-term strategic dangers for the region should the Soviets be allowed to absorb Afghanistan. From his perspective as a former Pakistani ambassador to Moscow, Sajjad Hyder points out the continuities of Soviet strategic interests in the region. Seyed Qassem Reshtia, a former Afghan minister and ambassador as well as a historian, traces the origins of Soviet strategies in Afghanistan to czarist geopolitical objectives. Selig S. Harrison raises the point that it is necessary to attempt to ascertain from evidence on the ground, especially the building of strategic bases, the future direction of Soviet policy. Eden Naby, Harmon Kirby, Zia-ul Islam Ansari, and others discuss the Islamic dimension of the conflict and its impact on Afghanistan, the region, and within the Soviet Union itself.

The Islamic dimension forms the central theme of Eden Naby's paper. Although analogies to other resistance movements, such as those in Algeria and Central Asia can be made, the Afghan jehad must be examined in the context of Afghan history and society. She examines the often drawn analogy of the Afghan *mujahidin* to the Central Asian *basmachi* resistance to the Bolsheviks and finds that the *basmachi* ideology was more nationalist and modernist than specifically Islamic in nature.

The Afghan resistance movement developed over time and today contains elements from virtually every sector of Afghan society and every shade of ideology, but the overwhelming majority of the resistance adheres to Islamic ideology and all use Islamic terminology. With few exceptions, they are dedicated to the establishment of some form of Islamic state. Divisions among *mujahidin* organizations are traced by Naby to sociocultural cleavages, differing histories and, most importantly, to the type of Islamic state they wish to establish. The "traditionalists" feel that such a state would develop out of the traditional Afghan tribal and religious situation as it had existed under the monarchy. The "revolutionaries" feel that even that system was a corruption of Islamic ideals, and thus seek a revolutionary transformation. This is not the same as the Iranian revolutionary model. The ideology of the Afghan jehad is being shaped by Afghan leaders, particularly Professor Burhanuddin Rabbani, and by the developments stemming from the course of the war itself. She thus believes that the dynamics of the military and political situation in Afghanistan favor the more revolutionary groups over the long term: they have greater mass appeal and appeal more to the youthful internal leaders who are emerging today.

External factors, such as the policies of Pakistan and support received from the Islamic world and the West will continue to have an important impact on the resistance. However, the resistance will continue, and in the process a new sense of revolutionary Islamic Afghan nationalism is being created in the new generation of fighters, in the refugee camps, and within the Afghan population.

In their comments, Seyed Reshtia and Seyed Majrooh emphasize that the factors unifying the resistance are far stronger than those pulling it apart. Reshtia feels that alongside the factors of religion and nationalism the Afghan resistance exhibits the traditional Afghan spirit of resistance to foreign invaders and their ability to cooperate through their tradition of democratic assemblies or *jirgahs*. Majrooh emphasizes the political unity developing inside Afghanistan based more on the practical needs of the struggle and the personalities of local and regional commanders than on formal adherence to a particular ideology or political group.

These remarks on the fundamental nature of the Afghan resistance are elaborated on by Louis Dupree, Charles J. Adams, and Sabahuddin Kushkaki. Adams emphasizes his agreement with Naby's point that each Islamic "revolutionary" movement must be examined in the light of the particular circumstances of the country in which it appears. In particular, the situations in Iran and Afghanistan are quite different.

Sajjad Hyder discusses the security and political aspects of Afghan refugees in Pakistan. Based on historical data, he believes it impossible for Afghan refugees to be integrated into the population of Pakistan. Noor A. Husain believes that the Afghan resistance will continue, but questions its ability to raise the price to the Soviets high enough to cause them to change their policy.

Peers Carter and Claude Malhuret focus on the broader aspects of the relationship of the Afghan resistance, and of guerrilla wars in general, to the international order. Such conflicts place heavy burdens on civilian populations. The brutality of Soviet tactics against civilian populations are deliberate, and can be confirmed by similar tactics in other such wars in which the Soviets are now engaged, such as in Kampuchea and Eritrea.

Marvin G. Weinbaum believes that although the future of Afghanistan will be decided most of all by events on the ground inside the country, as well as by decisions made in Moscow and perhaps in Washington, the ultimate outcome in Afghanistan may be significantly influenced by a number of international developments. The Soviets certainly erred in their underestimation of the international impact of their actions. The West erred in its expectations of the effect of the continuing international response on Soviet policies on Afghanistan.

On the broad level of East-West relations, an intensification of the worldwide tensions could make Afghanistan into either an arena for each side to test the other's resolve, or it could turn it into a bargaining chip for a superpower deal. A number of regional developments—instability in the Arab Middle East, political instability in Pakistan, the ending of the Iran/Iraq war, the future course of the Iranian revolution, and an improvement in Indo-Pakistani relations—would have major impacts on Afghan developments.

How these developments might alter the outcome in Afghanistan can be understood in the context of six possible options, ranging from the establishment of an anti-Soviet "fundamentalist" government to the absorption of Afghanistan into the USSR. In conclusion, Marvin Weinbaum states that any favorable outcome will be impossible without significant external support.

In her commentary, Katarina Engberg emphasizes the role of the international community in providing humanitarian aid to the victims of the fighting inside Afghanistan. She had recently verified these humanitarian needs through her personal experience in connection with a Swedish-supported medical clinic in Kunar province. Sajjad Hyder then examines the determinants of Pakistan's foreign policy and, in particular, the history and present state of Pakistani-Afghan relations. From this, he concludes that the Soviet-Karmal regime's unprecedented campaign of pressure and propaganda villification of Pakistan poses a threat to Pakistan's very existence, making a political settlement imperative. Such a settlement might come through the UN-sponsored indirect negotiations being conducted by Diego Cordoves. A political agreement would be greatly facilitated by an Indo-Pakistani agreement on a common goal and approach. Barring such a political settlement, Hyder believes that Pakistan cannot continue to support the Afghan resistance.

A number of conferees discuss the options raised in Marvin Weinbaum's paper. Selig Harrison discusses in detail the nature, internal and external, of a possible "Finland-type" solution. Sabahuddin Kushkaki examines the position of the resistance groups that would limit certain options. However, he states that there is a broad agreement that a future independent Afghan government would be nonaligned and not hostile to the Soviet Union. Zia-ul-Islam Ansari suggests that no outside power has a right to tell the Afghan people what form of government they should adopt, and this should not be a condition for any political settlement.

Laurent Carrel and Reinhardt Rummel both suggest that the international community and specifically the European nations have an important responsibility in keeping up pressure on the Soviets. Rummel notes that the course of recent events in Poland reveals that the Soviets have been sufficiently influenced by events in Afghanistan and the international reactions to these to be more cautious in their risk-taking. With reference to Sajjad Hyder's comments on Pakistan's exposed position to Soviet aggression, he makes the analogy to the geopolitical situation of West Germany: such a situation poses responsibilities that go beyond purely national or even regional considerations.

Two viewpoints, the official one presented by Harmon E. Kirby of the State Department and an unofficial view by Thomas E. Gouttierre of the Center for Afghanistan Studies of the University of Nebraska at Omaha, are given regarding the important issue of U.S. policy. Kirby declares that the United States opposes the Soviet occupation of Afghanistan out of a concern for the human tragedy this imposes on the Afghan people, as well as for reasons of broad strategic interests. "It is absolutely essential," he states, "that Soviet aggression in Afghanistan be checked and not succeed."

The United States is continually exloring, bilaterally, multilaterally, and through public diplomacy, how this can be accomplished. It is committed to endorse any political settlement consistent with the repeated UN General Assembly resolutions, and in this effort the United States and Pakistan, which is conducting indirect talks through the UN process, are in full agreement.

Kirby feels that there were some indications after Yuri Andropov's taking power of a changing attitude in Moscow, but that these quickly dissipated when the Soviets failed to provide a timetable for the withdrawal of their forces. On the ground, the situation inside Afghanistan shows every sign of intensification. The *mujahidin* are more effective, the Soviets have not been able to consolidate a stable and acceptable regime in Kabul, nor have they made the Afghan army into an effective instrument. Consequently, their military actions have become even more brutal in their bombings and reprisals directed at the civilian population for their consistent support of the resistance.

Gouttierre's contribution provides some interesting commentary on official U.S. policy. He deals with the current widespread perceptions regarding this policy and finds that these perceptions, whether true or not, may influence the outcome of the situation in Afghanistan. Some of these perceptions are: both the Carter and Reagan administrations have made commitments of military support to the Afghan resistance; the level of this support has been insufficient; the United States and the USSR have an informal understanding as to spheres of influence trading off Afghanistan for Central America; the United States is "fighting to the last Afghan" to embarrass and tie down the Soviets in another Vietnam; and the U.S. role is dependent on Pakistan, which does not wish to have unity among the Afghan resistance groups. He then discusses the negative impact of these widely held perceptions and raises the question as to whether American policy, which has widespread international and bipartisan support, would not be better served by more open demonstration of its military support for the resistance.

Selig Harrison holds that the primary American objectives in Afghanistan include military withdrawal of Soviet forces, the stability of Pakistan and the South Asian region, a healthy U.S. relationship with Pakistan, and the creation of an Afghanistan which would allow for a gradual noncommunist and independent evolution. None of these objectives, he holds, would be served by a military intensification of the conflict. He feels that the Soviets may be willing to accept a new form of political regime in Kabul, which would come out of negotiations between organizations dependent on the current regime and independent Afghan elements, including the *mujahidin,* but feels that the United States has been reluctant to accept such an arrangement. None of the choices facing Afghanistan is easy; the Soviets may not really want to withdraw, but this must be fully explored: "We have to aid the resistance as long as the Afghans are willing to fight and the Soviets are not willing to get out. But let us make sure they are not willing to get out before we go that route," states Harrison.

Kirby responded to a number of the questions raised both by Gouttierre's paper and by Harrison's remarks. He reemphasized the fact that the United States would like to see a political solution and he specifically denied that we have restrained the Pakistanis in any way in the course of UN negotiations.

Jiri Valenta, Sabuhuddin Kushkaki, Louis Dupree, and Laurent Carrel emphasized the crucial nature of the conflict in Afghanistan and its linkage to other global issues. This necessitated an increase in American assistance to the Afghan resistance movement. Claude Malhuret feels that humanitarian aid, military aid, and diplomatic support for the Afghan resistance must all be continued and increased, and that current Soviet support for political negotiations is aimed solely at obtaining international legitimation for the Karmal regime, not at a peaceful settlement. Several persons, including Marvin Weinbaum, Gerald Steibel, and Reinhardt Rummel, indicated that too little attention is being paid to historical examples of past Soviet withdrawals.

Noor Husain's contribution places the conflict in Afghanistan in the light of the geostrategic compulsions of the region. Afghanistan has traditionally formed the security zone of South and South West Asia, and whichever power seeks to control a quarter of the world's population and three-quarters of the world's oil will have to control the Hindu Kush region. This was the essence of Leonid Brezhnev's "Asian Collective Security System," which is now gradually coming into being based on Afghanistan and India.

Still, in four years a tribal society armed with small weapons has continued to fight. Currently, the Soviets are working to gain time for the Sovietization of the country and to flush out all opponents. This is why they are reluctant to give a timetable for their withdrawal. The most desirable option for Afghanistan would be for the Soviets to agree to this political solution, but this may not be possible.

An overwhelming majority of Pakistani experts forecast that, after waiting a few years following their final absorption of Afghanistan, the Soviets will move into Pakistani and Iranian Baluchistan to the Indian Ocean. A minority view is that Afghanistan could prove to be a Soviet "Vietnam," and the Soviets could lose all their Muslim areas within a few years.

Afghanistan offers a wealth of strategic options and the greatest possibility of strategic gains of any of the areas in which the Soviets have recently been engaged in coercive military diplomacy. The possibilities of a favorable option for Afghanistan will depend on the policies and strategy of the United States, the West, and the Islamic world.

Louis Dupree comments that the long-term outcome in Afghanistan will be determined as much by events outside the country as inside. In this connection, much needs to be done to make Soviet terror tactics known to the outside world. This theme is echoed by Gerald C. Steibel, who points to a number of the practical problems involved, including those of terminology, in making the Afghan jehad intelligible to the West. B. A. Hamzah, from the Islamic country of Malaysia, makes several practical suggestions as to how this might be accomplished, including the establishment of a special fund for the Afghan cause by Islamic countries and philanthropies. Robert Neumann agrees that such a fund would be most useful, but points to a number of practical problems. Peers Carter, who was Neumann's colleague when both were ambassadors in Kabul, emphasizes the need for greater publicity as well, particularly on television. Seyed Reshtia feels that part of the problem is the lack of a unified representation for the Afghan resistance. Such a representation, Marvin Weinbaum remarks, might well entail outside friends of the Afghan cause having to make a decision as to which of the many groups should be aided. Both Ansari and Noor Husain state emphatically that Pakistan is doing nothing to hinder the unity of the Afghan resistance.

Louis Dupree holds that it is the belief of the Afghan resistance, as well as his own, that the Soviets are not going to leave Afghanistan until they are forced to do so by military pressure, which in turn requires outside supply of arms. Ultimately, the Afghan *mujahidin* will evolve sufficiently politically and militarily to move into the diplomatic area. However, at this stage, to deny them the weapons they need is emotional, immature, and juvenile.

Since the conclusion of the International Conference on Afghan Alternatives, a number of events have demonstrated the importance and continued relevance of issues, options, and policies discussed in this volume. Soviet policies and pronouncements and, above all, their intensification of their military actions in the spring and summer of 1984 demonstrate the validity of the assertion often made in the course of our discussions that the most important events affecting the future of Afghanistan would be those taking place in the fighting inside the country. The hardening of attitudes which began in the last months of Yuri Andropov's tenure was intensified under his successor.

The press in the West has focused mainly on the Soviet offensive in the Panjshir region against the prominent *mujahidin* commander Ahmad Shah Mas'ud, but heavy fighting has taken place throughout the country, in part initiated by the Soviets and in part the result of *mujahidin* counteroffensives. This fighting has been particularly intense in Herat, Kandahar, Jalalabad, and especially along the entire main supply route of the Soviets north from Kabul over the Salang Pass to the Oxus River. In the course of this fighting, the civilian population has suffered heavily, as always, particularly from the new Soviet tactics of high-level carpet bombing by planes flying directly from the Soviet Union. However, the forces of the Karmal regime have demonstrated once again their ineffectiveness, as major desertions to the *mujahidin* continued even during the height of the Panjshir offensive.

The resistance demonstrated impressive ability to cooperate in counterattacks on Soviet bases and convoys. The effectiveness of these attacks was unmistakably demonstrated by new austerity measures announced by the Kabul regime regarding the distribution of petroleum supplies in early June 1984.

An interesting development in this period was the issuance of a direct appeal made by Commander Mas'ud to foreign humanitarian aid agencies for supplies and support in influencing their governments on the Afghan issue in anticipation of the Soviet offensive. That these appeals did not go unheeded was proven by the opening of new medical clinics inside Afghanistan supported by Swedish organizations and by increased activities of French medical organizations. Large new shipments of medicines were made also by U.S. governmental and private humanitarian aid agencies.

The Soviet Karmal regime continues, along with its military offensive, an intensified diplomatic and public relations campaign aimed at Western public opinion. They press their campaign to obtain international legitimation (despite negative votes in the UN General Assembly) by inviting foreign journalists to Kabul for carefully guided tours of the city and interviews with selected government officials.

Support for the cause of the Afghan resistance, however, remains high, both from the Islamic world and the West. Despite air raids by Soviet planes on border villages and refugee camps in Pakistan, President Zia-ul Haq continued to voice the support of Pakistan in an interview with the Saudi Arabian newspaper *'Uzak* (Jiddah): "The Russians forget that these attacks can never prevent us from helping our Afghan brothers and that in fact they increase our determination to support and care for them."[1]

In the United States, while President Reagan expressed his desire to resume arms limitation negotiations with the Soviets, he continued to stress the importance the United States places on Soviet actions in Afghanistan in the context of U.S.-Soviet relations. In May 1984, Vice-President George Bush visited Pakistan where he reassured both Pakistan and the Afghan *mujahidin* of the continued support of their cause, and delivered new shipments of humanitarian aid. In the area of so-called covert operations, *Time* magazine published a highly detailed and entertaining account of a CIA-run supply line stretching from Saudi Arabia to inside Afghanistan.[2]

A number of participants in this conference continued to be active in various aspects of the Afghan situation, both in the field and in print. Selig Harrison visited Kabul for eight days in the spring and reported on that visit and his interview with Babrak Karmal in the *Washington Post* of May 13, 1984. Many of the assertions he made in this article were subsequently challenged by Thomas Gouttierre (with David C. Champagne) in a letter to the editor.[3] Mr. Gouttierre was in Peshawar at the same time that Harrison was in Kabul. Seyed Majrooh also replied to Harrison in a supplement to the *Afghanistan Information Centre Monthly Bulletin* of May 1984.[4]

It was announced in June that the UN-sponsored "indirect" talks between the Kabul regime and Pakistan would resume in Geneva in August 1984. In this regard, Assistant Secretary of State Richard S. Murphy, in a letter to the editor of the *New York Times* printed on January 30, specifically took issue with an article entitled "Are We Fighting to the Last Afghan?" published in the Op-Ed section of the *Times* on December 29, especially the view expressed by Selig S. Harrison that the United States was hindering progress on the Geneva talks.

The conference did not reach a consensus, much less make any formal motions or votes in the course of the three days of formal and informal exchanges. What did develop, however, was an immense respect for the deeply held and forcibly presented views of our fellow participants, even when we disagreed with equal force. There developed as well an even deeper understanding of what we already believed to be the case—that there is no quick or easy solution to the problem in Afghanistan, that the continuation of the conflict presents a danger to international and regional peace as well as an unmitigated human tragedy for the brave Afghan people and, finally, whatever alternatives might exist for Afghanistan, none of these can be imposed by outsiders, even those who are most sympathetic to the cause of a free and independent Afghanistan.

Notes

1. "Zia-ul Haq Interviewed on Domestic, Foreign Affairs," *FBIS-South Asia, Daily Report 7,* no. 107 (1 June 1984), reporting on an interview with Muhammad 'Abd as-Sattar published in *'Uzak* (Jiddah, 28 May 1984):6.
2. Dean Brelis, "Carvans on Moonless Nights," *Time* (11 June 1984):38-40.
3. Thomas E. Gouttierre and David C. Champagne, "Free for All," *Washington Post* (26 May 1984):A-19.
4. "Selig S. Harrison in Kabul: An Unexpected Jump into Emptiness," *Afghan Information Centre Monthly Bulletin,* no. 38 (May 1984).

2

Soviet Aims, Policies, and Alternatives in Afghanistan

Jiri Valenta

The Soviet Union's 1979 decision to lend Afghanistan "fraternal aid," the Soviet euphemism for invasion and subsequent occupation of a country, conjured up what by then were the almost forgotten images of Hungary in 1956 and Czechoslovakia in 1968, reminding the world for yet a third time since World War II that the Soviets are determined to intervene militarily in neighboring Leninist countries when their governments are perceived as untrustworthy and lacking control. The official rationale for the invasion of Afghanistan was strikingly similar to the arguments advanced in November 1956 and August 1968. Each time the Soviets alledgedly responded to a call to "assist healthy forces" put down an impending "counterrevolution" supported from abroad. In Hungary and Czechoslovakia the threat was supposedly from the imperialist block, primarily the U.S. Central Intelligence Agency, neighboring West German "revanchists," and "Zionists" worldwide. In Afghanistan the United States but also Egypt and neighboring Pakistan and China were implicated. Following both East European invasions the Soviet leadership concluded treaties providing for the "temporary" stationing of Soviet troops which so far have not vacated the affected countries. To determine whether the occupation of Afghanistan will also be indefinite is one purpose of this essay.

First, however, it is necessary to assess the effects of the Soviet occupation of Afghanistan upon Soviet domestic politics and foreign policymaking in the five years since the invasion. The impact on the USSR, in turn, must be seen in light of initial Soviet objectives in Afghanistan and, assuming these have not been fulfilled, alternative Soviet choices and possibilities. This leads to the fourth concern: what options are open to the West and all those countries which oppose the

East Europeanization of Afghanistan and hope to end Soviet occupation.

Soviet Objectives

There is a tendency among Western analysts to play down the importance of knowing why the Soviets invaded Afghanistan. However, since the motives that induced them to act must also figure in the reasons for their staying in Afghanistan and might serve to motivate similar actions elsewhere in the future, the reasons for the intervention need to be carefully analyzed. Aside from the rather contradictory explanations offered by the Soviets themselves, Western analysts differ sharply about the nature of Soviet objectives. The school of thought espoused by George Kennan maintains that the "immediate objective" in Afghanistan was "primarily defensive." Accordingly, the traditional Russian preoccupation, if not obsession, with border defenses conditioned the Soviet response when developments became unpredictable along the southern frontier. Another school of thought championed by Richard Pipes holds that the invasion was an offensive operation conditioned by another historical trend just as viable as the first—the desire to enhance Soviet power and influence to the south, in the direction of the strategically important Persian Gulf.

Both interpretations are correct if taken as two sides of the same coin; the invasion of Afghanistan, like other Soviet moves vis-à-vis immediate neighbors, reflected internal as well as external considerations, all of which were affected by overlapping defensive and offensive concerns. In 1980 I argued for what a congressional report described as "a combined interpretion"[1] of Soviet motives for invading Afghanistan. By this interpretation the crucial factors in the Soviet decision to occupy Afghanistan can be classified according to whether they emanated from the domestic affairs of the country or conditions external to the nation.

Domestic Factors

In Afghanistan, like in Eastern Europe, Russian policies traditionally have been guided by the all-important search for "defensible" borders. To the Russians, the most easily defendable and thus the most secure borders are those where, as suggested by a czar's minister of foreign affairs, Russian soldiers stand on both sides. Soviet behavior in Afghanistan, as well as in Hungary and Czechoslovakia, betrays an inordinate concern about developments in the immediate geographic proximity of the USSR. Unlike in the remotely located Angola and

Ethiopia, in countries with which they share borders the Soviets are willing to engage their own massive force, without the assistance of proxies, to ensure stability.

On one level the invasion of Afghanistan perpetuated nineteenth-century czarist expansionism toward northern Afghanistan and the Hindu Kush mountains. The aforementioned interest in securing the southern border, as well as what Dostoevsky used to call Russia's "civilizing mission" to the Central Asian nations, propelled this thrust which, by the end of the century, had culminated in Russia's annexation of the northern Panjdeh district occupied by Turkmen tribesmen. The Bosheviks continued the efforts of their czarist predecessors to penetrate northern Afghanistan because of the same need to defend Russia's "sacred borders," this time against Muslim adversaries in Central Asia who sought refuge in northern Afghanistan where the Soviet army chased them in hot pursuit. The struggle waged by the Red army between 1923 and 1936 against the so-called *basmachi* (the Turkish word for bandits) and Muslim national communists was never forgotten by Soviet officials. With reason the image of Muslim terrorists from Soviet Central Asia seeking assistance and refuge in hostile Afghan sanctuaries was evoked in 1979 and thereafter by the Soviet press which has revived the term *basmachi* in reference to the Afghan *mujahidin* or freedom fighters of today.

After World War II the Soviets pursued more stable forms of penetration in Afghanistan—economic and military assistance, diplomacy, and, since 1965, political support for the gradual build-up of a Leninist party. The ultimate military penetration of the country in 1979 would have been impossible without the foothold established through these efforts. In spite of the Soviets' long effort to gain a legitimate presence, Afghanistan prior to 1978 never belonged to what is generally considered the Soviet sphere of influence. Indeed, to ensure Afghanistan's status as a neutral buffer state between the British and Russian empires, the British fought two costly wars in the nineteenth century. After World War II the United States persevered in the steps of the British and until 1979 this policy of economic assistance deterred the Russians from attempting a full-scale invasion of Afghanistan.

Ideology provided another important impetus to the Soviet invasion and occupation of Afghanistan as the Leninist notion of "international duty" superseded orthodoxy's "civilizing mission." After the 1978 seizure of power in Afghanistan by forces of the Leninist People's Democratic Party, consisting of the Parcham and Khalq factions which had reunited in 1977, the Soviets began to envisage Afghanistan as a "revolutionary" and "socialist-oriented" country developing according to the Leninist tenets of (1) 1-party system (the party being the "avant-garde of the proletariat"); (2) democratic centralism (Leninism's pyramidal ruling principle); and (3) proletarian internationalism (the pursuit of domestic and foreign policy in alliance with the Soviet Union). To be sure, ideology did not guide Soviet foreign policy, but since 1978 it did begin to shape Soviet behavior in a normative sense and to serve as a legitimizer. In a normative fashion, as soon as Afghanistan was classified as on the path of Leninist development, it attained preferred ideological status, becoming a country both to which the Soviet Union should make an ideological commitment and to which it was linked in the special relationship of proletarian internationalism. Unlike in Finland, which also borders the Soviet Union but is capitalist, in "socialist-oriented" Afghanistan a return to the pre-1978 status quo would have contradicted the Soviet-proclaimed irreversibility of communism.

Ideology also exercised a legitimizing function in Soviet domestic politics. In other words, the ascendancy of the Communist Party in Afghanistan was seen to boost the legitimacy of Soviet party rule to domestic constituencies in the USSR. By the same token, when Hafizullah Amin took control of the Afghan government in October 1979, his erratic policies—described by the Soviets as "nationalist," "left-wing" deviationist, and "petit bourgeois"—were viewed as more of an internal (Soviet) rather than external threat (given the new ideological status of Afghanistan discussed above). With his sui generis style of communism Amin challenged the Soviet model of a "proper" communist state. By extension, the Soviets probably also feared that in the long run a Soviet ideological setback in Afghanistan could undermine the legitimacy of Soviet-style communism among the Muslim groups of Soviet Central Asia (mainly Uzbeks, Tajiks, Turkmen, and Kirghiz, but also Kazakhs).

In spite of denials, Soviet perceptions regarding the potential ideological spillover from Afghanistan on Soviet Central Asia was another consideration which influenced the decision to invade and occupy Afghanistan. There is no evidence, however, that there was an imminent threat of Muslim rebellion or a recurrence of Amin's nationalist communism in Soviet Central Asia. Unlike conditions prior to the Czechoslovak invasion (when the presses of the non-Soviet republics of the West, particularly the Ukraine, were filled with apprehensions of the leaderships who feared the repercussions of Czech "deviationism" on their own inhabitants), in Central Asia in 1979 the threat of contagion was not immediate. Already prior to 1979 the Islamic revival in Iran and Afghanistan had failed to arouse significantly the Muslim populations of the Soviet Central Asian republics or the Caucasus. (However, the brand of Islam practiced by the Sunni of Afghanistan is different from the Shiite fundamentalism of Iran.) If Afghanistan posed a threat to Soviet domestic stability in 1979 it was only potential and then remote, in the sense that it would have to have been linked to long-term demographic and ethnic trends in the Soviet south and a growing sense of a separate Islamic identity among Soviet Muslims. The Muslims of Soviet Central Asia, mainly Turkic and Iranian peoples, do share geography and some historical experience with the same ethnic groups in the bordering states of Iran and Afghanistan. (In Afghanistan alone there are over 3 million Tajiks, 1.5 million Uzbeks, and 0.5 million Turkmen.) Because of these relationships, the long war in Afghanistan might eventually provoke the Soviet domestic instability which it was intended to curtail.

Bureaucratic politics among the Soviet elites probably influenced the Soviet decision on Afghanistan. However, we have little evidence of the existence of a preinvasion debate or bureaucratic pulling and hauling in the Soviet leadership as we did prior to the Soviet invasion of Czechoslovakia in 1968 (on which I focused in *Soviet Intervention in Czechoslovakia, 1968: Anatomy of a Decision*).[2] Though the Soviet generals and KGB officials appeared to play the dominant role in Afghanistan prior to the invasion, as opposed to Soviet diplomats, we do not have evidence that their reports and maneuverings swayed the Politburo. Nonetheless, it is very feasible that the military's interest in making Afghanistan a forward base, testing newly acquired military operational capabilities (particularly airlift), and putting into practice the doctrine of strategic surprise contributed to the decision.

External Factors

Among the most crucial external factors affecting the Soviet decision-making process on Afghanistan was the urge to safeguard threatened Soviet interests in Afghanistan. Apart from the Soviet investments already discussed and others that will be mentioned later, Afghanistan has sizable mineral wealth and is a major supplier of gas to Soviet Central Asia. By the fall of 1979 the threat to Soviet political, idological, strategic, and economic stakes was seen to increase rapidly.

Second, the Soviets did not view the internal situation in Afghanistan in a vacuum but rather within the overall regional context. In their calculations the situation in Afghanistan was very much complicated by the Iranian revolution, whose chaos could spread throughout the region and engulf other unstable countries. Ostensibly the Soviets were pulled into Afghanistan for reasons of defense, to curb the infectious dynamics of the region and Afghanistan's internal instability and thereby ward off spillover effects on the Soviet Union. The same defense rationale, however, could cloak more offensive purposes: By intervening in Afghanistan the Soviets gained a more forward position in Asia, which can enhance their strategic capability in the region and facilitate the realization of objectives in South Asia and the Persian Gulf.

The Soviets' estimate of the likely Western and particularly U.S. response was another substantial factor in Soviet calculations of the costs and risks of an invasion. Although they consistently courted the Afghans, first with economic and later military assistance, in the 1950s and 1960s the Soviets were extremely cautious about their overtures to that country. Direct military support for Leninist forces in Afghanistan came only after 1978 when in Soviet eyes the worldwide correlation of forces between capitalism and communism, symbolized at that time by the post-Vietnam decline of U.S. ability to counter the Soviets in the Third World, was shifting substantially in the Soviets' favor. This historical shift was accompanied by the Soviets' growing self-confidence as a mature global power and by perceptions of U.S. impotence arising out of domestic constraints, preoccupation with Iran, and vacillation of the Carter administration. Although the Soviets must have known that by invading they were breaking an informal understanding with the United States about Afghanistan's status as a neutral buffer state between the USSR and U.S.-allied Pakistan, they probably calculated that the United States would respond no more seriously to the Afghan occupation than it had to the invasions of Eastern Europe in 1956 and 1968.

To sum up, the Soviet invasion of Afghanistan was neither an exclusively defensive nor offensive operation. Of the many considerations that influenced the decision—geography, history, ideology, stability in the USSR, bureaucratic politics, internal conditions in Afghanistan, the regional context, and the U.S. response—all were, in different degrees, both offensive and defensive in their makeup.

In the short term the Soviets aimed at stabilizing a Leninist-type country with a deviationist regime impossible to ignore because of its proximity to the USSR. In the long term they hoped to pacify Afghanistan to forestall any unfavorable impact on the Muslims of Central Asia but also (although this was probably not their initial overriding objective) to better position themselves for exploiting future opportunities in the volatile Persian Gulf and Pakistan. In a pacified Afghanistan the Soviet temptation to take advantage of a forward position to continue their encirclement of China and South Asia would be enormous. Even

George Kennan does not deny that the Soviet Union might eventually exploit a pivotal position in Afghanistan to expand its power and influence in South Asia and the Persian Gulf. He only argues that the Soviet Union has no "immediate intention" of doing so.

The Soviet Occupation and Its Impact on the USSR

The previous section shows how the Soviet occupation of Afghanistan was shaped by the domestic context of Soviet politics as well as external factors of a regional and global nature. Here the reverse flow of influence will be shown—how the continuous Soviet occupation is affecting Soviet domestic politics and foreign policy formulation. A temporary strategic success, the Soviet invasion so far has been an ongoing tactical failure. The Soviets were able to achieve strategic surprise with a quick, decisive blow against the main vital centers of Afghanistan. However, they did not realize how protracted the war would be or how unpleasant its political and military consequences. The Soviets expected that several months into the invasion the Afghan resistance would crumble, whereupon the Afghan issue would become past history and Afghanistan would follow the path of Mongolia and Eastern Europe. However, as some of us foresaw already in 1980, "unlike Czechoslovakia, Afghanistan continues to be a source of trouble for the Soviet Union. . . . Though it is unlikely that Afghanistan will become the Soviets' Vietnam, the Soviets may find themselves in a situation similar to that of the Germans in Yugoslavia during World War II, holding the cities and roads but unable to control the countryside."[3] In mid-1984 at the time of this writing, the Soviets still control only the large cities first taken in 1979-80. They have been unable to pacify the countryside and the war has become one of attrition.

The war has underscored the weaknesses of the Soviet military machine: inflexibility, inefficiency in protracted military campaigns, and lack of mobility. In spite of continuous adjustments and adaptations and recent Soviet emphasis on preparing troops for mountain combat, Soviet training and military hardware are still more relevant for fighting on the plains of Central Europe than for waging protracted, low-intensity warfare against loosely organized guerrilla forces in mountainous terrain. (Afghanistan measures 260,000 square miles and has some 2,800 miles of frontiers.) Tight control is still exercised by higher headquarters over field units, with the result that Soviet junior officers are not fully able to make battlefield decisions.

After the invasion the Afghan armed forces disintegrated almost entirely and as of 1984 they are still not a viable force. Plagued with defections and low morale, they are unable alone to handle Soviet-made equipment. In 1979-80 the Soviets obviously miscalculated the role of their own military whose main projected task was to prod and help consolidate the Afghan forces, which would eventually become the main fighting force. As of January 1984 President Babrak Karmal still urges "all-around consolidation" of the Afghan armed forces,[4] implicitly admitting that this goal has not yet been accomplished.

The Soviets also have tried to unite the ranks of the Communist Party of Afghanistan, which remains disjointed. The feud between the Khalqis and Parchamis is far from healed and the party is still isolated from broad segments of the Afghan population.

Impact on Soviet Internal Politics

Evidence suggests that the unexpectedly long war and mounting casualties in Afghanistan (according to some estimates, at least 20,000 killed, wounded, or missing in action) are already having some detrimental consequences on the USSR, particularly as regards the Central Asian minorities and the morale of Soviet troops and their families. Furthermore, there are incipient signs of dissent in the Soviet establishment.

Because of the necessary last-minute nature of the call-up in fall 1979, the Soviet leadership had no choice but to tap reservists of low-combat readiness divisions (categories B and C) from Turkestan and the Central Asian districts. The mobilization of reserves from other districts and their transfer to the Afghan borders would have been detected and viewed as extremely alarming by Western intelligence. Already shortly after the invasion there were reports about widespread fraternization between Uzbeks and Tajiks from the Soviet Central Asian republics and Uzbeks and Tajiks from Afghanistan.[5] It is said that many Soviet Central Asian soldiers were more interested in buying copies of the Qur'an and other religious articles than fighting the *mujahidin*. Since many of the Central Asian reservists refused to fight the Afghans, during the course of 1980 most of these troops were replaced by Slavs (Russians, Ukrainians, Belorussians). By 1984 the Central Asians in Afghanistan were confined to construction and support units and to some Internal Security Forces special units. Nevertheless, Soviet press reports indicate that some of them still served in regular combat units.

The discussion above should not suggest that all Central Asian cadres, whether military or civilian, are unreliable. Both before and after the invasion the Soviet leadership availed itself of reliable Uzbek, Tajik, and Turkmenian party members to build new institutions, assist in the cultural and economic integration of Afghanistan with Soviet Central Asia, and cultivate other ethnic and cultural ties with their counterparts in Afghanistan. In particular the experience of the Soviet republics of Turkmenistan, Uzbekistan, and Tajikistan was viewed as a model for Afghan development. The Education Ministry of Afghanistan, for example, was modeled on that of Tajikistan.

Should the war in Afghanistan continue indefinitely, the flow of influence could begin to move in the opposite direction from Afghanistan to Central Asia, feeding a new and perhaps more powerful awareness among Soviet Central Asians about their religious and ethnic kinship with groups across the border in Afghanistan. In the long run one cannot entirely exclude a growing dissent and perhaps some yet unexpected form of support for the Afghan *mujahidin*. Over the long term the continuous war in Afghanistan may aggravate the situation in Central Asia which the invasion was supposed to stabilize.

There are signs that the Soviet war in Afghanistan is gradually but surely becoming a very unpopular war in the USSR. The Czechoslovak invasion and even the Hungarian invasion were quick police operations. The great patriotic war against the Germans in 1941-45 and the brief 1969 conflict with the Chinese at the Ussuri River were viewed as necessary defenses of the national territory. The war in Afghanistan, on the other hand, is apparently perceived by growing numbers of Russians as extravagant and unending. This is not to suggest that the war will become a serious domestic issue in the proportion that the Vietnam War was in the United States. Unlike their American counterparts, the Soviet media are not permitted to air the atrocities of the war on the nightly news. Nevertheless, even the censored and controlled Soviet media cannot entirely ignore and lie about the continuous bloodshed in Afghanistan. Although most of the reports in the Soviet media, particularly up to 1983, tried to create an impression that the "limited contingent" of Soviet forces in Afghanistan live more or less normal lives, more recent allusions to the heroism, struggle, and hardships of servicemen suggest to the careful Soviet reader that the opposite is true.

The unpopularity of the war appears pronounced among relatives and friends of servicemen. The impact on these groups is easily discernible in a careful reading of Soviet newspapers in 1983 and 1984. At times during this period the military newspaper *Krasnaia zvezda* and, to a lesser extent, other Soviet newspapers, detailed the activities of Soviet servicemen in Afghanistan as well as the "terrorist acts" of the *mujahidin* (even in Kabul), lauding Soviet soldiers killed in action as heroes and no longer trying to hide the fact that Soviet units suffered casualties. Some very revealing information is contained in these reports: hundreds of "counterrevolutionary" rebels can tamper with Soviet logistic supplies and mine the main roads, particularly in the southern parts of the country; Soviet units have to help Afghan troops protect the roads and escort convoys carrying supplies; "counterrevolutionary" operations affect at least 80 of 286 Afghan administrative units;[6] Soviet Mi-6 helicopters and pilots are employed in the northeastern provinces of Afghanistan to transport grain to Afghan villages where rebel activities make the use of roads unsafe.[7] On one occasion *Krasnaia zvezda* published a rather unusual letter of complaint from a Soviet mother eager to hear about her son's "fulfillment" of "international duty" in Afghanistan in "more detail" than is usually reported in the regular Soviet press. *Krasnaia zvezda* decided to satisfy the anxious mother by describing her son Igor's duties, admitting that his service was indeed hard and asking mothers as well as young women "to write the soldiers in Afghanistan more often."[8] Another report in the same newspaper described military service as "difficult" and "far from the motherland [where] anything can happen."

In early 1984, in another very unusual display of candidness, another Soviet government newspaper, *Komsomol'skaia pravda* (an organ of the Soviet youth organization Komsomol), published a letter from a Soviet soldier who complained that a soldier friend had received a letter from a girlfriend with some "irresponsible lines" in reference to the Afghan war. This girl reportedly wrote: "Whenever I see a soldier I start feeling bad."[9] This was called "downright insulting" by the newspaper. The same Soviet soldier was amazed at "how little is written about Afghanistan in the Soviet press," and declared that "no matter how depressed and sad we may feel far from home, Soviet soldiers will never break the glorious tradition of the army." Delays affecting mail from relatives for Soviet troops in Afghanistan (sometimes taking about two months and therefore often lost) were also severely criticized by another report in *Krasnaia zvezda*.

Reported interviews with Soviet soldiers captured by the Afghan *mujahidin* suggest a very low troop morale. New recruits are indoctrinated not to fall into the hands of the partisans under any circumstances since "the *basmachi* cut out the eyes and cut off the ears of every Soviet soldier they capture." The *dembels,* soldiers about to be demobilized and sent home, mistreat the *salaki* (small fish), which is the nickname for new recruits. Since regular Soviet soldiers receive only about 15 rubles per month spending money, in comparison with an officer's minimum pay of 250 rubles, the main concern of the simple, often hungry Soviet soldier is to secure victuals, often even if he has to sell some of his military equipment at the Afghan bazaar. It is no wonder that Soviet soldiers in Afghanistan are fighting "half-heartedly," acquiring a liking for Afghan opium, in some cases committing suicide, and disobeying their superiors.[10] (Some soldiers reportedly refuse to kill innocent civilians.) Though it is difficult to make a precise assessment of the impact of the war, judging from some unusually candid reports in the Soviet press, the morale of the Soviet troops and their relatives is far from jubilant and there is growing dissatisfaction with the war.

That there are some signs of dissent even among the Soviet establishment in Moscow became apparent on May 23, 1983 when Radio Moscow English-language newscaster Vladimir Danchev did something which had never been done before in the USSR. In several worldwide English-language broadcasts he called the Soviets' "fraternal assistance" to Afghanistan by its real name, "occupation," the Soviet soldiers "bandits," and the *mujahidin* "defenders of the country" against "Soviet invaders."[11] Interviews with a knowledgeable Soviet defector indicate that a serious blunder of this magnitude could not have occurred in the highly controlled Soviet Radio without Danchev's having had accomplices. Danchev was promptly banished from Moscow to an insane asylum in Tashkent.

True, five years after the invasion there are no visible signs of massive dissent in the USSR against the Afghan war, certainly nothing like the dissent rampant in America five years into the Vietnam War. The prevailing view of Soviet officialdom about the future of the war is still, as implied by the Soviet newspaper *Sovietskaia rossiia,* that despite all difficulties, the Soviets will not leave Afghanistan as the Americans left Vietnam.[12] But this view may not necessarily be irreversible should the war begin to exact a much heavier toll on the morale of the Soviet troops, public, and the economy which, according to estimates, has been drained of at least $12 billion since 1979 on account of the war in Afghanistan.

Impact on Soviet Foreign Policy

Five years after the invasion, the ongoing occupation of Afghanistan is continuing to affect Soviet foreign policy formulation. The sum of combined costs abroad has already proven to be quite high in terms of Soviet relations with the West. The war has hindered better Soviet relations with the United States, U.S. allies, and a number of developing countries. The invasion itself was one of the factors which delayed ratification of SALT II and led to a postponement of new START negotiations with the United States. In 1979 the Soviet leadership surely did not anticipate the high international costs of the invasion and ensuing war. In particular they misjudged the response of the United States and a number of Third World countries which, as of 1984, reportedly continue to provide military and economic aid to the Afghan *mujahidin*.

Soviet relations with the Islamic countries of the Middle East and Asia, could be immeasurably bettered were it not for the continuous bloodshed in Afghanistan. The same is true about Soviet relations with ruling and nonruling communist parties. In Eastern Europe, even among the most reliable ruling elites, the war in Afghanistan has few enthusiastic supporters. In the independent communist countries of China, Yugoslavia, and Albania, the invasion has increased already existing fears about Soviet threats to their independent variants of communism. As regards China, the ongoing war in Afghanistan is one of three serious obstacles to the normalization of Soviet relations with that country. Soviet relations with nonruling communist parties, particularly in Western Europe, also suffer as a result of the Soviet occupation of Afghanistan. The undeclared Soviet war in Afghanistan further strengthens the independent and anti-Soviet tendencies of the Eurocommunist parties, particularly the Italian Communist Party, the largest and most influential.

Finally, the Afghan resistance is keeping Soviet power pinned down and this affects policy formulation during international crises elsewhere. To cite a well-known example, Soviet preoccupation with Afghanistan very likely helped deter a direct Soviet intervention in Poland and kept the experiment with Solidarity alive for sixteen months. In early 1981, when the threat of a Soviet military invasion in Poland was particularly acute, the Soviets were forced to deploy an additional 20,000 troops in Afghanistan, bringing the total Soviet troop deployment there to 105,000.

The fact that the Soviets still try to sustain the war in Afghanistan with a just slightly higher level of deployment suggests that they are not insensitive to either the domestic or international costs of the war. As of 1984 it seems the Soviets are still convinced that they can afford the high price of the Afghan occupation. However, these costs could increase considerably over the long haul. War expenditures, coupled with the cost of Soviet involvement with client countries such as Cuba and Vietnam, the growing indebtedness of the East European countries, and serious economic difficulties in the USSR sooner or later could prompt a serious reassessment of Soviet policies vis-à-vis Afghanistan.

Soviet Alternatives in Afghanistan

The Soviets face three possible alternatives in Afghanistan: (1) continuation of present policies; (2) escalation of the war; or (3) "Finlandization"—a negotiated diplomatic solution similar to the Finnish-Soviet understanding after World War II, guaranteeing the neutral status of Afghanistan.

Continuation of Present Policies

After five years of occupation the Soviets are still resolved to win the war in Afghanistan by doing more of the same. Their plan for a long involvement in that country is suggested by a number of military projects (building permanent bridges on the river Amu Darya, upgrading Afghan airfields) and economic projects (construction of a new pipeline from Afghan natural gas fields to Central Asia, the new port city Jayratan on the Amu Darya). Other indications of unswerving Soviet resolve are efforts to strengthen ideological ties between Central Asia and Afghanistan by publishing in Tashkent a million copies of works by Marx, Engels, and Lenin in the Pushtu language. (Before they were published only in Urdu and Dari.) Soviet generals have found Afghanistan to be a useful training ground where for the first time since the end of World War II their officers can develop practical battle experience.

The Soviet Politburo still believes that eventually they will be able to exert various pressures to stifle the resistance. They are taking a long-term view and as of 1984 they appear to be committed to holding Afghanistan. By seeking to pacify by force rebellious minorities and movements within their borders, the Soviets are upholding a long historical legacy of the Russian and Soviet states. One example often mentioned in the Soviet press is the Red army's 10-year struggle against the *basmachi* in Central Asia in the 1920s and 1930s. There are other historical examples as well: the Russo-Caucasian wars in the nineteenth century, the Soviet struggle against Muslim mountaineers in the northern Caucasus in the 1920s. Perhaps the Soviets are calculating that it will also take about ten years to subdue the Afghan *mujahidin,* among whose ranks walk the same Turkmen and Uzbeks who swelled the forces of the *basmachi.* (Not surprisingly, the Soviets lately have published a number of novels in Central Asian languages whose main theme is the struggle against the *basmachi.)*

Time and technology may be on the Soviet side, as well as the willingness to recur to the most brutal means of warfare. In 1983-84 the

Soviets introduced a deliberate policy of extreme brutality against Afghan civilians suspected of helping the resistance. Among other tactics the Soviets try to starve the *mujahidin* by bombing their irrigation systems and killing their cattle. However, the total subjugation of Afghanistan will take more resources and manpower than the successful campaign against the *basmachi* in the 1930s. The ranks of the *mujahidin* far exceed those of the *basmachi* in number and they are of superior quality. Moreover, unlike the vast steppes of Central Asia, the mountainous terrain of Afghanistan is a paradise for guerrillas. So far the Soviets have been much less successful in their struggle against the *mujahidin,* although they have used tactics similar to those directed against the *basmachi*—creating local paramilitary organizations to turn against the guerrillas, coopting large numbers of the intelligentsia and middle class, bribing various tribes, infiltrating the resistance. In the 1920s and 1930s the Soviets were able successfully to play some Central Asian groups against others. In Afghanistan, the Soviets may succeed with the same tactics in areas populated by Tajiks, Uzbeks, and Turkmen closest to the Soviet borders (and even this is questionable), but not in areas to the center and south of the country populated by the fiercely independent Pushtuns. Afghanistan is a nation of tribal nationalism and so far the Soviet war has cemented national unity.

Another factor to be contended with, which was not a problem in the colonial era of the 1930s when the Soviets were engaged in the *basmachi* wars, is the independent Muslim countries in the Middle East and South Asia willing to assist the Afghan *mujahidin*. The Soviet war in Afghanistan is infinitely more difficult than the war against the *basmachi,* particularly because of the sanctuary offered by Pakistan, but also Iran, and because of other forms of Pakistani and Iranian aid.

Escalation

As the Soviets continue to win the battles but not the war, the Soviet leadership may decide to escalate the war in Afghanistan (deploying up to 500,000 troops) so as to achieve a rapid victory and avoid the deleterious internal and external effects of a protracted war.

This alternative is bound with serious risks. A massive escalation of the Afghan war would undercut Soviet military commitments elsewhere and hinder the goal of making the war an Afghan war—building an effective Afghan force to fight the resistance. A large escalation would also be politically dangerous as it surely would lead to more pronounced forms of dissent among the relatives of Soviet soldiers and youth, alienate the Muslims in Central Asia as well as those south of the Soviet borders, and harm Soviet relations with the West, other communist countries, and Muslim Third World countries.

Finlandization

Rising costs in Afghanistan may bring about a shift in the opposite direction, prompting a negotiated solution whereby the Soviets would withdraw their military in exchange for Afghanistan's agreement to remain a basically friendly, Nonaligned but non-Leninist border state. For lack of a better word this could be called "Finlandization." It is possible that some recent leaks and subtle hints by the Soviets that they would be prepared to discuss a withdrawal from Afghanistan (occurring in the summer of 1983 and probably ordered by Andropov) were testing the waters in this direction. However, these openings were later retracted as Andropov's health rapidly declined. Other Soviet officials were reported to have told foreign diplomats not to take these hints seriously—a likely sign of disagreement within the Soviet leadership. It appears that Andropov's successor, "Brezhnevite" Konstantin Chernenko, is less inclined and less able to experiment in domestic and foreign affairs than his predecessor was in the first months of his tenure.

A negotiated option is risk-laden for the USSR. If implemented, such an agreement would contradict the supposedly irreversible process of communism and show Soviet weaknesses in their commitment to "socialist-oriented" allies. Yet this alternative may be more palatable than escalation of the war. The Soviets themselves have not ruled out entirely such a solution. This is indicated by the fact that Soviet ideologists, when referring to Afghanistan, still carefully speak of "national democracy" and "socialist orientation" only and not yet "real socialism" as they do when referring to Eastern Europe, Mongolia, Vietnam, and Cuba. This implies that the socialist orientation of Afghanistan is not necessarily irreversible. However, the efforts of the West and friendly Third World countries are needed to promote a turnaround.

End to Soviet Occupation

One reason the West in general and the United States in particular have hesitated to give greater support to the Afghan resistance has been the incorrect assumption that Afghanistan is too close to the Soviet Union, in its shadow if not sphere of influence.[13] To repeat, however, Afghanistan, unlike Eastern Europe, is not and has never been in the Soviet sphere of influence. For more than 150 years Afghanistan has been a geographically important but ideologically neutral buffer state between Russia and the West.

The Soviet occupation seeks to change this, creating an unthinkable nightmare for the West but also for independent developing countries in Asia (including China) and the Middle East: the possibility of a dramatic change in the equilibrium of the Asian continent. The consolidation of Soviet power in Afghanistan would give Moscow a great geopolitical advantage, better enabling the Soviets to manipulate regional powers such as Pakistan and Iran (particularly given the instability in the latter), influence politics in countries around the Persian Gulf, and extend the circle of pro-Soviet regimes around China.

Ultimate dominion over Afghanistan would also reinforce Moscow's perceptions that military force is the best means for maintaining control over the Soviet periphery and thus encourage similar ventures in the future. By failing to provide effective support to the *mujahidin* in Afghanistan, the West and particularly the United States would seriously undermine their own credibility among other political groups resisting Soviet attempts to build new nuclei in the worldwide "socialist system." The confidence in Western resolve shared by many friendly developing nations will be eroded if the West does nothing.

To prevent the Soviet Union from turning Afghanistan into a Leninist satellite based on the East European model, the United States, in concert with its allies, other Islamic countries, and China, should pursue a 2-track policy combining imaginative diplomacy and increased military aid for the rebels. Unlike in Eastern Europe, the U.S. objective in Afghanistan should be to undermine the illegitimate puppet regime of Babrak Karmal and restore Afghanistan's status as a Nonaligned, non-Leninist state.

Recent private talks with resistance leaders indicate that they badly need to improve their defenses. They have proved their willingness and ability to fight without foreign advisors. However, if their struggle is to have a greater impact upon Soviet domestic and foreign policies, they need upgraded military aid, including advanced antiaircraft and antitank weapons. We must devise a way to increase the trickle of weapons that reportedly has been reaching the *mujahidin* through neighboring countries. Particularly we must try to augment the flow through Pakistan (without undermining President Mohammed Zia-ul Haq, whose domestic political position would be endangered if such aid moved openly through his country) and even through Iran.

All the countries which oppose the Soviet occupation should do their utmost to ensure that economic, medical, and educational aid gets through to the areas controlled by the resistance. Finally, we must help alleviate Pakistan's economic problems and upgrade military aid to that country, which faces continued Soviet intimidation, both by Soviet diplomats, who make threats and then quietly try to undercut Pakistan's opposition to the Soviet occupation with offers of economic aid, and dozens of unauthorized military overflights along the borders when Pakistani territory has been bombarded by MIG fighter jets.

The aim of upgraded assistance would be to further augment the domestic and international costs of the war for the Soviet Union. Soviet losses are considerable but not enough to bring Moscow to negotiate a settlement. Indirect negotiations between the Kabul regime and the Pakistanis being sponsored by the United Nations are designed to seek recognition of that regime by Pakistan and blunt the adverse international reaction to the war. Some observers expect these talks to produce a variant of Finlandization. They forget that the Finns were able to come to terms with Moscow only after their prolonged resistance persuaded the Kremlin that such a compromise was preferable to the costs of imposing a Leninist regime on an unwilling population. Moscow cannot be expected to negotiate in good faith with the Afghan freedom fighters until it faces a comparable choice. Though the Western upgrading of military aid to the *mujahidin* entails some risk of escalation of the war in Afghanistan, it is more likely to lead to an eventual Soviet reassessment of the costs and a serious willingness to negotiate.

This would be especially true if Western and Third World pressure were to be accompanied by efforts to engage the Soviets and the Afghan resistance leaders in direct negotiations. If we merely increased military aid to the resistance without making serious diplomatic overtures and offering economic incentives to the Soviets, we would risk serious military escalation and greater devastation. Only with a 2-track policy can we hope to bring about a Finlandized Afghanistan. Often this term is used in derogatory fashion, but at the moment Finlandization is the best we can hope for in Afghanistan.

Notes

1. For what remains the best summary and analysis of interpretations of Soviet motives for invading Afghanistan, see *An Assessment of the Afghanistan Sanctions: Implications for Trade and Diplomacy in the 1980s*, prepared for the Subcommittee on Europe and the Middle East of the Committee on Foreign Relations, U.S. House of Representatives (Washington, D.C.: U.S. Government Printing Office, August 1981), pp. 11-14.

2. Published by Johns Hopkins University Press (Baltimore) in 1979, 1981, and 1984.
3. See my articles "From Prague to Kabul: The Soviet Style of Invasion," *International Security* (Fall 1980); and "The Soviet Invasion of Afghanistan: The Difficulty of Knowing Where to Stop," *ORBIS* 24 (Summer 1980).
4. "Conference in Kabul," *Pravda* (Moscow, January 9, 1984):4.
5. S. Enders Wimbush and Alex Alexiev, *Soviet Central Asian Soldiers in Afghanistan* (Santa Monica, Calif: Rand Corporation Memo, N-1634-NA, January 1981).
6. Radio Moscow (World Series in English), January 4, 1984; FBIS-USSR. January 4, 1984.
7. "Editorial Report," *Krasnaia zvezda* (December 8, 1983):1.
8. Lt. Col. V. Skrizhalin, "In the Spurs of the Hindu Kush," *Krasnaia zvezda* (December 12, 1983):1.
9. "Letter Home," written by guards sergeant Viktor Tankin, *Komsomol'skaia pravda* (Moscow, February 10, 1984):4.
10. See interviews with captured Soviet soldiers, *Der Spiegel* (Hamburg, May 30, 1983):122-29; and *UPI* report about news conference with two captured Soviet soldiers at Freedom House on December 6, 1983, *UPI* (December 6, 1983).
11. Danchev's text was broadcast at 1100 GMT, 1200 GMT and 1300 GMT, May 23, 1983. He was replaced before the 1400 broadcast by another newscaster. See FBIS-USSR, May 23, 1983.
12. A. Khorobrykh, "From the Afghan Network: On the Road to Kabul," *Sovetskaiia rossiia* (Moscow, September 29, 1983).
13. This section is based on my article which appeared in the *New York Times* (December 27, 1983).

Commentaries on Professor Valenta's Paper

Marian K. Leighton

It is good that Dr. Valenta was chosen to present this paper because, although he is not an Afghan expert, he is one of the few people who look at Soviet foreign policy from a broad perspective. It is extremely important that we place the Afghan situation in the general context of Soviet foreign policy.

Dr. Valenta cited the 1978 Communist coup in Afghanistan as an ideological watershed. I think it was also a strategic watershed in that the Soviet Union created the preconditions for breaching the so-called Northern Tier that the West created in the 1950s to try to separate and contain the USSR from moving into the Middle East. The Baghdad Pact, renamed the Central Treaty Organization (CENTO) after Iraq withdrew in 1959, was the main vehicle for this containment. Iran, Pakistan, and Turkey were the Middle Eastern members of CENTO, but Afghanistan, chiefly at the urging of the shah, was being drawn into economic cooperation with these countries, and some regional development schemes were getting underway. In view of the sizable economic investment and military-strategic infrastructure that they put into Afghanistan, the Soviets regarded this situation with alarm. The fall of the shah sealed the fate of the Northern Tier and helped pave the way for a more aggressive Soviet posture in Afghanistan and elsewhere.

The long-term Soviet strategy in the Middle East is to isolate and neutralize U.S. allies, particularly Pakistan and Turkey, and to prevent Iran from returning to the Western fold. There has been a lot of talk about Afghanistan's role as a stepping stone to the Persian Gulf and also as a component of the Soviet attempt to encircle China. With regard to the Gulf, I would imagine that committing manpower and resources to Afghanistan would have been more of a diversion than a facilitator (although the improved airfields and other military infrastructure in Afghanistan obviously have potential value). There are easier ways to get into Iran than by way of Aghanistan. However, I do agree with Dr. Valenta's long-term outlook that the Soviets certainly want to expand their influence in the entire Middle East.

With regard to China, it already is pretty much encircled by Vietnam, Mongolia, India, and the Soviet Union itself, so I really do not see the role of Afghanistan as immediately relevant. As Dr. Valenta pointed out, Afghanistan historically has been a buffer state and also a gateway into South Asia, so I think that India and Pakistan loom foremost in Soviet strategic considerations. It is worth noting that in 1980 Brezhnev gave a speech to the Indian Parliament in which he connected Indian security directly with the situation in the Persian Gulf. His immediate proposal was a 5-point plan for neutralization of the Gulf—removal of the Western naval presence from there—with the result that the Soviet Union, by virtue of its geography, would become the dominant power.

The point of all these remarks is to place Afghanistan within the larger strategic context of a very big area and, again, I do agree with Dr. Valenta in terms of his portrayal of the long-term Soviet use of a pacified Afghanistan to further Moscow's objectives in South Asia as well as the Persian Gulf.

Dr. Valenta's contention that a combination of offensive and defensive motivations prompted the Soviet move into Afghanistan is in line with my own views. In order to feel secure, the Soviet Union traditionally has perceived the need to surround itself with buffer states on all its borders. Now that the USSR's southern periphery is pretty much wide open, Moscow is taking advantage of the new strategic opportunities there.

Turning to domestic affairs in Afghanistan, Dr. Valenta spoke of the Soviet Union's fears that Hafizullah Amin would betray the Kremlin. Amin was a leader of the Khalq faction of the Afghan Communist Party (the People's Democratic Party) and served as deputy prime minister and foreign minister in the Communist government created after the 1978 coup. He deposed President Nur Mohammed Taraki in September 1979 and was himself killed by the Soviets during their invasion in December. The major reason why the Soviets wanted to replace Amin was that his radical agrarian and social reforms threatened to spark a backlash within Afghanistan that would imperil the continuing existence of a Communist regime there.

With regard to Soviet military policy in Afghanistan, it is true that the Soviets went in somewhat unprepared. They put in a great deal of heavy equipment, they sent recruits from Soviet Central Asia to fight fellow Muslims, and so forth. A lot of these policies did not work out too well, but the Soviets learned from their mistakes. For example, they began to use helicopter gunships, which have proved much more effective than some of the earlier equipment they deployed.

I believe that the Soviets are in Afghanistan for the foreseeable future, and I think that we might usefully discuss the whole question of the so-called burden of empire: to what extent is the Afghan situation a burden on the USSR? I do not regard it as a major problem, whether in terms of economic difficulties, casualty rates, or the international reaction, which I do not view as excessively harsh.

Let me add one more point, and that regards putative KGB opposition to the invasion of Afghanistan. There is a new book by two Soviet émigrés entitled *Andropov's Secret Passage into the Kremlin*. It contends that Andropov, realizing that Brezhnev and a number of other top officials were either physically incapacitated or unavailable for some other reason, forged an alliance with the military and became a prime mover behind the decision to invade Afghanistan. The most interesting thing this book illuminates is how little we know about what goes on in the Kremlin.

Gregory M. Kortanek

I would like to address not only Soviet intentions but also the U.S. response to Soviet activities in Afghanistan. To begin with, after the extraordinary events in both Iran and Afghanistan during 1979, President Carter was moved in his 1980 State of the Union address to articulate what has been known as the Carter Doctrine, reasserting U.S. vital interests in the Gulf. Shortly after that (on 1 March 1980), a military organization came into being known as the Rapid Development Joint Task Force. It initially had a limited role to perform. Primarily, it was to be able to move forces to intervene militarily in those parts of the world where our vital interests were directly threatened. But because of the transitory nature of a joint task force within the military scheme of things, one of the difficulties we had was to convince friendly states within the region, notably Pakistan, that the U.S. commitment to regional security was a long-term and continuing one, and not simply a passing fad brought about by these extraordinary events.

In his September 1982 "peace initiative," President Reagan reconfirmed our commitment to resist further Soviet aggression within the region, in concert with our allies. We have taken steps to do that. On 1 January 1983, the Rapid Deployment Joint Task Force was replaced by the United States Central Command, of which I am proud to be a member. We have an 850-man headquarters in Tampa, Florida, three component headquarters, and a large military force designated for planning. I do not want to leave anybody with the impression that we intend to move that force into Afghanistan or elsewhere in the region any time in the near future; certainly not without prior consultations and discussions with our friends in the region. But concerning Soviet intentions for the future in Afghanistan, I think the creation of this new American military commitment to the region has to be factored into Soviet decision making. We now see, perhaps, a certain degree of caution entering into Soviet regional activities, and possibly a tacit acceptance of a stalemate within Afghanistan. I hope that during the discussion period we will be able to look at issues such as the Soviet quiescence concerning the moral support that Pakistan has been providing to the Afghan resistance, as well as the condemnation of the Soviet Union by a Nonaligned country such as Pakistan. The Soviets have done very little in response to this, perhaps aircraft border incursions and things of that sort.

I am not sure I would agree with Professor Valenta when he talked about the tactical failure of the Soviets. If their initial intention was the complete pacification and subjugation of Afghanistan, they have seen that it would require a much larger commitment of forces and resources than they had initially anticipated or were prepared to commit. But before we characterize that as a failure, we must look at the net results of Soviet activities in Afghanistan. They have been able to position themselves strategically much closer to the Persian Gulf region. I do not necessarily look for a Soviet drive to the Gulf using Afghanistan as an invasion route, but nonetheless, they do now have control over certain military facilities within Afghanistan which have improved their position. Additionally, they have created large potentially destabilizing refugee populations in Pakistan and Iran. Further, as a Pakistani diplomat observed, the Soviets may have sought to use Afghanistan not as a buffer state, but as a glacis state. That is, just as glacis plates on a ship are designed to deflect assaults of naval gunfire, so do the Soviets view their activities in Afghanistan as a means of deflecting the threats posed by the potential expansion of militant Islam to the Muslim populations of the Soviet Union itself. They have done all this at a relatively modest cost, both in lives spent and world opinion. Afghanistan has pretty much moved off the front pages of major papers around the world. If that is in fact a failure, it is perhaps the obverse of a Pyrrhic victory—maybe it is a "Pyrrhic failure." One more "failure" like that for the Soviets and we may be undone in Southwest Asia.

The Soviets must be concerned about the possibility of a U.S.

response to any increase or escalation of their activities in the region. Over the last three years we have conducted exercises with some friendly nations in the Southwest Asian region. We know that these exercises have been monitored and have been of great concern to the Soviets. They were very concerned to see what sort of capabilities we have, and I think these are now being factored into the decision-making process.

One of our challenges now, not only in Afghanistan but regionally, is to look at future possibilities in Iran. This is an important state in the region from a standpoint of population, resources, and potential military power. And it is very much in the U.S. interest to look for rapprochement with a post-Khomeini Iran. I would like in the discussion period to have an idea of just how such a rapproachement might be effected without providing the Soviets with an opportunity to exploit ethnic divisions and other causes of potential disruptions within Iran, not only to maintain their position in Afghanistan, but also to ensure that Iran remains at least in the neutral camp. Their intention could then be to orchestrate an Iranian shift toward the Soviets. They might attempt to block any rapprochement between the United States and Iran that could allow Iran to cooperate with the United States as in the past. Normalized U.S.-Iranian relations certainly would be in our interest, and it would be a challenge to effect that without providing the Soviets an opportunity to use their present position in Afghanistan to exploit potential instability in Iran.

DISCUSSION

Stephen A. Garrett: I would suggest, in line with Professor Valenta's presentation, that we concentrate in a broad sense on these three major questions he has introduced: the initial intervention, the reasons, the motivations for that action; the military and political situation on the ground in Afghanistan as it affects Soviet policy; and the biggest question of all, the future. What are the ultimate Soviet aims and goals in Afghanistan and adjacent region and how does this situation affect Soviet foreign policy in general? As Marian said, one of the most useful aspects of Jiri's presentation is putting the Afghan situation into the broader context of Soviet foreign policy. This is particularly important for the international community. The floor is open for observations.

Robert G. Neumann: Indeed Professor Valenta has put before us virtually every conceivable and possibly some less conceivable motives for Soviet actions. What we need now is to put priorities on one or the other. Having spent a little over half of my professional life in academe and a little under half in government service I am impressed by the overestimation of theoretical aspects. Bureaucracies by their nature are operationally oriented and leap upon the immediate events requiring action.

As Professor Valenta said, the invasion of December 1979 did not come out of the blue. The options available to the Soviet leadership were very limited at that time. I doubt that there was a great deal of discussion, though none of us will ever know, about all these other strategic, theoretical aspects, although for a trained Communist these are already present in the mind and perhaps need not be specifically emphasized. There are different views around the table as to the Soviet involvement in the 1978 coup. But even those of us like myself, who consider the Soviet involvement considerable, have not, at least I have not, reached a clear understanding as to whether this was a response to an opportunity or a long-conceived approach. I always opt in favor of the opportunity or the correcting of a mistake rather than the other way around.

I had hoped Professor Valenta or others in the discussion might establish some priorities on these various aspects. As to military calculations about equipment and so forth, there seems to be an operational tendency to underestimate the difficulties. If the Soviets, despite their way considerable presence in Afghanistan for many years, underestimated their problems, so did the Israelis in Lebanon.

Jiri Valenta: I indicated that the most important factor in the Soviet decision-making process, which has been missed by people on both the Left and the Right, was the internal conditions in Afghanistan. There was a certain logic in the situation of 1978 and 1979 which is somewhat analogous to what occurred in Vietnam in 1964-66. For example, in March 1979 Soviet advisors and their dependents, estimated at sixteen to forty in number, were killed in Herat. The Soviets retaliated by sending in a limited force which proved to be ineffective and had to augmented. This illustrates how, in some ways, they were enveloped in the conflict.

If I were to rank the factors influencing their decision, the most immediate would be the need to stabilize volatile internal conditions in an important neighboring country. But there was a related long-term consideration, certainly in the eyes of the military, and that was to enhance the Soviet position for dealing with unpredictable regional developments.

I do not believe that Andropov was opposed to the invasion. At the same time, I would not be surprised if Soviet officials responsible for domestic affairs were apprehensive about its impact on Central Asia, whereas others responsible for foreign policy were concerned with the global impact. Still others, such as Michael Suslov, would have been concerned with interparty relations and repercussions on Soviet standing in the international Communist movement. Unfortunately there is no hard evidence on the bureaucratic organizational aspect of the decision-making process in Afghanistan as there was, for example, in the case of the Soviet invasion of Czechoslovakia in 1968. Furthermore, the Soviets are doing their utmost not to tell us the facts and when they do tell us something, it is veiled in deception.

Louis Dupree: I must admit to everyone that I was wrong about the entire situation. I did not think the Soviets would go into Afghanistan. I was thinking like an Afghan, of course, and so recently I have started to think like a Soviet. And that is more difficult for us non–Soviet specialists. I shall never forgive my advisor when I was a graduate student who advised me not to take Russian as a second language because it would never be of any use in the Middle East and particularly in South Asia and Afghanistan.

I would like to make a few comments on Professor Valenta's superb presentation. Hélène Carrère d'Encausse's study of Soviet Central Asia (*Decline of Empire: The Soviet Socialist Republics in Revolt,* trans. M. Sokolensky and H.A. LaFarge [New York: Newsweek Books, 1979]) and most of the non-Slavic ethnic groups in the Soviet Union indicate that by the year 2000, 53 percent of the population of the Soviet Union will be non-Russian, and that approximately one-third will be Muslim or of Muslim origin. With the potential, at least, of their subversively following Mohammed instead of Marx, you may find a little dissension developing over the long run. As an anthropologist, I have always thought over the long range of 1,000 years; I now find myself being compressed into twenty or thirty years. We must realize that the Soviets have been patient in moving out of the heartland into Central Asia and now down to Afghanistan on the edge of the South Asian area.

I would like to give you the worst possible scenario for the future. We all know that history and culture take different patterns and directions and continue along certain lines unless something different is introduced from the outside to change the direction of these patterns, be they historical or cultural. As I look at the patterns as they are developing now in the Afghan area I feel that we cannot stop aggression, but must drive it back from whence it came. The Soviets are in

Afghanistan now, and I agree completely with Dr. Valenta that they are not planning to get out. They are turning Afghanistan, especially in the urban areas and military zones, into a concrete jungle. It is amazing the number of buildings going up as cantonments, the number of runways being extended, and so forth. So I do not think they are planning to leave for a long time. What I call the choreography of diplomacy, which is what the Geneva conferences are turning out to be, will continue as long as anyone will dance with anyone else. But I am in favor of these conferences, because they do provide a door which can be opened at any time that anyone happens to be serious about a peaceful solution to the Afghan situation. You may remember that the Vietnam War at its end had a number of problems because in Paris delegates were arguing about the size of the table, the shape of the table, who should sit where, for months. Now that Geneva door can be opened at any time.

But let us look at this worst possible scenerio. If nothing is introduced, and of course things *will* be introduced, I see the Soviets using Afghanistan as a springboard—not to launch an invasion to the south, not to move a single Soviet soldier across the border into Pakistan or Iran—but as a springboard to increase the tensions that are already there. We all know that Pakistan from the beginning has had the problems of regional autonomy within the minority provinces—the Northwest Frontier Province, Baluchistan, and Sind—and these problems are still there. They can be accelerated and increased. They are being increased by Sovietized Pakistanis and Afghans who are coming across the border now, making contact with the dissidents in these areas, looking forward to a possible explosion in the future. We cannot forget the Afghan refugees in this equation. After five or ten years the Afghan refugees, those 3 million or whatever, decide they cannot go home. What are they going to do, become good Pakistani citizens? I do not think so. In all probability they will join with dissidents in the Northwest Frontier and Baluchistan, and possibly create an independent Baluchistan and an independent Pushtunistan. Sind, itself, will tend to break away, and Punjab will become the Lichtenstein of Asia. If that occurs, friendly nations to the south and west can effectively control, block, dominate if you would, the Persian Gulf oil. And the Soviets are obviously going to create dissension in Iran at the same time. The Arabian peninsula itself is not that stable. So by the year 2000 the Soviets could conceivably be the dominant economic and political factor in South Asia and possibly even in the Middle East.

And what does this do? This effectively blocks the energy requirements of Western Europe and Japan. Here Afghanistan becomes an important economic as well as strategic factor. We all know that Afghanistan floats on natural gas in the northern part of the country; quite a bit of oil is unexploited in Afghanistan, and the gas from Afghanistan is now powering most of the important industrial complexes east of the Urals. This releases the natural gas from the Yamal peninsula in Siberia for other purposes. What are the Soviets doing with the acquiescence of Western Europe? They are building a pipeline straight to the Atlantic Ocean. So when West European energy requirements are above what the oil states can produce, the Soviets can have ready energy supplies for Western Europe. This will ultimately destroy NATO, Which I think is the ultimate Soviet goal.

I do not think the Soviets are thinking in these terms. And I am thinking in terms of an evolutionary process which has already begun, and which cannot be altered unless something is fed into the situation. This, of course, is one of the problems we have—what do we feed into the situation? I agree with Dr. Valenta. We should increase effective quality and quantity of weapons going to the *mujahidin* inside Afghanistan. At the same time, and this will be most controversial, we should guarantee the territorial integrity of Pakistan. This will not make our Indian friends too happy, but it is about time we made our Indian friends unhappy about certain things—they make us unhappy all the time. The lack of such a guarantee is one reason why the Pakistanis are not permitting more arms going across the border. If all of a sudden an escalation of fighting takes place inside Afghanistan, who will be punished? Pakistan. And the Pakistanis are not too sure the Americans will respond to defend their interest if this occurs. They look at the American track record and they are not too satisfied with American defense of friends in times of crisis over various areas of the globe.

Noor A. Husain: I think I cannot do better justice to Pakistan's case than my friend Dr. Dupree has done. But I would just like to offer a few comments on the very thorough paper of Dr. Valenta. He noted that the Soviets already have a very fine or very strategic border with Iran. However, by moving into Afghanistan they gain about 700-800 miles of very open flat land ideal for use of motorized rifle and armor formations. This area is very dissimilar to what they already have in Azerbaijan, between the Black and the Caspian seas and east of the Caspian Sea. This is a far more open flank for the employment of rapid motorized, mechanized, and armor formations than Iran's northern flank. Regarding the question of alienating the Muslims of Central Asia, one must not forget that the Turkmen, Uzbeks, and Tajiks have been involved in building up institutions inside Afghanistan during the last two decades. They will probably get more sucked into the so-called economic, political, social, and cultural development projects for Afghanistan, and thereby some of the animosity or alienation will be diffused when they see themselves as building up new institutions in neighboring Afghanistan—in ethnically homogeneous areas.

Afghanistan has been, apart from being in the past 200 years a buffer between two imperial powers, the British and Czarist, the traditional security zone of Central Asia, South Asia, and West Asia—what Toynbee has called "one of the world's two roundabouts." One is the area north of Kabul—the Bagram area. The other is what we have in Lebanon, the Tripoli area. Most of the world's civilizations, conquerors, and adventurers have revolved around these areas. That was probably an important input in Soviet decision making in coming into Afghanistan.

The military decision to move into Afghanistan was made by a class of Soviet generals who are more in the military managing class than military commanding class. Marshal Ustinov, if you check the record of World War II, was not a combat general. And a noncombat general is more likely to blunder into a thing like this, against a freedom struggle in a mountainous area. As long as the five important elements of insurgency are there it will continue. Maybe a new class of military managers has taken over in the Soviet Union, and they may well keep on blundering with the tactical and strategic side of military operations of Afghanistan.

There have been recent reports that the Soviets have introduced another 30,000 troops. I could not verify this before leaving Pakistan, whether this was a part of the relief program or whether these troops were in addition to the 105,000 already operating inside Afghanistan. I think that there is far more Soviet presence around the borders with Iran now than a year ago—in the areas of Herat, Farah, and Shindand, and this is the open terrain to which I was referring.

There was a remark about Pakistan hindering the unification of the refugees. I am not sure what sort of hindering Pakistan is doing, but please do not forget that we have had over 1,000 violations of our air space in the last four years. No self-respecting nation would tolerate such a situation. I may add that our air force youth flying 1950 vintage MIG 19s and until recently F86s, have been straining at the leash to have a go at some of these Soviet planes with Afghan markings or Soviet planes with no markings that come over. But you can appreciate the technological gap that exists and is certainly not being made up by the introduction of six F16s. So if there is a degree of caution, there are very good reasons for debate among the policy and decision makers. I do not think having headquarters of the Central Command on the other side of the globe in Tampa, Florida, really helps either in image or confidence building as far as our region is concerned. You may have very good reasons for doing that, but you have to look at it from the angle of a person who can feel the Soviets breathing down their necks.

Gregory M. Kortanek: In response to that, I was wondering whether you are offering us a site for a headquarters.

Noor A. Husain: You have every right to ask that. Our official policy is quite clear—no bases of any kind. If I may take another minute or so regarding refugees, yes, there are about 3 million and they keep coming in at a rate of anything from 5 to 15,000 a month. Three million are in Pakistan and about 1 million in Iran, which is anything from one-fourth to one-third the population outside Afghanistan. And our western borders are being crossed by these refugees from scores of places. Neither of the two superpowers has either the capability or the strength to stop this movement. Pakistan has put all its efforts behind a political solution to the problem, which would guarantee the return of these refugees back into Afghanistan with honor. If we look at the problem of refugees historically in this region, we will find that they returned only in the wake of victorious armies when conditions were created in their own land guaranteeing them a degree of security.

Sajjad Hyder: Professor Valenta had set 1978 as the date for the Soviet decision. I would like to say that the date goes a little earlier to 1973, when King Zahir Shah was overthrown by Sardar Da'ud. Da'ud came to Moscow incognito before he overthrew the king. We should also take into account that in October 1975 President Nikolai Podgorny flew all of a sudden from Moscow to Kabul to reason with Da'ud. He said: "Do not go after the Left after the promises you made to us in 1973." I met Da'ud in the Kremlin in April 1977. We were having trouble in Pakistan at the time, but I thought his troubles were greater than ours. I never met any president as troubled as he was. He told me: "I don't like what your mullahs are doing in Pakistan," and I could gauge by that what was really bothering him. When Tariki came to the USSR for the first time after the 1978 coup, the usual party was held for him in St. George's Hall of the Kremlin by Brezhnev. He was surrounded by a number of young military officers with special badges on their chests. I, being an ignorant old soldier, could not make out what they stood for. But a very clever Rumanian ambassador took me aside and told me that this man went to a Soviet tank school, that man went to a airborne school, etc. You see, these are factors which have to be taken into account—it was a long process. Whether it was an opportunity or a long-term plan, I agree with Ambassador Neumann that it was really the bureaucracy going for opportunity. But there has been long-term thinking, right from 1929: from the time King Amanullah Khan was overthrown and they created Tajikistan into a full republic—that was a notice to the Afghans, to the Chinese, and to the British.

I think the word *defensive* in your formulation, Professor Valenta, has a very wide connotation. This is an explanation that the Soviets have been giving over the last century for the forward policy of the people on the other side. In the nineteenth century it was the British forward policy. Now they are talking about the American forward policy. Hafizullah Amin was not only thrown out because he might have turned out to be another Tito, but because he was thought to be the harbinger of the American forward policy.

I want to note in passing Mr. Dupree's comment about what the Soviets can do in Pakistan. I think we should ask Mr. Harrison how many Baluch are being trained in Afghanistan today with Soviet money. He has made a study of it. These are the problems that really concern Pakistan. But I do not think that the solution Professor Dupree advocates is workable. We are talking about your force, your 900-man headquarters. Have you some idea of the reaction in Pakistan after your RDF exercises last year? You see, it is not so easy, as he says, to guarantee Pakistan's territorial integrity. Both in 1965 and 1971 you did nothing insofar as our territorial integrity was concerned. And therefore the people of Pakistan, and I speak for the people of Pakistan, have had no faith in your guarantees. You say that Pakistan should be made to let more weapons go through. Most people in Pakistan, not everybody, do not welcome the idea of being a weapons trail, because they know what happened to weapons trails in other countries. As for Professor Valenta's statement that Pakistan is hindering the unification of the Afghan resistance—can anybody hinder the resistance leaders from unifying?

Gregory M. Kortanek: I wanted to distance myself somewhat from Professor Dupree's suggestion that Pakistan become a weapons trail. I would like to make a couple of comments about the creation of USCENTCOM and the tie with the old Rapid Deployment Joint Task Force. The Rapid Deployment Joint Task Force was created in response to extraordinary factors. The U.S. Central Command is geared to look after the ordinary events of our military interests in the region—which was, prior to the creation of this command, divided between two separate military commands within the U.S. military structure—the European Command and the Pacific Command. Although those commands did the best they could with their available resources, the region was never the primary focus of either command. The Pacific Command primarily looked at Korea, for example, and the

European Command looked at NATO commitments. The purpose of creating a permanent, unified command is to send a signal to our friends in the region that the U.S. commitment is not a passing one. It is not merely a reaction to the Soviet intervention in Afghanistan, but is a long-term commitment. Although our headquarters is in Tampa, Florida, we are rapidly improving our ability to, if necessary, move forces into the region if requested. We do not seek to permanently station combat forces in the region. We seek only to work in cooperation and in consultation with our friends in the region to ensure their security. Only as last resort, if diplomatic and noncombatant military efforts fail to deter aggression, would combat forces be introduced. These forces would be withdrawn immediately upon accomplishment of their objective.

Jiri Valenta: I would suggest that the United States has equally valuable friends on both sides of the Afghan-Pakistani border. Therefore it is important to broach the question of whether assistance to Afghan freedom fighters via the south is being hindered. This is what I hear from my Afghan friends. However, I am not that familiar with the situation; therefore I would welcome a response from our Pakistani friends as to how we might improve that cooperation.

Sajjad Hyder: I think the important thing would be to say who is hindering whom.

Eden Naby: I wanted to comment on the issue of Central Asians. I think there are some questions that need to be dealt with. First of all, in terms of the scholarship that has been done on Soviet Moslems in general and Central Asians in particular, the work has been done mainly by French scholars, because these are the people who were trained, prior to the current crisis, in the languages of the area. There were very few people in Central Asian studies prior to 1978; many more have entered the field since. But the projections that these scholars have put forward are often misinterpreted. It has been said that they project a violent political explosion in Central Asia. I have not seen this in the works of the several scholars known in this field. Rather, what they have attempted to point to are the problems in Central Asia and among Soviet Muslims that the Soviets are aware of and need to confront. I think this is where the Central Asian issue relates directly to the Afghan case, and it is perhaps here that I should like to focus some attention.

The two main problems of Central Asia stem from demography and from the increased awareness of Central Asians—Central Asian Muslims and Central Asians who have perhaps not identified themselves strictly as Muslims. The increased awareness among these people is of their separate identities, their heritage, and these are the areas in which the problems lie for the Soviet Union. These are not insurmountable problems, but they are problems that must be handled by Moscow.

I am not going to talk about the use of Soviet Central Asian support troops in Afghanistan. It is a complex issue, but Professor Valenta's point that the Soviets simply withdrew Soviet Muslim forces because they were unreliable needs some discussion. I think that the Soviet's Central Asian problems could be diffused by using Afghanistan in a way I would like to outline. We know that since 1978 the Soviets have made a great effort to increase use of Central Asians in Afghan institutions. Particularly important are the select ethnic institutions they have attempted to develop. Since the invasion these institutions have fallen by the wayside, but in theory they still exist. It was the Soviet Central Asians who staffed these. Why do they staff them, aside from the fact that they had been sent there and had the grand opportunity to be outside the Soviet Union? They are glad to fill these positions and enthusiastically support Soviet policy in Afghanistan in terms of ethnicity because they see themselves helping their fellow "oppressed" ethnic Uzbek, Tajik, and Turkmen countrymen. This help contributes to their own sense of self-identity as cultural and kin entities, aside from politics. For example, Soviet Uzbeks feel they are increasing the Uzbek presence in the area by helping the Uzbeks in Afghanistan to confirm their own identity.

The second way in which the Soviet Central Asians may be recruited in the future, and perhaps even now they are being recruited to help in the Soviets' case to pacify the country, is by relocation of population. We know that one of the main problems in Central Asia has been an oversupply of labor within the republics which cannot be induced to voluntarily move non-Muslims to areas where labor is needed. This problem has been extensively discussed in the Soviet press and by Western scholars. Opinion is divided as to whether this labor force will have to be moved through force or whether the answer lies in increasing industry in the area. In recent months we see an attempt to relocate Tajiks forceably, for example, out of their own republic into an area where manpower is needed. One way to diffuse both the Afghan resistance in the north and help with the Central Asian labor problems would be to relocate some of the excess Soviet Central Asian population into Afghanistan's north. Soviet Muslims are reluctant to relocate into predominantly non-Muslim areas. But they may not be so reluctant to relocate, for example, to Mazar-e Sharif, Qunduz, Faizabad, or Miamana. They would be among their own people. And they would possibly, particularly the more secularized ones, be in a position to justify this move by saying that they are strengthening their coethnic identities in those areas. I think we cannot ignore this possibility. We have spoken on and off, and probably will speak more, particularly when discussing Marvin Weinbaum's paper, about annexation of Afghanistan or its incorporation in some form or other into the Soviet Union. This might create demographic problems. Why would Moscow wish to increase the number of Muslims in the Soviet Union? Where should the border with Pakistan be drawn? There is a reasonable alternative in terms of ethnicity. That is to draw the line along the Hindu Kush. This is the natural ethnic boundary. What does that mean for Pakistan? It means the creation of a Pushtun, an Afghan, entity. I think we should keep this line in mind in our discussions, particularly when examining the ethnic and Central Asian issue.

Selig S. Harrison: Major Kortanek referred to the fact that the control of military facilities by the Soviets resulting from their occupation has improved their position in the region. Louis talked about concrete jungles, runways being extended and tunnels being built. I hope we can focus a little on where we stand with respect to the degree of Soviet military capability that is being built and has been built during the occupation addressed to strategic military objectives. It is very important to have a clear fix and as much agreement as possible on the facts, because they are elusive. I understand that the Soviets inherited some facilities that could give them the opportunity to bring small numbers of Bisons and Bears into airstrips in Afghanistan for stopovers enroute to the Gulf and surrounding countries. But they have not been doing many of the things which would make these facilities useful as strategic bases, such as building runways clearly designed to handle large numbers of Bisons and Bears, or the kind of parking facilities, "hardstands," for that purpose. They are taking full advantage of what they inherited from the Americans and the Soviet facilities built prior to 1979 to prosecute the struggle against the *mujahidin,* but they have not fulfilled the prophecy that they want Afghanistan for strategic purposes. Most evidence indicates that they do not now have bombers like SU-24s in Afghanistan with the kind of reach that extends into the Gulf and the Straits. Are they improving their capability for the struggle in Afghanistan itself as it would appear, or have they reached the point already where they are committed to a policy of developing a base structure primarily intended for strategic military purposes in surrounding countries? I would welcome comments and guidance on this from people who are in a position to know, recognizing the fact that some of these things cannot be spelled out in detail. At the point where we can clearly say that the Soviets are seriously developing their facilities in Afghanistan with larger strategic purposes in the region in mind, the talk of a political solution becomes irrelevant. Their investment will certainly grow to the extent that they become committed to strategic bases in Afghanistan, so to me it is a watershed issue.

Now I would like to make one or two more comments about what has been said this morning on the destruction of the monarchy in 1973. Clearly, I think, from all my encounters with Soviets individually and in the literature, this was the point of departure—as Ambasssador Hyder says. Having removed the one source of legitimacy and unity that had, historically, made Afghanistan as a state possible, the anxieties of neighboring states, whether it was the Soviet Union, Iran, or others, were bound to grow. An entirely new situation was created. Certainly, in operational terms in 1975, it is clear from the evidence that the Soviets began to give a kind of support and recognition to, and become involved with, the Communist movement in Afghanistan in a way that had never been true before. This was a qualitative change in their whole approach. They were trying to create the opportunity for a Communist regime in Afghanistan if they felt the situation required it, and they felt the situation probably would. This is very important, not only with respect to the minutia of what happened in 1978, but also in terms of the present situation. With the monarchy gone, it seems to me that the Soviets do not believe in the capacity of any Afghan regime to be viable or stable or, from their point of view, a reliable partner with which to deal without a very substantial infusion of their influence and control. The degree and nature of that control are issues that may still be open for negotiation. But the removal of the monarchy created an inherently unstable situation in the eyes of the Soviets and changed the whole ball game. In this context, Hafizullah Amin was not seen merely as a leftist deviationist whose policies stimulated the insurgency. He was seen as unreliable in a much broader sense—as an unpredictable Pushtun nationalist, as a leader who, and this is really a key point, had a strong personality and organizational ability. He represented an important human factor in the situation. He had created a machine in the army that was much more viable and important as an instrument of control than anything that the Parchamis had been able to create within the military. As the Soviets saw it, the fact that this personal loyalty structure existed within the army made it impossible to deal with the situation in any way other than through the introduction of Soviet forces, quite apart from all the other things they did not like about Amin. It was not enough to get rid of Amin alone, because you had the whole army to worry about. To this day, it has not been purged of many Khalqis.

Finally, on the point that Major Kortanek made that the Soviets had not yet engaged in hot pursuit and punitive military measures in Pakistan, one very important reason for this restraint is the fact that they entered into the UN negotiations, whether or not you take these seriously. They are intended, by Pakistan certainly, to restrain such punitive action. And the other side of the coin is that the Soviets are increasingly frank in explaining that if this is not going to go anywhere, that kind of restraint will not hold. I have heard a very prominent Soviet at the UN say to me (call this disinformation or whatever you want, but the fact that it has been said is worth relating): "If they decide that nothing is possible at the diplomatic level, they will not rely entirely on Afghan forces to deal with the camps in Pakistan." They are making threats of hot pursuit, not only by the Afghan forces but by the Soviet forces. They say they will take out the camps that are being used by the *mujahidin* in Pakistan.

Louis Dupree: That means at least 300 camps.

Selig S. Harrison: Well, whatever the number, they talk of about eighty.

Thomas E. Gouttierre: The whole question of this division of a north/south Afghanistan has a lot of relevance when we consider what might be some of the alternatives. The first time I got involved with this kind of discussion was at the MESA (Middle East Studies Association) meetings in Washington in the fall of 1980. There, Jack Shroder, who is a geologist from our center and who has been quite interested in developments in Afghanistan, made some suggestions. He said we would likely see a number of things develop over the next couple of years. The Soviets had a particular interest in harnessing the watershed of the Amu Darya, because it had a flow comparable to the Nile. They were concerned with the drying up of the Aral Sea and Kara Kum canal. He feels strongly that the development plans in that area, which would include northern Afghanistan, the effort they are putting into development, and the dependency they seem to be developing on things like gas, for their industries in Soviet Central Asia, are indicative of this approach.

The matter relating to the Soviet Central Asian peoples is always an interesting one that gets discussed at various panels and conferences. We were just at one in Chicago where Professor Alexandre Bennigsen made some very enlightening comments. But you find a certain on again, off again, or black and white kind of perspective. Some people feel that the emphasis on the Central Asian peoples relating to the question of Afghanistan itself is overdrawn, both as a reason for why the Soviets may have done what they did or what they may do later.

Others feel that this is a very important question for both of those considerations. Are you talking, Eden, about some kind of timetable on the relocation policy? Is that going on now to any significant degree, or do you think that Tajiks, Uzbeks, or Turkmen could be introduced in northern Afghanistan right now with any degree of security? If not now, when would this be an active policy? Is this a part of the Soviet scheme or is this something they are using for the short term that will eventually have some kind of long-term benefit?

Eden Naby: I spoke of relocation in two spheres. First, there is currently under way what is the first, at least in recent years, attempt to more or less forceably relocate Tajiks within the Soviet Union outside their own republic—outside the Muslim areas. And second, I spoke about the possible future relocation of Soviet Central Asian Muslims, particularly from the rural areas where there is overpopulation and not enough agricultural jobs at present, into northern Afghanistan. This is not a policy that we see in operation now, and I do not think we will see it as long as the resistance movement is active in the northern part of the country. It necessarily calls for the development of rural agriculture areas along Soviet collective models. I do not see it occurring now, but I see it as a very real possibility, particularly in view of the fact that Central Asian support troops continue to be used in the country and that there does not appear to be reluctance to use Central Asians in Afghanistan.

Sabahuddin Kushkaki: The Afghans have fought the Soviets for four years, if you just count the time when they invaded Afghanistan, although we started fighting the Communist regime since 1978. It is longer than the Soviets fought in World War II. They have brought in all their sophisticated weaponry, yet with all the problems the Afghan resistance is facing, the Soviets have not been able to break the backbone of the Afghan jehad. It is not correct to say that the Soviets are winning. We should not assume that a superpower, although as strong as the Soviets, is successful in Afghanistan. Certainly, all the reports we have had from the resistance movement groups from inside Afghanistan indicate the Afghan resistance has conducted one of the best periods of their fighting this last summer. All the reports indicated that the Afghan resistance was more successful than at any other time. But this does not mean that we should be overconfident. The Afghan resistance is suffering from disunity; it is suffering from lack of equipment and weapons. The Afghan resistance is not really becoming a sophisticated kind of organization which will sustain itself for a longer period. It is largely deprived of the intellectual and educated elite of the Afghans, who are mostly now living in the West. But at the same time, to assume that the enemy can have it own way in Afghanistan just because it is a superpower is incorrect. The Afghans have proved that it cannot.

As an Afghan who has witnessed the Soviet penetration in Afghanistan over many years, at least over the past three decades, I would also like to point out that we should not look for too fast and too hasty actions on the part of the Soviet Union. The Soviet Union's policy is a very patient and long-term kind of policy. What they are trying to do right now is consolidate their position in Afghanistan without alarming or signaling to the outside world that they are going to penetrate further. They are not going to, for example, create trouble for Pakistan immediately. That is probably why they are having negotiations with the Pakistanis. They do not want to give the outside world—the international community—the impression that Afghanistan is a first step forward for the Soviets and the next step is going to be Pakistan or Iran.

Once they consolidate their position in Afghanistan, they will not penetrate to neighboring areas by overt military action. They did not wish to come into Afghanistan militarily. They wanted to have their way in Afghanistan in a very quiet and discreet manner. Over all these years they worked to make Afghanistan militarily and economically dependent on the Soviet Union. At one stage the Soviet leadership, and this is documented, even gave promises to the Afghan leaders that they have nothing to do with the "hooligans," meaning the Communist Party in Afghanistan: "You can do anything with them you want—we want to have the best kind of relations with the government of Afghanistan." They were at one time trying to tell the Afghan leadership that they had no interest in recruiting Communists or developing or helping to develop the Communist Party in Afghanistan. But when Afghanistan started its democratic reforms the Soviet Union—it is also proved by facts and the actions of the Soviet Embassy and KGB—actively engaged in recruiting a Communist Party in Afghanistan. The Soviet Union is doing its work in a different way than our friends in the West think. They are doing it in a very quiet, sophisticated manner, so that it should not cause too much alarm among the outside world. They are trying to consolidate their position in Afghanistan first. And you will see what they will do eventually to Pakistan and Iran.

Marian K. Leighton: I am interested in what you said about consolidating their power. Consolidation does not necessarily mean that the Soviets have to pacify the country completely. Should some opportunity arise in Iran or Pakistan, the Soviets probably would wish to take advantage of it, even if the war in Afghanistan is still underway. The fact that the resistance is still active in Afghanistan would not necessarily prevent the Soviet Union from using Afghanistan as a springboard for adventures beyond its borders. The country need not be completely pacified, so long as the Soviets have certain installations where they can deploy their weaponry and troops for use outside Afghanistan.

Sabahuddin Kushkaki: Yes, it can be like that. But what the Soviet Union would like to do would be what I told you, because they don't want to create greater alarm among the international community. They want to do it patiently and on a long-term basis. Maybe there will be opportunities for them to grab—and they will grab them then.

Laurent Carrel: I appreciate that we opened the discussion with the presentation of Mr. Valenta, because he has a thorough understanding of the Soviet military doctrine and military strategy. Every time we discuss Soviet policy, whether in Afghanistan or somewhere else, there are very few people who have that understanding.

My first remark deals with the decision-making process before the invasion. I think one point which has not yet been raised, is that not only did the Soviets miscalculate the strength of the resistance forces within Afghanistan, and the bravery of the *mujahidin,* but also they did not foresee the fast decay of the regular Afghan army. They did not anticipate that they would have to take over a very large share of the ground fighting. This was a very important factor why they did so badly in the beginning.

The second point concerns the statement of Mr. Valenta that they want to win the war—this is their goal. Mr. Valenta estimated that they would need about 500,000 men to do so. I could agree with both statements, and indeed the Soviets are aware that they would have to commit much larger forces to win militarily. At present not only the military price but also the political price they would have to pay in terms of loss of presige in Third World countries is too high for them. Presently the Soviets are not trying to occupy or pacify the countryside. Instead, they want to keep the war cheap and nasty; they resort to scorched earth tactics; they subvert the resistance; they infiltrate informants. In other words they are trying to win the war by attrition of the freedom fighters.

With my third remark I would like to challenge the opinion raised by Dr. Leighton that we cannot talk about a tactical failure of the Soviet ground forces. Militarily speaking, one can talk about a tactical failure in every respect—even taking into consideration the modifications they made, the tactics they changed, and the new weapons they introduced. In terms of counterinsurgency operations, of command, control, and communications (C3), small-unit actions, night operations, and low morale, poor training, and lack of competence of their noncommissioned and junior officers—their battle effectiveness has to be considered a tactical failure. The Soviets—after four years of fighting—are still unable to cope with the Afghan situation. This is one reason why they have to resort to their cruel policy against the civilian population.

It is true that they are still there and the costly fighting goes on. I agree with Mr. Kushkaki's statement that the resistance fighters are doing increasingly better, especially during the summer operations. One thing we should not forget is that the Soviet Union repeats one mistake the United States made in Vietnam. They have a fast rotation system; they may have rotated over 500,000 military personnel in Afghanistan. Officers may serve as little as six months in Afghanistan. When you read interviews of captured Soviet soldiers or unmailed letters found on casualties, you realize that what they experienced is totally different from what they expected. Nobody can tell me that this is not going to have an impact. Certainly the returning witnesses of the war are not going to have the same impact on Soviet society as Vietnam veterans did in the United States. But within the Soviet military forces they may eventually have an impact. More and more people are going to tell the Soviet people that the fight is still going on, and that it has been going on now for four years and may well continue.

Seyed Qassem Reshtia: Dr. Valenta was correct when he said that there is no single factor, or two or three factors, which prompted the Russians to invade Afghanistan. I too, avoid the views of offensive and defensive motives. Rather, I would say positive and negative. Let me address the point of view and the version of the Afghans about these reasons and factors.

First, it should be remembered that throughout their troubled history the Russians' main foreign policy objectives have been consistent and unchanging. This is caused by their geographic position, a vast country spreading across two continents surrounded on three sides by powerful neighbors. This situation has not changed significantly for the last three centuries, despite the profound changes which have taken place since the Soviet Union achieved the rank of a great world power. Even after the October Revolution of 1917 the main foreign policy objectives remained as before. Although this may appear strange, it is nevertheless understandable. Despite many changes in the regions and changes in the USSR's frontiers in Europe after World War II, the country still remains hemmed in on three sides, and as far from warm waters as before with only limited access to the high seas.

It is in this context that Afghanistan acquired a special significance for Moscow in recent years. Afghanistan's geographic and strategic position, as well as its geopolitical importance, can be decisive in the realization of the twofold objectives of Soviet foreign policy in this region. These are, first, free access to the high seas, the warm waters of the Indian Ocean, and the oil fields of the Persian Gulf, which would presumably result in countering and neutralizing American and other Western influence. And second, to contain and effectively restrain the People's Republic of China. With these objectives in mind, the Soviets began penetrating Afghanistan with economic help a quarter of a century ago. From the fifties onward the Soviets have tried to change Afghanistan fundamentally. They invested over $3 billion to develop—for their own ends—transport and communications systems and to train technical, military, and civilian personnel under Soviet instructors. After all these preparations the Soviets have decided to resume their march toward the Indian Ocean, halted a century ago by the battle of Panjdeh in 1885 on the northern frontier of Afghanistan. (A battle fought on 30 March 1885 between Afghan and Russian forces north of Herat in what is now the Turkmen SSR. The crisis following the Afghan defeat brought Great Britain and Russia close to war, but ultimately resulted in the demarcation of the Russo-Afghan border from Iran to the Amu Darya river in 1887.)

First, Afghanistan had to be physically occupied and brought soundly into the Soviet orbit. To this end the monarchy was overthrown in 1973, as five years later was the republican government headed by Prince Da'ud, which had replaced the monarchy. Both coups d'état had been prepared and led by Marxist groups and Soviet officers. The hastily prepared and ill-conceived programs of turning Afghanistan into a socialist state undertaken by the first Marxist government of Afghanistan ran into unforeseen and serious opposition from the traditional Muslim population. Toward the end of 1979 the Kremlin leaders were suddenly faced with the first failure of their Afghan adventure. They had planned on a fairly long period of transition under the direction of Afghan puppet leaders to prepare the country for full absorption into the camp of the socialist countries. Faced with the total bankruptcy of the Kabul regime, the Soviets realized they had two alternatives only, either to abandon their Marxist puppets and watch them be replaced by Muslim nationalists, or to intervene directly to save the regime which presented the first step toward the broader Soviet objectives. The Soviet party Politburo and the Soviet government opted for the second alternative. Red army units invaded Afghanistan on December 27, 1979, and overthrew the Marxist government of Hafizullah Amin. They replaced it with that of his rival Babrak Karmal, who had been living in exile in Prague for a year.

This is the present position of the Soviet plan of action, which, far from being completed, is merely in its first phase—albeit an important and decisive one. Before detailing this plan, the implementation of which is now under way, it must be remembered that since the reign of Peter the Great and Czarina Catherine II up to the October Revolution, whenever a southward march for the conquest of India and for gaining an opening to the Indian Ocean was considered, Afghanistan was regarded as the only route to the successful realization of such a plan. Despite the great changes of the last sixty years this view has not changed. Today, as yesterday, Moscow strategists believe Afghanistan to be the key to the success of such an undertaking. Therefore, Afghanistan is extremely important in Soviet global strategy, because as a base and springboard it would allow large-scale operations to any place within the region. Thus the Soviet Union would secure a total superiority in Asia.

This was a complete departure from the status quo policy followed by the USSR in this sensitive region since World War II. However, it was the only logical outcome of a long preparation and it would be a mistake to think that that decision was made without prior consideration of its consequences. Moscow was well aware of the weakness and lack of experience of the young Afghan Communist Party and the obvious hostility of the Afghans toward communism. However, after a complete break with President Da'ud, the Soviet leaders saw no other solution except to try this policy. The international situation and to a certain extent the internal problems of Afghanistan's neighbors favored such a decision. It should not be forgotten that in 1978 political life in Pakistan was overshadowed by the crisis caused by the trial of ex–prime minister Zulfikar Ali Bhutto. In Iran warning signs of a popular revolt against the autocratic regime of the shah had began to appear, slowly paralyzing the machinery of government. India itself, a potential victim of Soviet expansionism, was suffering from political disputes within the ruling Congress Party. Thus, an atmosphere of uncertainty and ambiguity was created which might encourage the new leaders of Peking to try an opportunistic reconciliation. However, earlier preparation for bringing Afghanistan within the Soviet orbit began long ago, and nothing had to be done except to fix its timing, and this depended largely on the international situation.

Zia-ul-Islam Ansari: I would like to add two points to the background which has been given to us by Professor Valenta. One, I would like to remind you of the conversations between Seyed Jamal-ad-Din al-Afghani (1838-97, a leading Islamic scholar and political activist of the nineteenth century known primarily as the ideologist of pan-Islamic thought) and Randolph Churchill in 1887. Afghani told Churchill that if the Russians were allowed to stay in Merv and Panjdeh for five years, in the future there would be no India, no Afghanistan, no Iran, and no Anatolia. Now as Professor Dupree has painted the picture of 2,000 years, we come to the same conclusion. There are two aspects to their actions, one the danger to their own security given by the Soviets, and the other, expansionist design particularly aiming at the Gulf area. Professor Valenta mentioned that both arguments had to be taken into consideration. I think the ideological factor is more important than the Gulf factor. In 1930, Dr. Mohammed Iqbal (1873-1938), in his speech giving reasons why Pakistan should be created, stated that the only solution to the communal problem of India was that these five Muslim majority provinces should be grouped together to form an independent state. When this state came into being, Dr. Iqbal visualized that it would provide a defense for the subcontinent from invasion from the north. This to him was a factor which was coming in the wake of the creation of Pakistan. I draw your attention to the situation which erupted in 1979-80. Mr. Kushkaki has pointed out that apparently it was an abrupt action. Why? Because we have not studied the factors as deeply as the Soviets. The problem of the past in the subcontinent was that the invaders were allowed to pass through to Delhi; Iqbal visualized a new role for this area. Pakistan will provide the defense for the subcontinent from the invasions coming from the north. And this is why, in 1947, Afghanistan was the only country, under King Zahir Shah's government, to oppose Pakistan's entry into the United Nations.

Professor Valenta has suggested that if they leave, the understanding given to the West by the Soviets will remain true—that this will be a buffer state. The fault lies with the rest of the world for believing that the Soviet Union will keep or will be contented with this buffer state. It reminds me of a speech in 1976 by David D. Newsome, who was undersecretary of the State Department. He made reference in a speech at a university that the United States considered this area as within the Soviet sphere of influence. This document was published in Pakistan, supplied by USIS, and widely circulated and published by all Pakistani newspapers.

It was mentioned by Major Kortanek that we should have a rapprochement with the post-Khomeini regime in Iran. The Soviets must have done some homework on the Iranian revolution. The latter was not a phenomenon that came up abruptly in 1978 or 1979, but had been going on for the past decade. This is a type of revolution which is in many fields attractive to the Muslims of Central Asia. The concept of the Islam prevailing in the world today, or a few years ago, was that of an ideology or a religion maintaining a sort of status quo. But the sort of religion coming up in various Islamic countries, including Pakistan and Iran, is a different kind of philosophy, a different kind of thinking. In the Iranian Revolution, Khomeini and his colleagues described what Islam stands for: upgrading, uplifting the have-nots. The Muslims in Central Asia, where the Soviets say the danger to their security lies, are after all citizens of a so-called superpower. In 1980 it was reported by *The New York Times* Moscow correspondent that the official organ of the Communist Party of Kirgizistan mentioned in an editorial that the feeling of Muslim nationalism was gaining ground in these regions and must be nipped in the bud—otherwise you would have a serious problem. Mind you, this was a comment by an organ of the Communist Party of Kirgizistan warning the central Communist Party, so this is not to be brushed aside. The Iranian Revolution was taking place in the same decade as the invasion of Afghanistan and with the slogan that Islam was not a religion for maintaining the status quo. With this sort of thinking current, the Soviets were doing their homework.

Harmon E. Kirby: Leaving aside what Undersecretary Newsome may or may not have said (I think the quote is inaccurate), I wanted to come to the Iranian factor. In the Department of State we do not pretend, any more then this group has pretended this morning, that we know why the Soviets wandered into Afghanistan. We spend a lot of time now looking at these things, I think largely for the same reasons that we are having this discussion in the belief that, if we can get some clues as to why they went in, somehow that might provide a clue to how they might be persuaded to get out. I tend to identify with the thesis that we heard from Ambassador Neumann this morning on the incremental nature of decision making and the way that bureaucracies frequently blunder into decisions. Within almost any bureaucracy there are groups with their own sort of private agendas. As opportunities arise, some will say, "Let's go for this reason," "Let's go for that reason," and so on. My hunch is that if this were an academic examination with the following question: "Did the Soviets go in for the fourteen reasons that we have heard this morning?" I would probably mark the box "all of the above," with some things counting for them more than others.

The Iranian factor has interested me a great deal during the past year. We, in conversation with Soviet diplomats and academicians, around the world and here, where it seems that it is never quite carefully explained, find it coming out of these Soviet interlocutors more than any other single word, phrase, or idea. It comes in a variety of ways. They may be blowing smoke; they may be trying to find a retrospective reason for putting the best face on something that to a considerable extent had turned out to be untenable. But I remember private discussions we had with some Soviet academicians about a year ago. They talked about the uncertainties in Iran in 1979, and their concern appeared twofold. One, that somehow, in some mysterious way, if they did not move at a time of perceived uncertainty and weakness in the West, the West might get itself together and make a comeback into Iran. But more importantly, they were worried about the implications of the Khomeini revolution, "fundamentalism," first of all Afghanistan and then in their own Central Asian republics. One of these prominent academicians argued in these words: "Why doesn't the world let us alone in Afghanistan? Can't you understand that we are doing the world's business? A fundamentalist Afghanistan would not be in the interest of the Soviet Union; it wouldn't be in the interest of the United States; it wouldn't be in anybody's interest. So leave us alone." Well, we had some rather sharp rejoinders. We replied that he seemed to be offering for the people of Afghanistan, and indeed the world, the peace of the grave, and we found this unacceptable. We felt very strongly on that. Again, there were strong indications that from about the late spring of this year, in various captials around the world, Soviet diplomats, whether under instruction or not I do not pretend to know, indicated that they would like to find a honorable way out: "We would like to arrive at a negotiated settlement that would allow us to withdraw. But even if we were successful through the UN negotiating mechanism or otherwise, even if we were successful in finding a negotiated solution with Pakistan, that still wouldn't take care of the Iranian problem." Usually, the argument then trials off, and you get some fanciful things about *mujahidin* who are not now over in the Iranian sector going over the way and hitting Soviet troops and DRA (the Democratic Republic of Afghanistan—the official designation of the Kabul regime) forces in Afghanistan through Iran. At that stage, the argument intellectually tends to break down. The subject of Iran keeps coming up, with all its uncertainties, in almost every conversation about which you hear. I do not know how profound this is with the Soviets. I would like to leave the question with those of you who are nearer to being Soviet specialists than I whether this is profound or whether it is just a rationale.

Thomas E. Gouttierre: I wanted to ask just one question of Jiri: To what degree do you think the Soviets are willing to subjugate Afghanistan, given all that we have talked about? Particularly in light of what Dr. Carrel said here today.

Zia-ul-Islam Ansari: The United States should accept and have a rapprochement with these countries, Pakistan and Iran, and take their ideology as progressive Islam—not as militant Islam. This will ultimately prove a threat to the Soviets through the Muslims of Central Asia, and will give you a real alternative in the future. Somehow to achieve good relations with Khomeini and try to persuade him not to describe the United States as "Satan number 1" and the Soviet Union as "Satan number 2," but to get him to reverse the order.

Jiri Valenta: I hope I did not leave the impression (and I do not recall saying so) that I adhere to either of the two interpretations—that the invasion of Afghanistan was either exclusively offensive or exclusively defensive in motivation. Both are misleading and tend to blur other considerations, particularly developments "on the ground." Both explanations neglect the nature of the 1978 coup, that it was a Communist takeover. What we are discussing is *why* and *how* the Soviets invaded, and we are continuing to learn about it. But we should not forget that our concern over Afghanistan began only after the invasion and not in 1978 (the year of the coup).

If there is any pattern emerging from Afghanistan, it is *how* a country merits "fraternal assistance." This is a phenomenon made possible by the takeover by Leninist forces and the Soviets' ability to commit themselves militarily, the later depending upon a number of circumstances. Something that we can also study here are past U.S. mistakes. During the invasion of Afghanistan we were preoccupied with Iran. So, for U.S. policymakers and diplomats, the question is, can we manage two crises at the same time, and how?

3

The Afghan Resistance Movement

Eden Naby

A well-known Afghan patriot many years prior to the events that led to the Soviet invasion of his country used to take pride in the invincibility of his fellow Afghans by pointing out that one of the earliest historic conquerors of that region, Alexander of Macedonia, fought long and bitter battles to secure the geographic entity now forming Afghanistan. Afghans, as this poet would have it, then and throughout history have evicted intruders or absorbed them.

This attitude, rather than being manufactured in the imagination of a twentieth-century poet, was handed down to him and others from past generations as Afghans have resisted pressures, especially during the last centuries, from outsiders. In recent history the pressure has been exerted by the two chief rival colonial powers of the region, the Soviet Union and Britain. The traditional Afghan attitude of independence, wedded more or less successfully to religious principles of holy war and holy terrain, forms the psychological basis for the Afghan resistance movements today, both in the political and military spheres.

There exists a more cynical argument for why the Afghans had remained independent until the Soviet invasion of December 1979: This argument, put forward especially in India, states that the Afghans remained relatively untouched by colonial powers because little military, economic, or political gain would accrue from possession of their country. Today the Soviet Union sees advantages to controlling Afghanistan: Easy access to the Persian Gulf, greater ability to pressure Iran and Pakistan and thereby gain leverage over the West, are but a couple. Therefore, the argument would have it, Afghans face for the first time an invader both powerful enough and determined to posses their land. For this reason, past history of successful Afghan ejection of intruders cannot determine the outcome of this confrontation. There are many among the Afghan elite who suspect that the Soviets are less interested in Afghans than in Afghanistan: that Soviet reasons for entering Afghanistan arise less from the ideological need to defend a nascent (1978) socialist regime than from the military and political advantage gained from possessing Afghan territory. The pursuit of a policy that aims at depopulating Afghanistan through terror and wholesale devastation referred to as "migratory genocide" would appear to support this reasoning.[1]

Although there appears to be much truth in the arguments put forward predicting the early destruction of any Afghan resistance to Soviet aims, the Afghan resistance has continued with very little outside encouragement for as long as either world war and on a scale unprecedented in previous Russian experience in Central Asia or Eastern Europe. This resistance continues despite considerable suffering from dislocation (about 5 million internal and external refugees), disruption of lifestyle (caused by the Soviet scorched earth policy among other things), death, disease, and starvation, and widespread execution and torture in Soviet-administered prisons. The explanation for the strength of the resistance appears to lie in the nature of Afghanistan and the characteristics of its inhabitants. Regional politics and international tensions, although significant to the rhetoric of the conflict, would not in themselves sustain this drama for this many years. Therefore I would like to examine the Afghan resistance movements from the historical perspective of the past twenty years, and to explore the tactics, leadership, and psychosocial profile of participants less in light of guerrilla movements in general than in light of Afghan character.

Information and Propaganda

Information about the Afghan resistance is scarce. Soviet-dominated Kabul bars Western reporters with the exception of either those known to be sympathetic to Moscow or those willing to move under close supervision and remain confined to Kabul.[2] International agencies such as the Red Cross and Amnesty International are barred altogether. Reports from the countryside where resistance is highest, generally come from journalists, some experienced and others clearly intent on the personal adventure involved in making the harrowing walk into the Afghan countryside under fire or threat of fire.[3] Most Westerners entering the country have no knowledge of any of the languages spoken by Afghans and conversely, few Afghan fighters know Western languages. Communication remains at a primitive level from several perspectives.

Supplementing these meager sources are the field reports from humanitarian organizations, especially French medical teams that have been entering the country illegally since 1980 to minister to the ill and wounded. Thanks to reports from Médecins sans Frontières, Aide Médicale Internationale, and Médicins du Monde, a considerable amount of information about specific regions such as the Panjshir valley northeast of Kabul finds its way to the West.[4] Much of the combat area however, remains shrouded in secrecy lifted only sporadically by reports appearing in the Peshawar resistance press. Particularly unknown are the areas of Afghanistan bordering on Iran in the west and the Soviet Muslim areas to the north. Although we hear of heavy fighting in the north, especially the use of Soviet aircraft and troops stationed in the Soviet Central Asian republics not part of the official 110,000 contingent in the country, few Westerners have ventured so far from the relative safety of the Pakistani border to report on the war in that region.[5]

The Afghan resistance press, both from Peshawar and from various points inside the country, has served only to inform about conditions from the Afghan perspective. This press has largely been unavailable to the world community however, due to the language barrier. With the exception of some materials in Arabic (for the Gulf region), little appears in languages other than Pushtu and Afghan Persian (Dari).[6] None of these publications can hope to replace the video and radio reporting that helped to make the Vietnam war so vivid and repulsive.[7]

Confronting these meager sources of information stands the vast array of information from Moscow and Kabul intended for outside consumption. The *Kabul New Times,* the English-language newspaper that continuously carries articles and pictures claiming success for the puppet regime and the Kabul army, is not available in Kabul except to diplomats.[8] Likewise the Soviet internal press only began publishing articles about the Afghan front after 1982 when it became clear that the war would continue for the near future and that controlled news to counteract rumors and adverse information from the West was necessary to shape Soviet opinion in the accepted direction. Outside the Soviet block, use of the pro-Moscow leftist press to sway opinion in the West has been in effect since 1981.[9] In sum, information about the Afghan resistance, in particular about internal fighting, has been sparce due partially to the nature of guerrilla warfare and to the inaccessibility of Afghanistan geographically, and now, politically.

Afghans, Middle Eastern Guerrilla Movements, and Soviet Muslims

The Afghan resistance is unusual in that it pits a small, fragmented society only gradually beginning to enter the portals of modern technology against an industrialized, technologically advanced nation geared psychologically and materially to conduct war. Most nonregional specialists, particularly experts on Soviet affairs, predicted a quick defeat of the Afghans and the absorption of Afghanistan into the Soviet sphere. Some of these same experts regarded such noncommunist-nation tactics as the Olympic boycott and the grain embargo as so much empty gesturing. Nevertheless international censure of Soviet action has lent greatly to the resolve of such organizations as the Islamic Conference and to Pakistan's firm position vis-à-vis internal threats and Soviet blandishments. Moreover, the censure has aided Afghan morale despite the lack of positive action such as continuation of the embargoes and effective supply to the resistance of usable, sophisticated arms.

Despite the four years of Afghan resistance, many Soviet studies experts continue to view it as an ephemeral aberration that will succumb to superior force at any time.[10] Belief in the inevitability of this outcome is based on the Eastern European experience and on Vietnam. Two facets tend to be disregarded in this analysis: first, superpower experience with Muslim societies has generally shown that intrusion of an alien force or culture has, over time, led to a backlash. This backlash has often been based on religio-national ideology, been popular with both intellectuals and masses, and has swept away or eroded political domination from the outside. The case of Algerian resistance to French absorption may be cited as an example. The phenomenon, however, has earlier antecedents during the early twentieth century under the influence of Arabs and non-Arabs such as Muhammad Abduh (1849-1905) and Jamal-ad-Din al-Afghani (1838/39-1897).

Nor does the Russian and Soviet confrontation with Muslim society provide the example of pacification of religio-national resistance that some would view as a model for termination of the Afghan crisis. Long-term prospects for retaining Soviet Muslims in subservience by granting them equal status with Russians as the new "Soviet man" appear dim.[11] Aside from the demographic challenge that Soviet Muslims pose to the currently dominant Russian population of the Soviet Union, there are indications that Moscow feels a need to intimate use of force, or actually use force in Soviet Central Asia even now to quell popular unrest over religious issues. Frequent articles in the controlled Soviet Muslim press recounting the defeat of the Basmachis (the Bolshevik era indigenous resistance to Soviet absorption) and glorifying both the KGB and the Border Guards indicate concern during the last five years about disquiet over internal matters.[12] The confrontation between local Kazakhs and the military in Alma Ata over the internment of Muslim casualities of the Afghan war forced the use of tanks to quell unrest.[13] Indications are that new generations of Soviet Muslims, though seemingly Russified in that large numbers are bilingual in Russian, sense their separateness, are more assertive regarding control over their affairs, and insofar as the Soviet state structure will allow have begun to express their assertiveness. Both Islamic spirituality and pride in their Islamic heritage contribute to their self-confidence.[14]

The second factor militating for the continuation of the Afghan resistance lies in the nature of guerrilla movements, in the Middle East in particular. Where guerrilla movements are based on a combination of large numbers of refugees living on foreign but friendly soil and on the popularity of the resistance (and unpopularity of the imposed regime) among the populace, they have been hard to overcome. The Palestinians, though fragmented and beleaguered, have neither been absorbed by their Arab coethnics nor erased from the political map of the Middle East. The Kurds continually rise to threaten Iran, Iraq, and Turkey partly because of the popularity of their cause among the masses. These examples, drawn from contemporary history of the Middle East, are but two that provide a perspective on the Afghan resistance movement. Early-twentieth-century history yields other examples of resistance movements against superior military force: the Indian independence movement is one and Muslim resistance to inclusion in the Soviet empire is another. The latter proved unsuccessful at the time due to reasons still only vaguely understood in the West. Moscow's restrictions on research on this topic by outsiders would indicate its sensitivity to the issue despite regular allusions to the similar fate awaiting Afghan resistance.[15]

Soviet historians and international experts who cite the apparent success of the Soviet Union in suppressing the Basmachis as reason for their certain eradication of the Afghan resistance probably share with Moscow the belief in the similarity of the two movements. From the little we know about the Basmachi movement however, it would appear to differ in key respects from the Afghan resistance.

While both movements are aimed against the Soviets, the Basmachis were fighting a colonizing power while the Afghans focus on the communist nature of the Soviet presence. Probably as a consequence of this, the Afghans base their opposition on Islam, adopting the reestablishment of a traditional or revolutionary Islamic state in their country as the positive reason for forcing the departure of the Soviet military. The Basmachis, on the other hand, were badly divided among those who were mesmerized by relative Russian modernity, the old elite who feared the loss of status, and a tribal rural element who merely wanted freedom from Russian encroachment. The use of religious terminology by the second and third elements did not imply an understanding, let alone an aspiration, for the establishment of an Islamic state. Thus, whereas the Afghan resistance, divided though it is, typically espouses one form or other of Islamic ideology and is united in this goal, among key elements of the Central Asian resistance there were deep divisions based on outlook as well as sociocultural backgrounds.

For these reasons the Soviets were able to manipulate one element of the Central Asian population against the other quite successfully in the armed forces and as figurehead leaders. The contrary is true in Afghanistan. In the latter, therefore, they are forced to use other tactics also used previously: the attempts to coopt children and the killing of the old intelligentsia and leadership.

In the international and regional spheres too lie contrasts between the two resistance movements. During the 1920s there was no widespread Muslim insurgency or self-assertiveness as there is today. Afghanistan and Iran, the front-line states, were engaged in emulating Western-style modernization and secularization. They viewed the Central Asian struggle as remote and aided little their largely Turkic and non-Iranian-speaking neighbors. This situation too differs considerably today, as does the influence exerted by large numbers of Afghan refugees in neighboring countries.

Of great importance too is the independence and relatively wealthy status of Muslim countries. Moral and material support from these countries are signficant to the Afghan resistance. They were nonexistant during the Basmachi period. In the same manner, the international attention focused on Afghanistan aids the resistance as does the Sino-Soviet confrontation.

Without continued world attention to the Afghan resistance however, the practical differences between the Afghan and the Central Asian opposition to the Soviets would be virtually meaningless. For this reason the Soviets harass journalists and prevent, to the extent possible, information about the Afghan resistance from being disseminated. The Basmachis disappeared after about fourteen years (1932), leaving few written records of their goals and accomplishments save for adverse materials available from their opponents. The Afghan resistance, whatever its final outcome, has understood the power of the press. A preliminary bibliography of the resistance press lists about 305 published items, excluding the periodical press.[16] Their own efforts together with those of foreign humanitarians, journalists, and others may turn out to be the critical point of difference between the Afghan resistance and Basmachis.

The Mujahidin

The motivation of the Afghan resistance has varied with time, region, and political group. But, as the Soviet invasion of their country approaches its sixth year, the primary motivation has crystalized as a struggle waged to free Muslim Afghan land from an atheistic enemy. For this reason the resistance uses religious terms such as *jehad* (holy war) for its struggle against the Soviet Union and its Afghan communist supporters, and calls the individual who fights a *mujahid,* the plural of which becomes *mujahidin*. The person who dies for the cause becomes a martyr *(shahid)*. All these terms are based on Islamic usage and are therefore of Arabic origin and widely used in all Muslim countries. Iranian Marxist revolutionaries opposed to Khomeini, such as the Mujahidin-e Khalq, use similar terminology as does the current Iranian government which calls those who fall on the Iraqi front *shahid*. All factions of the Afghan fighting resistance use this terminology whether they belong to the zealously religious groups or to the moderately pious ones. Since the only claims to anti-Soviet fighters that are not Islamically motivated come from obscure Maoist forces whose existence can only be corroborated in the Kabul press, all the Afghan resistance may be correctly called Mujahidin.

The Afghan resistance came into being over a period of several years prior to the actual Soviet invasion of the country in late December 1979. The stages in which the resistance developed reflect to a large extent the political differences that continue to divide it. These stages are as follows: the period before the 1973 palace coup by Muhammad Zahir Shah's (r. 1933-73) cousin, Sardar Muhammad Da'ud (d. 1978); the period from 1973 to April 1978 which marked the beginning of the republican era in the country; the period following the bloody PDPA (combined Khalq and Parcham) coup of 1978; the period between the coup and the Soviet invasion in 1979; and finally two stages following the Soviet invasion. The progression from one stage to the next demonstrates the emergence and growth of the resistance, the forced politicization of a large segment of Afghan society previously untroubled by national political concerns, and most important, the expanding role of Islam as a motivating factor for resistance.

The Afghan political experiment in democracy (1964-73) ushered in a euphoric period when hopes swelled for governments better attuned to meet the developmental needs of the country. Not only did two small pro-Soviet parties rise among sections of the military and intellectual establishments, but a third Marxist group, as well as large numbers of centrist and rightist political groups, also emerged. The effects of this experiment in relatively democratic expression were observable in the high schools and colleges, through the printed media, and in the legislature. A very important group formed at Kabul University which dedicated itself to the ideals of restoring an Islamic society in the country. The republican coup of 1973 that toppled the monarchy was led by a man (Sardar Muhammad Da'ud) supported by the elitist pro-Soviet Marxist Party—the Parcham. The authoritarian regime in power from 1973 to 1978 regarded the Islamic groups, the non-Soviet Marxist groups, as well as the democratic groups, to be hostile to its existence. Thus the members and leaders of these groups were hunted, imprisoned, killed, or driven into exile. The seeds of one of the most significant of the political parties active in the Afghan resistance were planted during this period. Three leaders active at this time were Professor Burhanuddin Rabbani (head of the Jamiyat-e Islami Afghanistan—Islamic Society of Afghanistan), engineer Gulbuddin Hekmatyar (heading the Hizb-e Islami Afghanistan—Islamic Party of Afghanistan), and Professor Abdulraouf Sayyaf. Based in Pakistan, Rabbani and Hekmatyar attempted to stem the political direction of the Kabul regime through military and propaganda means but to no avail.

The pro-Soviet joint Khalq and Parcham coup of April 1978 fulfilled the fearful predictions made by the Islamic groups about the threat of a Communist takeover of the country. The bloody reprisals taken against most elements of society by the Communist regime together with the virulent anti-Islamic propaganda emanating from all branches of the government convinced large sectors of Afghan society that resistance to these changes was the sole means of preserving themselves and their society.

By the end of the summer of 1978, the Communist regime began to focus directly upon prominent religious leaders and arrested seventy members of the Mujadidi family alone, including the Hazrat-e Shor Bazaar, who was a leading sheik of the Naqshbandiya order of Sufis. In alarm several other Sufi leaders fled the country and formed nuclei for resistance. The second phase therefore yielded leaders who came from the traditional religious establishment and who had standing among large sectors of the Afghan population because they represented the leadership of such important Sufi orders as the Qadiriya, the Chishtiya, and the Naqshbandiya. Professor Sibqatullah Mujadidi, Pir Ahmad Gailani, and Mauvlana Muhammad Nabi Muhammadi emerged during this period.

The Soviet invasion during the last week of 1979 marks a turning point in the resistance. While prior to this the resistance had attracted ardent Muslim revolutionaries and traditionally religious elements, the invasion stirred all but the most zealous Communist Party members into action of one form or another. Relatively secularist nationalists from all walks of life—students, bureaucrats, technocrats, teachers, and professionals—took action in one of three ways. They fled the country to join the existing resistance groups in Peshawar or Iran, they joined the resistance in the countryside (especially true for military men), or collaborated with the resistance in the towns while they continued holding their jobs in the private or public sector. It is in this period, the months following the Soviet invasion, that dramatic defections took place in international forums such as the meeting of Non-aligned nations at the United Nations in New York[17] and the Afghan wrestling team in Europe. Important national figures found excuses to leave, sometimes it would seem, with the collusion of their friends, families and relatives well placed in government. Perhaps Kabul would have found persecution of Afghans of established international reputation such as Abdul Rauf Rawan Farhadi (a diplomat and scholar) and Abdul Rahman Pazhwak (a diplomat and poet) embarrassing. Remaining to staff the administrative bodies of the country are the young party recruits, and increasingly, Soviet citizens.

Over the past three years, since 1981, others have fled the country who represent a different group of persons. As tensions between the two factions of the PDPA have intensified despite Soviet efforts, Khalq faction members have also sought refuge in Pakistan or India. These include not only military men but also middle- to upper-level bureaucrats who found themselves not important enough to be protected by the Soviets (as has been Assadullah Sarwari, now exiled to the ambassadorship in Ulan Batur) while threatened especially by the Parchami-controlled Khad, the secret police.

As well-placed Afghans have left in considerable numbers so have large numbers of ordinary men and women, both from the countryside and the towns. In one way or another, the refugees have added to the ranks of the resistance.

Afghan Nationalism

All the political entities that now form the Middle East took shape relatively recently in the form that we see them today. Notwithstanding the hoary antiquity of select cultures (Egyptian, Indian, Mesopotamian, and Iranian), the present boundaries of all these states were carved under European pressure, sometimes exclusively so and at other times decisively. In many cases the boundaries are not based on geographically meaningful terrain such as rivers or mountains. Afghanistan's boundaries demonstrate this problem quite well. In Afghanistan as in many other countries, the political boundaries divide ethnic groups among two or three political entities. Lack of incentives for mobility has meant that ethnic groups straddling international borders have not moved elsewhere in the country but have remained on the border, often carrying on their seasonal routines with little regard to the paper boundaries. When the ethnic group has been small enough in any one state, it has been ignored by the ruling circles, at times oppressed and deprived from participation in the developmental infrastructure. In sum, border ethnic groups, with little exception, have not been affected by positive nationalism.

Unlike neighboring Iran where the Persians have dominated the culture and administration (if not the ruling posts) of the country for over a millenium, in Afghanistan the situation has not been as clear-cut. While true that Pushtuns (or Afghans) have dominated the area generally now forming Afghanistan, theirs has been political domination accomplished by virtue of military ability based on their tribal structure. Culturally the country has been fragmented between Persian speakers who have controlled the administrative offices as well as the literature, various Turkic speakers shared with Soviet Central Asia, and other minor groups who have maintained separate cultural, and at times political, existence, from both the Persian and Pushtu speakers. The picture is further clouded by the fact that all of Afghanistan's various ethnic groups are related to coethnics across international boundaries. In addition, Afghanistan has disputed its southern boundary with Pakistan, and has land and water disputes with Iran on the west that have barely been settled. It holds grudges against the Soviet Union which, as Czarist Russia, annexed a corner of northwestern Afghanistan in 1885. All these factors have contributed to lack of the basic elements that contribute to the development of national consciousness. The chief reason that the resistance has been unable to form a government in exile, and thus improve its bargaining position vis-à-vis the Soviets and the rest of the world, has been the lack of strong national consciousness among the major portion of the Afghan people. It is partially for this reason too that religion comes to play the major political role in molding the resistance.

Like many people of the Middle East, it is chiefly among the new generations of Afghans, particularly those born during the 1950s and 1960s, that any kind of national feeling capable of overcoming regionalism, tribalism, and ethnic affiliation occurs. These persons have been affected by the slowly activated rural education program of the 1960s—they grew up after the communications infrastructure that finally began to lay the basis for communications between the rural areas and the cities, especially Kabul, came into being. This generation also benefited from public health measures together with relative peace and prosperity. Thus it survived childhood in large numbers, and forms a substantial portion of the population. The portion of the Afghan population therefore, that has a modicum of education and a sense of identity aside from that of their forefathers is proportionally larger now than ever before. This is the generation of men and women in their twenties and thirties which carries the arms and holds the key to the present resistance.

It is also this generation that forms the basis for the membership of the PDPA, in particular its Khalq faction, currently out of power. Khalq concentrated its efforts on rural, newly educated youth, both in the military and school systems. Parcham on the other hand, began as an elitist leftist group mainly tied to the urban centers, Kabul in particular.

This generation of Afghans, although exposed to Afghan nationalism sufficiently to harbor fewer suspicions and prejudices based on ethnicity, still needs an ideology as well as leaders to maintain themselves, either as resistance or as supporters of Babrak and the Soviets. For some, Marxism and a future Afghanistan developed economically on the model of the Soviet Central Asian republics holds attraction. But increasingly, the Soviets appear to be pinning their hopes on the next generation of Afghans, whose indoctrination may be better assured through Soviet-style education at home or abroad.

In addition to a new generation of Afghans, the Soviets (and Kabul regimes since 1978) have sought the allegiance of minority ethnic groups which they have wooed with promises of cultural autonomy.[18] Their efforts in this area have been thwarted less by the sense of national indignation at the invasion than by the aversion of Turkic groups in particular to atheist Marxism. Many among Afghan Uzbeks, Kazakhs, and Turkmen, as well as Kirghiz (many of whom have been resettled in Turkey) are descendants of those who fled the Bolsheviks and collectivization in Soviet Central Asia.[19] Nonetheless, radio and television programs, publications and other opportunities for cultural expression have been granted to ethnic groups such as Turkmen, Uzbeks, Baluch, and Tajiks. Clearly this activity will not enforce Afghan nationalism but factionalism that Kabul, without Soviet might, would be hard-pressed to control. But because such opportunities increase anti-Pushtun feelings and therefore are expected to diminish support for the resistance, they have been pursued.

The appeal that Moscow and Kabul have directed toward Afghan women is reminiscent of attempts made in the 1920s to form a "surrogate proletariat" of Central Asian women to replace the undeveloped indigenous proletariat in that region.[20] Kabul's efforts in this area began under Nur Muhammad Taraki with several laws aimed at changing the customary Afghan position of women. This thrust has been modified as in recent years Kabul has attempted to build a base among the traditional tribal and religious elements through such efforts as the National Fatherland Front. Thus for example, Dr. Anahita Ratabzad, longtime mistress of Babrak Karmal, has withdrawn from the public eye while Mahbooba Karmal has been elevated to public attention. The attempt to gain the allegiance of women however, or at least the effort to create the impression for outside consumption that Kabul is seeking to improve the lot of women, continues in the English-language press. For example the latest population estimate claims that about 8.5 million women live in Afghanistan (over half of the population) and that they enjoy equal opportunities in many spheres such as work, education, and social insurance. No mention is made of the controversial attempts to change family and customary law of the pre-Soviet period.[21]

Following the Soviet invasion, Kabul has found it very hard to appeal to Afghans on the basis of patriotism and nationalism despite constant use of this theme in its various propaganda organs. Whether Kabul's loss translates into gain for the resistance however, is a question complicated by issues such as leadership and the role of Islam in the resistance.

Resistance Leadership

Past Afghan resistance to outsiders has been confined to the Pushtuns insofar as past invasions have occurred from the south, east, and west. (The Czarist annexation of Panjdeh might have been avoided had the area been occupied by Pushtuns rather than Turkmen.) Resistance has taken the form of the mobilization of tribes under their military leader, a leader of family standing with skill or charisma. Thus one sees Afghans during their history following leaders rather than pressing causes. Such successful leaders have been politically astute enough to offer their followers material incentives in addition to political preference. The limited number of institutions contributing to nation building and to the evolution of leadership from such institutions necessarily hindered the availability of leaders other than tribal or in some cases religious ones.

Among the Afghan resistance movements we can see clearly reflected the various stages of development of Afghan political society. We see tribally (or ethnically) based leaders whose followers are monoregional or even monotribal. We may also find persons of traditional religious standing whose appeal is somewhat broader. And finally we find those whose leadership role has evolved from nascent (nation-building) institutions such as the university and other schools of higher education. We may even venture to say that the absence of a military leader who has gained a wide following demonstrates how the Afghan army never fulfilled its role as an institution for integrating ethnic diversity or promoting the evolution of leaders.

Given the lack of a unified political front among the exiled groups and the impossibility of conducting country-wide political arrangements internally due to war conditions, there is no single person whose leadership of the resistance is recognized. Commander Mas'ud (Ahmad Shah Mas'ud, b. 1954) of the Panjshir valley, is regarded by many as an able person but his position as an active military commander in the field, his youth, and non-Pushtun background make him an unlikely leader for the entire resistance. The former king, Zahir Shah, also remains only in the background, in Rome, although many of the traditional and nationalist elements, and possibly even the Soviets, view him as a likely candidate for figurehead leadership of a transitional government. To date no single leader has emerged. Should one emerge, he will in all likelihood come from among those active in the resistance inside the country. Such an event may take place when the field commanders realize the extent to which the Afghan resistance negotiating position is weakened by the lack of a government-in-exile with status to reach agreement on the international level to end the bloodshed.

The leadership vacuum together with a sense of nationalism still in its infancy has left but one other force to rally the Afghan resistance: religion. The paramount question is whether Islamic solidarity combined with a growing sense of Afghan national indignation can provide the motivation for protracted struggle.

Islamic Ideology

The struggle to build an Afghan national identity began a century ago with the emergence of present-day Afghanistan. Although Pushtun dominance of politics and culture has never been challenged effectively, with the rise in urbanism and the educational and communications infrastructure, particularly over the past three decades, a new generation of Afghans was emerging who were literate in one or both of the official languages of the country—Dari (Afghan Persian) and Pushtu. Moreover, these young persons were becoming detribalized and loosening their regional ties in favor of all overall Afghan identity. For the large majority of the population, however, tribe, ethnic group, and region of origin formed the basis of identity under normal circumstances. On the whole, however, the Muslim identity of the overwhelming majority of the population (99.9 percent) dominates most relationships. The situation in the country since the Soviet invasion, however, is special. Thus even though Afghan nationalism may not provide the catalyst for continued resistance, religious fervor does.

Afghan religious zeal does not manifest itself in the same fashion as in neighboring Iran. Partially due to their predominantly Sunni rather than Shi'ite Islam, Afghans perform their religious duties without the display and emotionalism associated with contemporary Shi'ite Iran. Field experience, however, demonstrates the intensity of their faith as does the resistance practice of allowing Soviet POWs an opportunity to convert to Islam, as well as its practice of insistence on calling Marxist Afghans "nonbelievers"—infidels like the Soviet Marxists themselves.

The appeal of Islamic ideology, though widespread, is not universal, even in Afghanistan. Although much of the resistance gives some lip service to the violation of Islam as motivation for fighting the Taraki, Amin, and now the Soviet-Karmal regimes, few emphasize the necessity to liberate Afghanistan from atheists and heretics as do those groups frequently lumped together in the West as "fundamentalist." The illusion has been created over the past few years that these "fundamentalists" are relatively uniform in their uncompromising attitude toward the Soviet Union, their lack of vision for a progressive society, and their reliance on the superstitions of a dull peasantry to gain their cause. This cause is seen variously as an attempt to roll back the delicate democratic beginnings of the 1960s, put women in medieval seclusion, and create an Islamic tyranny to match that alleged to function in Iran currently. Such popular views of the Afghan resistance grow in part from the fear raised by the success of the Iranian effort to overthrow rankling Westernisms, but they are also fed by Soviet propaganda efforts aimed at destroying the ideological base of the Afghan resistance.

Negative assumptions about a significant sector of the Afghan resistance are probably based on the paradigm that any attempt to subject state to religion is reactionary. This assumption is shared by many secular Afghans, especially functionaries who have been Westernized and Western-educated. Whether this assumption has a basis in fact cannot be discussed here. However, it is important to recognize the reality that most Afghans, especially those in the resistance, see the state and Islam is inseparable. Moreover, they see their religious faith as their only salvation from the physical and material problems they face.

In recognition of the depth of Islamic commitment among Afghans, both the Soviets and Karmal have adopted three tactics to replace the tarnished religious image of the invaders and their puppets. First, they have given emphasis to the personal piety of Babrak Karmal to overcome his well-recognized nature as a profligate womanizer. Second, they have created a role for religious leaders in support of the regime, have called conferences of religious leaders and clergymen in Kabul, created avenues for exchange of religious leaders with Soviet Muslims, and have embarked on a well-advertised program to pour money into clerical salaries and reconstruction of mosques.[22] Third, Kabul has attempted to portray the resistance as un-Islamic.

Since religion plays an important role in the morale of the resistance, in its sense of purpose, and to some extent its fractured unity efforts, and since Kabul and Moscow recognize the importance of the religious issue, it would be well to analyze to the extent possible the role of religion among the resistance.

Generally the Afghan resistance falls into three categories when viewed from the Islamic perspective: the revolutionary Islamic parties, the traditional Islamic parties, and the secularists. (Among the latter may also be found certain shades of Marxist-Leninists who avoid the religious issue altogether: Rahaie (Liberation) is an example of such a group.) Although most sources for this analysis of the religious issue come from the Pakistani presses of the resistance, some publications also emanate from Kandahar. Much of the important but relatively independent internal fighting leadership allies itself with one or the other Peshawar parties. Mas'ud belongs to Rabbani's Jamiyat-e Islami as does Zabihullah who commands important sections of the guerrillas along the northern part of the country. Amin Wardak, commander in the Wardak, south of Kabul, is allied to Gailani's party, and so forth.

The revolutionary Islamic parties claim the longer history of resistance. Under this category are included the three major groups of Rabbani, Hekmatyar, and Younis Khalis, with smaller breakaway factions that have joined these three coming from the younger elements of the traditional camp. The revolutionary Islamic parties have at various times over the past been united among themselves or have united temporarily with the traditional groups. Unity among themselves has proven elusive largely because of their inability to consent to the leadership of any single party leader. Attempts to promote leadership on a rotational basis have also proven unsuccessful. Nevertheless, a degree of cooperation exists among the groups, especially in the field. In fact most of the pressure for unity comes from fighters in the field. In the Panjshir, where Soviet and world attention has been focused, party members were "ordered" by Peshawar to cooperate under the leadership of Mas'ud. Among the revolutionary Islamic leaders, Rabbani has gained greater prestige over the last few years than his more eccentric colleagues. Perhaps as a mark of his growing prestige, he was received at the French foreign ministry, an event that drew the ire of Kabul.[23]

Rabbani's position may be more easily determined than that of the other revolutionary Islamic leaders, and since he appears to represent the middle ground between the ambitious dogmatism of Hekmatyar and the unsophisticated rural spunk of Khalis, it may be useful to examine some of his ideas.[24] First, it must be kept in mind that Rabbani and much of the revolutionary Islamic resistance appeals to the young, newly educated rural youth. Rabbani, who is a non-Pushtun from Faizabad (near the Soviet Tajik border), attracts ethnic minorities especially, as well as Pushtuns.

One of Rabbani's fellow professors at the Faculty of Islamic Law in Kabul, Professor Abdulraouf Sayyaf, began to rise to a position of leadership following his release from prison by the Soviet troops that poured into Kabul in late 1979. Sayyaf made his way across the Afghan-Pakistani border, and due to his pre-Da'ud leadership of the revolutionary Islamic groups, he was regarded as a possible unifying force among the competing political parties. To a certain extent he has achieved this goal, at least among the revolutionary groups, and has also attracted Muslim funds from the Gulf region, adding further leverage he can exercise. Although marred by kinship with Hafizullah Amin (regarded as the reason for his having escaped death), Sayyaf holds the advantage of age, scholarship, and recognition in the Arab world over his younger contemporaries. Owing to his Pushtun ethnic identity he attracts disgruntled members from the traditional camp to the revolutionary Islamic camp.

The revolutionary Islamic parties have insisted on calling themselves "revolutionary" although they are frequently lumped together by outsiders into categories such as "fundamentalist" and "revivalist." The two latter terms have Western religious associations that may make the position of these Afghan groups less well rather than better explained. Therefore, it is more helpful to use the terminology the Afghans themselves use.

The parties that have emerged around figures such as Rabbani, Hekmatyar, and Sayyaf, rose as semiunderground movements in one of the few Afghan institutions that fostered cross-cultural and cross-regional contacts, Kabul University. The aim of both the Jamiyat-e Islami and Afghan Youth was the transformation of Afghan institutions and society in two ways: technological modernization and Islamization. To accomplish these goals, it was deemed necessary to discard existing institutions, by force if necessary. Thus the groups may be rightly called revolutionary.

One of the chief targets of the revolutionary groups had been the inertia exhibited by the Afghan learned body of Islamic scholars, the ulama, which for a variety of reasons had never been either an intellectually stimulating community of men nor particularly independent politically.[25] Like other restless Muslim groups such as the Muslim Brotherhood (with which the Afghan revolutionary groups have certain philosophical affinities), for many years the Afghan groups viewed the internal threat to Islam coming from entrenched institutions as only slightly less threatening than foreign cultural and political intrusions. The degree to which they view foreign or internal threats to Islam the greater is what has separated the Jamiyat-e Islami from the Afghan Youth of Hekmatyar. For example, Rabbani has found it less onerous to cooperate with traditionally oriented groups such as those of Gailani and Mujadidi than has Hekmatyar who views both, especially Gailani, as the epitomy of decadent, superstition-ridden, and self-seeking men that have corrupted religion among Afghans.[26] Prior to the Soviet invasion, Rabbani's chief target used to be the foreign influences in the Afghan school system: Russian, American, and Chinese.[27]

Despite their having staked out their political and philosophical positions in rudimentary terms, no religious theologian of substance nor political thinker with impact has emerged to clarify, explicate, and advance the ideological position of the Islamic revolutionary resistance parties. During its first years, the resistance turned to Iranian ideologues such as Ali Shari'ati (d. 1977) and to Ayatollah Taleghani (d. 1980) for serviceable and inspiring thoughts. As their ardor for the Iranian clerical regime has cooled however, Afghans have come to rely on their own leaders for more philosophical guidance. Rabbani remains the closest figure the Afghans have produced to a philosopher of the resistance. Yet clearly he is encumbered with administrative, political, and military tasks and rarely, at least in recent years, takes the time to clarify his position in writing.

A speech given to students in 1982, however, reflects his ideas in outline. Foremost he stresses the need to live in the "electronic age" while upholding the principles and values of Islam as understood during the age of the Prophet and the four Rightful Caliphs. The main principles are viewed as justice and equality, seeking knowledge, election of leaders rather than hereditary elevation, government through a consultative council (here equated with parliamentary institutions), and freedom of speech.[28]

The disagreement of the revolutionary Islamic groups with the traditional Islamic groups runs deep. The chief problem lies in the fact that all three leaders of the traditional groups (often called "moderate" in the West as opposed to the "immoderate" revolutionary Islamic groups) come from a section of the religious establishment: Gailani heads the Qadiriya Sufi order, a position acquired on a hereditary basis and much contested due to the material gains associated with it; Mujadidi belongs to the politically active family of the Hazrat-e Shor Bazaar upon which has devolved leadership of the Naqshbandiya Sufi order, although Sibqatullah Mujadidi is a trained philosopher and intellectual and not the sheik of any *tariqa* (mystical order) currently; lastly, Mauvlana Nabi's support, though numerically widespread and large, is based among Pushtun tribes exclusively and derives partially from hereditary leadership position and partially from the esteem in which he is held as a Sufi.

Therefore by background alone, the traditional group leadership runs counter to the ideals of the revolutionary Islamic groups. Moreover, the traditional groups appear to have no goals and aims save the liberation of Afghanistan, a return to the status quo of the pre-1973 period, and, with the exception of Mujadidi, the restoration of former King Zahir either as figurehead leader or possibly the actual monarch.

The traditional groups have appealed for support to Pushtun tribes, Kabul bureaucrats and intellectuals, Western-educated and West-oriented technocrats and diplomats, and others of the *ancien régime*. In the face of continued adversity, the hardship of life as refugees in Pakistan, and the opportunities available to trained personnel outside the region, many of the supporters of Gailani in particular are gradually melting into exile. While Mauvlana Nabi's supporters continue to fight and increase in numbers with the influx of new refugees, his appears to be the only party of the traditional camps that shows signs of long-term endurance.

The revolutionary Islamic groups, on the other hand, have increased their influence even as they quarrel among themselves. Their position is augmented by educational institutions that have been established over the past years in the Northwest Frontier Province of Pakistan that encourage an Islamic education based on revolutionary ideology. The Bara Pir Madrasah begun in 1981 by a Pushtu speaker from Kunduz boasts over 200 students. The Darra Adam Khel Madrasah, an older institution, supports and educates about thirty students with Arab help. In the city of Peshawar itself two other *madrasahs* have been formed, both supportive of, or directly affiliated with, the revolutionary Islamic parties. Should the Afghan situation not be resolved to the satisfaction of the Islamic revolutionary parties, there remains a possibility that enough members of a younger generation could be mobilized to sow strife for a government in Kabul. Rabbani has emerged over the past three years as the leader with the most potential. His position is somewhat undermined, however, by his status as a non-Pushtun. His appeal to the young, among Muslims outside the region, and even increasingly to the Western world have advanced him as one of the key potential architects of peaceful negotiation, should the opportunity arise.

Options and Alternatives

As the largest refugee population in the world, the Afghan situation appears to be stalemated not only on the military and diplomatic fronts, but also shows no easy solution over time. Not only is the refugee population growing as new refugees arrive, but the birthrate in the camps appears to be very high as well. Thus the potential supply of resistance fighters could begin to grow rather than diminish from a purely demographic perspective.

There are other considerations of course. A key factor is the role of Pakistan and another the political compromises that Moscow-Kabul are willing to make, particularly with regard to the refugees. Can Pakistan continue to support the resistance movement? Can it afford not to? At present resettlement of refugees outside the bordering countries has been limited to individual resettlement in the West or the group resettlement program for some Turkic speakers to Turkey.[29] Given the large numbers involved, mass resettlement does not appear to provide the answer to the Afghan refugee problem either. Should Kabul make the necessary compromises to coax the refugees back to their homes, the resistance would be underminded considerably. Currently, however, Moscow seems intent on emptying the countryside of resistance supporters. Therefore prospects of even wanting them back appear dim.

Indications are that the war and the resistance will go on without major political shifts in the region. The resistance, especially the revolutionary Islamic resistance, appears to be preparing for such prospects by setting up permanent institutions to train and educate the young. The likelihood is that the sense of nationalism fostered over time in the refugee camps will blossom forth to create a new generation of fighters in whom "Afghanness" will overcome increasingly ethnic and regional exclusiveness. The prospects for this kind of breakdown of traditional affiliation may even affect the Pushtuns and thus render more likely over time the acceptance of non-Pushtun national leaders. Such prospects may not materialize except over several generations.

In the meantime, the resistance will be forced to administer civilian populations both inside and outside the country in addition to simply fighting. They will need to replace the institutional structures destroyed after long years of unrest. Steps taken in the Panjshir valley by Commander Mas'ud to organize the schools and so forth indicate recognition of the need to deal with civilian matters. In other parts of Afghanistan, such as Wardak, similar projects are undertaken by the resistance leaders.

With or without a settlement of the Afghan crisis and a withdrawal of the Soviet forces, however, it is clear that Afghanistan's political life will include large groups of people who will demand an active voice in their own administration. No longer will politicians and perhaps even religious leaders face politically inert populations because the experience of the turmoil in which the country has been embroiled has polarized many and politicized most. The emerging resistance institutions for civilians will provide an opportunity for them to make practical use of their ideas for an "electronic age" Islamic society and will give the outside world a microcosm to examine for successes and failures of such efforts.

Notes

1. This term was first coined by Louis Dupree to refer to Soviet tactics in the countryside that caused and continue to cause large exodus of refugees. The Afghan refugees form the largest group of refugees in the world.
2. Patricia Sethi (*Newsweek* [June 11, 1984]), Antero Pietila (*Bangkok Post [March 25, 1984]*, reproduced in the *Afghanistan Forum* 12 [June 16, 1984]:15), and Selig Harrison (*Washington Post* [May 13, 1984]:32) are three recent visitors. While the first two published accounts skeptical of Soviet-Kabul claims of success over the resistance, the latter accepted the Communist version of events without reservation.

3. Edward Girardet, writing for the *Christian Science Monitor,* continues to enter the country regularly and report with more insight than most on the issues.
4. See for example Claude Malhuret, "Report from Afghanistan," *Foreign Affairs* 62 (Winter 1983-84):426-435.
5. Regular reporting on the north appears in the *Afghan Information Centre Monthly Bulletin,* published by Sayed Bahauddin Majrooh in Peshawar. These reports are based on interviews of fighters coming to Peshawar to secure arms, visit families, and consult with political leadership.
6. My preliminary study of the Afghan resistance press has appeared in "The Mujahidin Press," *Afghanistan Forum* (formerly *Afghanistan Council Newsletter*) 8, no. 3 (1980):28-29.
7. Television reporting on Afghanistan, difficult as it is, loses much of its effectiveness by the Afghan insistence on refusing photographs of women (and sometimes children) and insisting that Afghan bravery and steadfastness be stressed rather than the poignant scenes of suffering. I was faced with the difficult choice between respecting the wishes of Afghan elders in refugee camps who wanted to protect the honor of their women by insisting on their seclusion, and trying to film the plight of Afghan widows and orphans. We chose the first option. See CBS, *60 Minutes* (April 6, 1980). Kabul sources, however, regularly feature women and children in the *Kabul New Times* to demonstrate happiness with the regime. But on the other hand, this reflects the bending of cultural mores to political will.
8. See *Afghanistan Forum* 12, no. 3 (1984):16.
9. For example Marilyn Wexler, editor of the *World Marxist Review,* was an early visitor to Kabul and has written laudatory articles about the Soviet invasion since then. Fred Halliday, a member of the Transnational Institute, was another early visitor whose Marxist point of view affected his reporting from Kabul. "Revolution in Afghanistan," *New Left Review* 9, nos. 2-3 (1978):12-19.
10. Thomas T. Hammond's *Red Flag over Afghanistan: The Communist Coup, the Soviet Invasion, and the Consequences* (Boulder, Colo.: Westview, 1984), pp. 193-95, remains the most detailed analysis of Soviet motives and options in Afghanistan to date. Hammond, a specialist on Soviet advances into Eastern Europe, concludes that Moscow will continue its military presence while endoctrinating future Afghan generations to play a greater role in the country's administration as a pro-Soviet communist state.
11. Alexandre Bennigsen and Marie Broxup, *The Islamic Threat to the Soviet State* (New York: St. Martin's, 1983) describe five Soviet/Muslim confrontations, including those in the Caucasus and Soviet Central Asia. Bennigsen remains the earliest and most ardent proponent of the theory that Soviet Islam has been and will continue to be a political threat to the stability of the Soviet regime.
12. The coincidence of this preoccupation with issues that have been dormant for sixty years with the rise of the Khomoeini regime and the growth of the Afghan resistance has been discussed by several writers including Bennigsen.
13. Bess Brown, "Alma Ata Clash over Muslim Burials," *Radio Liberty/Radio Free Europe Research Reports* (November 12, 1980):24-26.

14. Rebuilding of *madrasahs,* mosques, and saints' shrines for use as religious structures with and without official sanction has been occurring in Soviet Central Asia over the past decade, particularly in Turkmenistan and Uzbekistan. Mosques continue to be crowded with older men (obviously not the same retirees who were observed during the 1950s) and during the past few years especially, a virulent internal attack on Islam has been launched by the authorities. All these indicate both a resurgence of interest and concern by the indigenous Muslims and a fear of this development by Moscow.
15. Marie Broxup in a preliminary article has examined a large number of Soviet-published sources on the Basmachis. "Basmachi," *Central Asian Survey* 2, no. 1 (1983):57-82.
16. Abdul Bary Ghairat, *Athare Chapi Dar Mo'zilah-ye Afghanistan* ("printed works on the problem of Afghanistan") (Peshawar, 1362/198).
17. Abdul Rahim Ghafourzai, a middle-level diplomat representing Afghanistan at the Nonaligned Meeting chaired by Cuba, managed to denounce the Soviet invasion of his country while forcing the chairman to cable Kabul to plead for the release of his family. These were later whisked out of Kabul by the resistance. *Afghanistan Council Newsletter* 8, no. 2 (March 1980): 8, 28, 62.
18. Eden Naby, "The Ethnic Factor in Soviet-Afghan Relations," *Asian Survey* (March 1980):237-56.
19. Audrey Shalinsky has written extensively on this subject based on dissertation research in northern Afghanistan prior to the 1978 coup. See for example "Islam and Ethnicity: the Northern Afghan Perspective," *Central Asian Survey* 1, no. 2-3 (1983):71-84.
20. Gregory J. Massell has concluded from his study of Soviet attempts to undermine Central Asian Muslim society through use of women that the effort was not rewarding. *The Surrogate Proletariat: Moslem Women and Revolutionary Strategies in Soviet Central Asia, 1919-1929* (Princeton: Princeton University Press, 1974).
21. *Afghanistan Forum* 12, no. 3 (June 1984):32.
22. Ibid., pp. 32-33. The reference is to "religious" leaders, and although the officers of the organization appear to be Muslims, there is some question as to whether in fact other religious leaders may not also be included. Bakhtar Information Agency news releases for example emphasize the official celebration of Hindu, Sikh, and Shi'ite holy days as well.
23. *Afghanistan Forum* 12, no. 3 (June 1984):36.
24. For a more detailed historical analysis of the evolution of the revolutionary Islamic parties see Eden Naby, "The Changing role of Islam as a Unifying Force in Afghanistan," forthcoming in the SSRC publication on Islam, ethnicity, and state.
25. During the 1920s religious leaders did unite with disgruntled Afghan tribes to overthrow King Amanullah. However, Afghanistan has never developed a system of Islamic educational institutions that promote either theological excellence or the development of leaders with a cadre of followers. For a fuller discussion of these historical issues see Hassan Kakar, *Government and Society in Afghanistan: The Reign of Amir 'Abd Al-Rahman* (Austin: University of Texas Press, 1979); Leon B. Poullada, *Reform and Rebellion in Afghanistan, 1919-1929: King Amanullah's Fail-*

ure to Modernize a Tribal Society (Ithaca, N.Y.: Cornell University Press, 1973).

26. Personal interview, March 14, 1980, Peshawar, Pakistan.
27. *Shahid-e Zahdi,* no. 6-7 (1361/1982):4.
28. *Mirror of Jehad* (March-April 1982):9-10.
29. The resettlement program began as an effort for the Kirghiz but has included other Turkic speakers from Afghanistan. See Nancy Hatch Dupree, "The Afghan Kirghiz in Turkey," *Afghanistan Forum* 12, no. 2 (March 1984):21-22, 27.

Commentaries on Dr. Naby's Paper

Seyed Qassem Reshtia

Dr. Naby concentrated on two factors behind the resistance; one of these was nationalism and the second Islam. She minimized nationalism in Afghanistan, which she described as nascent and immature. But she is forgetting another factor which I consider to be the most important of all. This is the spirit of liberty and independence of the people of Afghanistan. I have before me something which was said a century ago by Lord Lawrence, who had been the Viceroy of India. On the eve of the Second Anglo-Afghan War (1878-80) he said: "The Afghan will put up with poverty and even insecurity of life but he will never tolerate being governed by foreigners."

These words reflect even more sharply today the truths about the character and mentality of the Afghan people. This fact has been well demonstrated by the Afghan resistance since the massive invasion of the Red army in the unequal but unrelenting combat undertaken by the whole population of the country against the invaders equipped with the most up-to-date weapons. This is the main force of the resistance and the hope of the Afghans. They will fight to the end. There are people who believe that the war is finished and that encouraging the Afghans to go on fighting and be killed is neither wise nor human. You cannot give this advice to the Afghans—they will fight. This is part of their life and they have done it throughout their very long history—from the time of Alexander the Great down to the British. This is why the struggle of the people of Afghanistan is, first and foremost, a patriotic struggle—for their independence, their way of life, and to preserve their Islamic faith.

The Afghans, 99.9 percent of them, are Muslims; therefore there is no need for them to prove that they are Muslims or Afghanistan is an Islamic country. As far as nationalism is concerned, recently I was reading the debate between Seyed Jamal-ad-Din al-Afghani and Ernst Renan. During this debate Renan, referring to Afghanistan remarked that "after Japan, Afghanistan is the only other country in the whole of Asia where one can find most of the component elements of nationhood." This is the opinion of the great thinker and philosopher of the nineteenth century, which was published in *Revue des Deux Mondes* in 1893.

Let me present some more details regarding the background of Afghan nationalism. In the beginning of this century Afghanistan was still a British protectorate. At that time the only newspaper of Afghanistan, *Siraj al Akhbar Afghaniyah* ("the lamp of the news of Afghanistan," 1911-1919) was published by Mahmud Tarzi (1866-1936), the father of journalism in Afghanistan. In this newspaper Afghan nationalism was one of the main topics. Recently a foreign journalist wrote that if we search for a positive side to the Soviet invasion of Afghanistan, we can say one thing: it has cemented the nationalism of the Afghans. Today, if you ask any person in Afghanistan who he is, he will not say, a Tajik, a Pushtun, or Uzbek; he will say, "I am an Afghan." Modern Afghanistan came into being in the middle of the eighteenth century. In 1747 Ahmad Shah Abdali (1722-72) founded the Durrani dynasty. Since then there as always been an Afghanistan and an Afghan nation. Afghanistan is a mosaic of ethnic groups of different peoples and languages, because it is a crossroad between East and West. But over more than two centuries (since 1747) it has been welded into one nation. We cannot deny that.

Now I want to say a few words about the two main groupings of the resistance. In Europe and the United States some people think that they are different, but both are basically Islamic groups. One is called "moderate" and the other "fundamentalist," but this is a creation of the imagination of some Western reporters or scholars. Mujadidi (Sibqatullah Mujadidi, leader of the Jabah-e-Milli-e-Nejat-e-Afghanistan—National Deliverance Front of Afghanistan—and considered the leader of the moderate grouping of the *mujahidin*) is a more devout Muslim than is, for example, Hekmatyar (Gulbuddin Hekmatyar, leader of the Hizb-e-Islami, Islamic party of the Afghan *mujahidin*, and considered to be one of the leaders of the fundamentalist grouping). Hekmatyar does not come from a religious family; he is an engineer. But Mujadidi comes from a very important religious family. The Mujadidi family has long been associated with the Nakshbandiya order of Sufis in the Indian subcontinent and Afghanistan. The head of the family in Afghanistan, known as the Hazrat of Shor Bazar, was killed by the Communist regime. Nabi and Gailani (Muhammad Nabi Muhammadi, leader of the Harakat-e-Engelab-e-Islami Afghanistan—National Liberation Front of Afghanistan—and a leader of the Qadiriya order of Sufis) are religious leaders.

The difference is not in their approach to Islam. The fundamentalists want to introduce another type of Islam into Afghanistan, which has never been there before. Islam in Afghanistan is of quite another type. When the Arabs came to Afghanistan, the Afghans were mostly Hindus; they fought with the Islamic army for two centuries. Only when they found out that the principles of Islam were very similar to their own traditions and way of life, they accepted them and made them part of their culture. They became zealous Muslims. Later on they introduced and spread Islam to Pakistan and India, as far as Calcutta and Dacca (Bangladesh). Thus, no other Islamic people can claim to be better Muslims than the Afghans. But the type of Islam in Afghanistan is a distinct one, different from others, from Iran's, for example. In Iran, besides the question of Shi'a and Sunni, the practice is quite different. There the clergy can claim the country's leadership, while in Afghanistan the spiritual and temporal powers are separated; religion and government administration work separately, though closely together. In the long history of Afghanistan, never has a religious leader claimed the throne. Even a brigand succeeded in occupying the throne of Afghanistan for nine months in 1929, but never a religious leader—not even those who were the instigators of the change of ruler. This is why we say Islam in Afghanistan is different from that in other countries. Even if the fundamentalists succeed in bringing another type of Islam in Afghanistan, the people will fight against it as they fought against the Iranians and Moghuls (both of them Muslims) in the seventeenth century. They will not accept it, and they will have their own way.

The second group, the moderates or traditionalists, are also Islamic. But they are trying to follow the traditional pattern. Afghanistan is basically a tribal society, with all its peculiarities. A traditional society is an inward-looking society where any reform will be rejected unless it is adapted to the traditions and introduced slowly and step by step. In looking for a future settlement in Afghanistan one should follow the same way, the traditional way. The Afghans have an unwritten law, called *Pushtunwali*. I am not speaking here about any specific tribe or ethnic group. This unwritten law is today understood and accepted everywhere in Afghanistan. All the different ethnic groups in Afghanistan are divided into tribes, including the non-Pushtuns. This law is based on the *jirgah* (tribal assembly), through consultations and consensus. Every time there arises a national problem it is resolved in a *jirgah*. We saw this when the Safavids occupied Herat and Kandahar. A *jirgah* decided to take arms against the Iranians and Mir Wais was elected to lead the liberation movement (1705-15). Once again when Nadir Afshar (Ruler of Iran, 1736-47) was assassinated, Ahmed Shah referred to a *jirgah*. As a matter of principle everyone is free to speak and participate in this institution. But when a consensus is reached it is binding on all. This is its democratic character. It is the traditional way to solve problems; all major problems of Afghanistan have been solved by a spontaneous or an organized *jirgah*. If there were to be a settlement in Afghanistan, it would have to follow the same line. This is the shortest and surest line to reach agreement. A leader also emerges from the *jirgah*. At the Kandahar *jirgah* of 1747 the leading candidate was the chief of the biggest tribe, the Barakzai, but this man was not elected. Instead the leader of the smaller Sadozai, Ahmad Shah, was accepted as the ruler. The traditionalist groups are following the teachings of Islam, but they are also taking into consideration the traditional pattern of Afghanistan.

Sayed Bahauddin Majrooh

The Afghan resistance has two sides: one is internal resistance in Afghanistan, the other external resistance organizations, mainly established in Peshawar. The external resistance has an organization, a political language, and also some differences in political philosophies. There are two distinct tendencies there. There is one which we could call "revolutionary" Islam, and the other we might call "traditional" or "moderate" Islam. But even inside this traditional Islam on one side and revolutionary Islam on the other, there is only one Islamic party which is really revolutionary along the lines of the Iranian revolution. There are more common points among them, and I am sure that if the situation is ripe they will come together. The differences are less important than the common points. Many think that even their political differences, their political tendencies, really do not have a very important impact on the resistance inside Afghanistan. Whenever a resistance fighter comes outside and you ask him to which group he belongs, he will just give you a card. But he will say, "I have more." He will show me two or three cards of different political groups. The value of the Peshawar groups for the resistance fighters is in the efficiency of military aid or other assistance. That is why we think Afghan resistance inside is different; the problems are different. It is mainly a military resistance, and they have more practical problems. They have no time for political theories.

In these four ycars of resistance much has changed inside Afghanistan. The one factor concerning internal resistance is that a new leadership is arising. This new leadership is, practically, the resistance commander. He belongs to any of the groups independently and is the important personality inside. He takes the initiative for operations. He has the initiative in decisions of alliances. That is why there are alliances inside Afghanistan which are quite different from those outside Afghanistan. They depend on the personality of the commander and also on local, social, and military conditions. Since last year and particularly during this year, very strong commanders have emerged. These commanders have extended their influence. Before it was more localized—a valley or the province. As they were able to extend their influence to other provinces, they were able to integrate and coordinate their activities.

Another interesting fact is that in the beginning these same commanders were more concerned about the immediate task of war and fighting. Over the last year some of these commanders are thinking about nonmilitary problems. For instance, they are thinking about how to administer the civilian population. They are thinking about the organization, the economic life, and the food supply of the civilian population. And they are even thinking about schooling. Some of them will try to establish at least some primary schools. Of course, they do not have the means to do this, but still the change in attitude is very important. The resistance commanders are becoming aware that they cannot fight only militarily. They have to fight on other fronts, such as the educational and economic fronts. They are also thinking about how to counter the subversive activities of the government. This increasing cohesion and unity among the resistance commanders inside is one of the main factors of pressure coming from inside—from the groups outside of Peshawar. This pressure is increasing, and it will be one of the factors which will force the outside groups to come to some kind of unity and alliance.

We must not misunderstand this. There is not a gulf between the groups inside from their affiliation with outside groups. We must not separate the resistance commanders inside from their leaders outside in Peshawar. They have affiliations, especially the commanders. Sometimes I have seen exaggerations that there were some resistance commanders who did not care about their leaders. This is not true; they are affiliated with their leaders, and this affiliation is useful. Even in this military phase of the resistance these groups are useful, efficient, and could be made more efficient if they had the means.

You know that the Soviets have problems in Afghanistan. There are some weaknesses, and, if we are able to exploit these weaknesses, the resistance is not hopeless. It can be effective in convincing the Soviets that a free, Islamic, and nonaligned Afghanistan will be more in their interest than all this trouble they now have. The Russians have military weaknesses. Still, they have learned much over the past three or four years about how to fight a war in a country like Afghanistan. They had never had this experience of mountains, extreme climates, and difficult conditions. They have learned, but I think they are still slow to learn. The resistance has been quicker to learn its lessons than have the Russians. The Russians are still moving very heavily. For instance, in land convoys they are very vulnerable. Their only superiority is in the air, and they are still using this. They have not been very efficient in learning land operations.

Their other problem is the ruling party. The government is split and the split is deepening. The Soviets are unable to unite the party, and the situation is worsening.

Yet a third problem for them, and their third weakness, is the Afghan army. They tried hard to rebuild this army. They thought when they built the army, as Afghans are known as good fighters, they would make a good army which would be able to win. It would be doing the job. The Soviets would not be forced to win by themselves. However, even with those people who were trained in Moscow, even with the equipment they were giving the Afghan army, they were surprised to find that it was not efficient. The equipment was regularly lost to the resistance; one of the main sources of supply of military equipment for the resistance has been arms captured from the Afghan army. The Afghan army is disintegrating. Forced recruitment did nothing. Soldiers of the army are defecting, massively, to the resistance. The Afghan army is not only not helping the Soviets but it is a problem for them. The Soviet army is trying to keep it, at least to show that there is a national army for the sake of propaganda. But the resistance considers this a victory. They are unable to build an army, and their administration in Kabul, their Marxist administration, has not been able to establish any kind of administration or government in the country. The Soviets were forced to do the job themselves even though they are now involved in the smallest administrative jobs in Kabul. They are involved in fighting the main military operations. We consider this an achievement. We forced them to come out themselves and not to show a kind of government, legitimize their government, or provide an efficient Afghan army.

That is why I think there is hope for the resistance. The resistance is more experienced and could become more efficient; that is one side of the story. Of course, we have weaknesses, but on the other hand the Soviets have their own. Even though the Soviets have had some subversive activities against the resistance, they have not really had successes. They have tried to infiltrate the resistance groups. Sometimes they made one group fight against the other, or sometimes the infiltrated groups defected on the order of the government. Then this group was shown on television and radio, but these were all the agents who had infiltrated. They could not extend that. Now the *mujahidin* have their own intelligence sources inside the government, and they now know who is sent out and who is doing what. The other subversive activity was to bribe tribal chiefs to recruit militia, but the Soviets were very surprised when this same militia and tribal chiefs turned their guns against them. They did understand one thing, one institution of the tribe. As long as the whole tribe was neutral, a chief could operate against resistance. But the moment the whole tribe decided to move against the government these militia groups were automatically absorbed. And they were disarmed automatically. Lately this happened in Pakhtia. Two or three tribes decided on a joint operation against a government base. There are many groups, many clans, which had cooperated with the government. Immediately after this decision all these groups disarmed themselves, or they went with their tribes to fight against the Kabul government and the Soviet army. And the Soviets did not understand this institution of the tribes in Afghanistan. And they will not understand it, because of their own ideological conditions. They don't see the nature of the society. They don't see the political nature of the resistance; they are blind to that. That's the other weakness that could really be exploited by the resistance very efficiently, if the resistance had the means to do it.

DISCUSSION

Noor A. Husain: I have no doubts that the resistance will go on in various degrees and levels of intensity. The point is whether it can extract a heavy enough price from the Soviets to force them to cut their losses and resort to a political settlement. That is what we are really concerned with. As far as the resistance itself is concerned, there are five essentials, which we are all aware of. As long as those five essentials are present it should go on in various degrees. But if two or three of those are absent or get knocked out, we are in for a different type of ball game. Number one is ideology. We know that Islam is a very strong factor—its concept of jehad makes it obligatory to fight both oppression and in self-defense. Then there is the question of leadership. It is fairly divided; there is leadership within and outside the country. In spite of best efforts, we have not been able to get them under one flag or one leader. Maybe that has something to do with the type of tribal society that prevails—what anthropologists call an acephalous society. The third essential is weapons and supplies, the logistic aspects. We are aware of the shortfalls there, and what the difficulties are of supplying or keeping a certain level of supplies going to these people. The fourth essential for any resistance is secure bases. You cannot have those people just operating from nowhere. We are aware that there are perhaps more bases inside Afghanistan than outside. But then comes the problem of keeping these bases supplied not only with weapons but with food and medicine too. The fifth essential for any insurgency or resistance movement to keep going is a good intelligence system. You should be able to anticipate what the Soviets are planning to do where and in what time frame, so you can be waiting for them at the right time and place. As long as these five essentials are there we would have an insurgency oscillating between peaks and low periods. The point remains whether it will be strong and widespread enough to extract a price from the Russians which they may not be prepared to pay.

Recently the Soviets withdrew an official book titled *The World of Islam*. This was an official Soviet publication. I am not sure why they did this, but it appears that even an official publication had been creating an impression or effects unfavorable to Soviet interests. Why should they withdraw an official publication called *The World of Islam* from distribution? One perhaps has to take into account both short- and long-term aims and policies. It is now emerging clearly that both the factors of necessity and opportunity will prevail as far as Soviet policies are concerned in the present and the foreseeable future. So where necessity and opportunity marry up, they would not hesitate in going ahead with their policy or an alternative in Afghanistan or the region.

Charles J. Adams: There are several brief points I should like to make concerning the role of religion in Afghanistan and among the Muslims of the world more generally. This morning there was a discussion of the role of ethnicity in Central Asia. The suggestion was made that there may be a polarity of forces in that area, with ethnicity tending to divide the people of Central Asia and their common Islamic commitment tending to unite them. On the basis of personal observations during a short visit to the region—and I am not a Soviet specialist—I am very inclined to discount the role of religion among the younger people of Central Asia. It is not only the case that the Soviets, over many years, have conducted vigorous campaigns to suppress Islam and that most of the institutions for the propagation of traditional Islam have been completely destroyed; one has only to visit Bokhara, formerly a center of world importance for Islamic learning, for instance, to see this vividly. But it is also true that the whole spirit of the modern world is antireligious. To the extent that the technological revolution continues to be pursued and people continue to see their good—economically, militarily, and the like—to lie in aligning themselves with that revolution, any religious establishment is seriously threatened. I am not convinced, especially with regard to the younger people of Central Asia, that religion can serve as a motivating force that will override other loyalties. Ethnicity—or incipient nationalism—on the other hand, is very powerful among them, as far as my observation goes. And along with the sense of identification as Turkmen, Uzbeks, Tajiks, etc., is a strong latent, if not manifest, anti-Soviet feeling. That sense of ethnic identity might affect the kind of policy that was suggested as a possibility this morning—one of Central Asian people being transplanted from the Soviet Union into northern Afghanistan as a kind of colonists. Such a policy might have a possible negative effect from a Soviet standpoint by reinforcing the sense of ethnicity which poses some threat to the Soviets. If the policy were carried out successfully, however, it would undoubtedly represent a gain for the Soviets.

The second point I wish to make has to do with Iran and its importance for Afghanistan and the Soviet Union. I do not think that much of importance for the Afghan situation and the Soviet Union can be extrapolated from the Iranian case. The circumstances are so peculiar—such things as Ithna 'Ashari Shi'ism being the ideological base of the Iranian revolution, the unique developments in the religious history of Iran in the past two centuries, the victory of the Usuli school over the Akhbaris, the emergence of the doctrine of the marja'-i taqlid, and so on—that the position of Khumayni is not understandable apart from that history. Furthermore, in the Iranian case it was not the religious leadership which was the ramrod of the revolution. The ideologists of the revolution were fundamentally secularists. They were people such as 'Ali Shari'ati, and the religious leadership came into control of events almost by accident. Their role is partially explained by their possession of bases outside Iran (in Iraq) where they were safe and could carry on their propaganda more or less freely. The Shah's police were able to destroy the intellectual elite and political dissenters within the country or, at least, sharply restrict their activities. The ulama, in contrast, had a safe haven outside Iran as well as a large and loosely coherent organization within the country. They fell into the lucky situation of becoming the point of crystallization of many different forces of resistance to the Shah's regime. These peculiarly Iranian circumstances do not exist either in Afghanistan or in the Soviet Union, and for that reason I do not see the Iranian revolution as a readily exportable commodity to those two countries.

The last point has to do with what is going on religiously in the Islamic world. Here I am afraid I may say something that will offend some of my Muslim friends—I trust not. Professor Naby rightly rejected the term *fundamentalism* as a name for the resurgent Islamic movements of our time. What is happening is the emergence all over the Islamic world of an increasing appeal to religious symbolism in public life, a growing resort to Islam for the purposes of establishing legitimacy, identity, dignity, purpose, and direction for various Muslim societies. We must emphasize strongly what Professor Naby also said to us, that these religious movements in different countries are motivated in each instance by the peculiar circumstances of that particular locale. They do not bear, and are not capable of bearing, a single description, nor is there a single set of characteristics that apply to them all. The close relationship between the resurgence movements and the Soviet occupation of Afghanistan as a case in point is abundantly evident to all. If there is anything that these movements have in common, it is only that they demand a greater place for Islam in public life, that they seek a closer association between religious and political loyalties. But what is the future of these movements? Do they really hold the possibility for the Afghans, for instance, or for any other Muslim people, to recover some of the glory of the Islamic past or to bring about the changes in society that will ensure the elements of economic, military, and political strength which all the peoples of the Muslim world are so eager to have?

It seems to me that these religious movements are quite capable of mobilizing people *against* something. They have not yet proven their ability to mobilize their people *for* something. I would hazard a guess that there will be a degree of unity among Islamic groups in the Afghan resistance so long as there is a clear enemy to fight against, though it must be said that even in the present circumstances that unity has proven difficult to consolidate. The example of Pakistan, however, shows that religious loyalty is not necessarily a sufficient basis for nationhood when independence and power have been won and people face the task of determining what the society will be like. Many of these movements that have been characterized as "resurgent," "revivalist," "fundamentalist," or whatever, do not, in the final analysis, have much profound intellectual content. This will mean in the long run, though not perhaps in the immediate future, that they will prove unable to provide the ideological base and the dynamic engine for real social, economic, or political development for many parts of the Islamic world. Since their leadership is, by and large, uninstructed in the ways of the more developed parts of human society, it has yet to come to terms in any deep way with the implications of the attitudes that go along with the technological revolution and the processes of modernization that have put such great power and influence into the hands of one particular segment of the human race. I do not think that in the long run the Islamic resurgence movements have the real answers to the problems of the Islamic societies. I would not want to hazard too much on the possibilities of their long-term influence. What is radically needed is a group of Muslim teachers who would emerge as real philosophers of religion, but I do not see such personalities, with exceptions that I can count on the fingers of one hand, anywhere in the Islamic world today.

Sajjad Hyder: Professor Naby has posed some brain teasers with her paper, and with womanly instinct has put them at the end of her presentation. She asked two questions. Can Pakistan afford to continue to support a resistance movement, and in the same breath, can it afford not to? These two questions should be answered tomorrow when we talk about alternatives. My own answers are to the first question: no; to the second: yes. I shall explain that tomorrow. I now want to lay the ground for what I am going to say tomorrow.

Two things which are fundamental to this question have been mentioned. One is the Hindu Kush. This was discussed in the context of relocation of population, which in Afghanistan is not the name of any new game. In the 1880s Amir Abdur Rahman relocated the Ghilzais. He took them to the Tajik and other areas, and he thought this was the answer to his political problem: take the Pushtuns from the other side of Afghanistan to the north and they will be in a new habitat and unable to trouble him. The Russians have sent out 3 million Afghans, mainly Pushtuns; the same thing applies to them. They are not going to allow them to come back. Ambassador Smirnov told me in Islamabad: "You can keep all 3 million." When it comes to the Hindu Kush, when you say that they want to divide Afghanistan into two, I am reminded of what Jawaharlal Nehru said in 1946. The prime minister of Afghanistan was Sardar Hashem Khan. He sent for Sir Giles Squire, who was a British minister working for India in Kabul, and said to him: "You tell your foreign minister that the choice for him and for Lord Mountbatten for the referendum in the Frontier Province should be not only to ask whether the Pashtuns want to join Pakistan or India, but whether they want to join Afghanistan." When this was conveyed by Sir Giles to the Ministry of External Affairs in New Delhi, with his own hand Jawaharlal Nehru sent a telegram to Hashem Khan, saying: "If you use history to claim a part of India, then by the claims of history the boundary of India lies on the Hindu Kush." This telegram can be seen in the British Foreign Office in London. He said: "The frontier of India, the natural frontier of India, is on the Hindu Kush"—not on the Durand Line (established in 1893 by an agreement between Sir Mortimer Durand and Amin Abdur Rahman Khan, and forming the boundary between the British Indian Empire and Afghanistan). And now, if the Soviets also say the same thing, that will be that empirical evidence to set out and use tomorrow to explain those two abrupt, very abrupt, answers that I have given to your question. You said that this was relocation.

The other thing you asked was whether the Islamic groups would integrate with the peoples of Pakistan—you said this was a very big question. This is a question which only Pakistan and its people can answer. If you look at the history of Pakistani-Afghan relations, it has not been possible for the Pakistanis to go to Afghanistan and integrate there with the people of Afghanistan. Three times in the last 100 years, the last time in 1920, some 20,000 came back from Afghanistan in rags. They were given land in Jebal-as-Seraj (a town in Parwan Province at the foot of the Salang Pass, about 50 miles north of Kabul)—three acres for each one of the 20,000 to till. They lost everything; they came back heartbroken and in rags. I have been in Tajikistan and have met Punjabis who settled in Tajikistan after being pushed out of Afghanistan in the last century. These things are more easily said than done. The reality is that Pakistanis, or what are now Pakistanis, were not able to integrate with Afghans. The reverse is also true: the 3 million Afghans will not be able to integrate easily with Pakistanis. I have just come from Peshawar where I held a seminar at the University. I met the people of Peshawar, and they told me of all the social and economic problems there. They say: "If a Pathan wants a job for 20 rupees, the Afghans immigrant does it for 5 rupees." Just yesterday 15,000 came; we have this problem. They buy identity cards for 500 rupees. One Pathan said to me: "I challenge you, you bring me a picture of Babrak Karmal. For 2,000 rupees I'll make a Pakistani identification card for him." They pay 500 rupees and they get a Pakistani passport, and they also get on the plane and come to the United States. These are real problems. They came and started buying property in Peshawar. They are buying property in Islamabad and Karachi. I was shocked when I came back after retirement, and so was the editor of the *Indian Express,* who had handled the problem of refugees from East Pakistan in 1971. He was in Pakistan two weeks ago. He said to me: "You haven't run a ring around them like we did in 1971 and confined them to camps?" I said, "Good heavens, George, what are you talking about? They're all over the place." This question of integration is not easy, and the desires, feelings, and sentiments of the people of Pakistan are a very important factor. You talk about the Palestinians—whether the Afghans will have schools, settlement camps, and resistance weapons like the Palestinians. You know what it means to the people of Pakistan? It means that we are going to have Palestinian-like fighters among us—3 million of them—upsetting and turning our society upside down. Already they are a factor in our political situation today. There are many opposition leaders who have stated that because of the Afghan refugees there is no opposition movement in the frontier provinces. Each one of them is armed. Who can take them on? Who can send them back? This is what the opposition is saying now. I am not saying that this is the situation. But this tells you that already they are a problem to us economically, socially, and now politically. Abdul Wali Khan, leader of the National Democratic Party in Pakistan, gets up and says: "Only Jamiyat-i-Islami has access to the refugees, nobody else." Therefore, they are a pro-Jamiat and anti-everybody-else factor in Pakistan. Hence, for anyone of us to talk, for me to talk, glibly of their becoming a Palestinian resistance over one decade or two is unrealistic. This is what one must bear in mind all the time. These two questions which you have posed can only be answered by the people of Pakistan. Whether we can continue to support this resistance movement, and at what cost. Secondly, can we afford not to do it—that I shall address tomorrow.

Eden Naby: I am very glad I did not try to answer those questions. If I seemed to have said that the Afghans are going to be integrated, it was a misstatement. This is a Soviet option, impossible to implement as long as the resistance continues. I do not think that the Afghans can be integrated. But there are ways in which this may be attempted, the primary one being to appeal to the Central Asians' sense of ethnic cohesion.

Peers Carter: I was happy to hear Dr. Majrooh draw the clear distinction between resistance groups inside and outside Afghanistan. We tend, in the West, to be mesmerized by the quarrels and disagreements of the resistance groups in Peshawar. This is for two reasons: first because we have more information about it, and second because the Western media love disagreement. I could give you a vivid example of that from our last Anglo-French summit meeting in London, where I was present throughout: a quarrel was invented by the media which had not taken place at all.

The other point I wish to mention is, certainly, the resistance is fighting and will go on fighting a long time, but we have not paid enough attention to the state of the noncombatant population of Afghanistan, which is being terrorized, especially by the helicopter gunships. This is intended precisely to withdraw from the resistance the natural element in which they live. The resistance *is* the population, and if the population is deprived of shelter, the crops burned, and the manpower gone, cultivation becomes impossible. With the shooting of flocks and transport animals movement becomes impossible. This is a much greater danger to the Afghan resistance than the military dangers to the *mujahidin* themselves.

And then again we come back to the need for more information, for more publicity about it. We simply don't get any, because with rare exceptions Western reporters don't get in. We have the admirable bulletins coming from Dr. Majrooh's Afghan Information Centre, but because they are not written by Western reporters and because they take several days at best, and sometimes several weeks, to get out, nobody in the international press will ever react at all. I feel sometimes a sense of near despair at the impossibility of getting publicity for the Afghan cause in the West, and I am concerned because we are mainly a humanitarian agency: no publicity means no private funds coming in.

Sabahuddin Kushkaki: It is very important to see that the Afghan problem is solved, so that the refugees return back to their home and the Pakistanis can attend to their own affairs. What is happening, as Dr. Majrooh was pointing out, is the emergence of a new sort of alliance within Afghanistan among the various commanders throughout the country. But that alone is not going to solve our problems of resisting the Soviets, both on the battle front and the diplomatic front. The *mujahidin* of Afghanistan are greatly in need of a very sophisticated and elaborate political institution as well. Due to Afghanistan's geographic situation and their vulnerability in the many areas within the country, it has so far been impossible for the Afghan resistance to establish this political institution or leadership within Afghanistan. Therefore they have to be maintained and sustained within Pakistan. It is essential to see what kind of political leadership is developing, or has so far developed, in Peshawar. As Professor Naby pointed out, there are two groups or alliances in the Afghan resistance movement. One is what she described as the Islamic progressive. I share her concern not to call these groups fundamentalist because, first of all, they hate to be called that, and then they are not fundamentalists in the sense that this term conveys to Western ears. They are mostly progressive. Of course, you have to argue about what kind of progressives, but they are progressive people. And then there is this so-called moderate group or the traditionalists.

I think that the Soviets are going to continue to resist any kind of withdrawal from Afghanistan, or the emergence of a government based on the will of the people of Afghanistan. The future of the Afghan jehad and the Afghan resistance lies with the Islamic progressives. They are the people who have the will and determination to continue this fight, but the main drawback for them is the lack of a dynamic political leadership.

It is one of the tragedies of Afghan history in the past twenty years that a gap has existed between the leadership and the emerging younger aspiring generation. What I have seen in Peshawar and in Pakistan during my stay there is that the same kind of situation, unfortunately, is developing now between the progressive Islamic groups and many of the people who fight on the front or work in their offices. As a result of the Soviet occupation in Afghanistan, as a result of the established Communist regime in Afghanistan, and even before that during the time of President Da'ud and the latter parts of King Zahir Shah's reign, a new generation of Afghans has emerged. This new generation is deadly opposed to communism, on one hand, and at the same time deadly opposed to Western materialistic ways of life, to a kind of civilization which they think will eventually wash away their Islamic beliefs and ideas. They fought this. They emerged as a group during the latter part of the monarchy. This young emerging generation forms the majority of those who are fighting inside the country and giving their blood, and are in the offices in Peshawar working for these various groups. They do not see their aspirations personified in the leaders of existing groups, whether they are from the moderate or the fundamentalist groups. They want some different kind of leadership, one which will chart a diplomatic program for them on the one hand, and accelerate their efforts to fight the Soviets on the other. Neither of these is being provided for them. Therefore one can find this gap between the leadership and the emerging generation of the Afghan jehad. This is what we have to be concerned with if we are going to help the Afghan majority and the Afghan leadership—how to help provide the kind of sophistication, the kind of intellectual infrastructure for these people who must be counted upon to continue the Afghan resistance against the Soviets.

The Soviets, saving some kind of drastic change either in their domestic affairs or in the international situation, will not withdraw from Afghanistan. We have to continue this fight. The people who are going to do the fighting are these people who are dead set against the kind of society which existed in Afghanistan at one time. Most considered Afghanistan a feudal type of society dominated by religious leaders, dominated by a number of khans, *maleks* and *arbabs,* to use their own terminology. They want the kind of Afghanistan in which the common man can see his aspirations fulfilled. These are the kind of people who have emerged in the Afghan jehad, and we have to keep them in mind. They are doing the fighting on the battle front, but they are looking forward for a dynamic political institution to be established. The role that can be played by the people of Pakistan and the Islamic world as a whole, and other friends of Afghan resistance in the West, is to see how we could strengthen the infrastructure of the Afghan resistance. This is one of the fundamental points that I wanted to make in regard to the Afghan resistance, because it is so important that a new generation has come about and is looking forward for a dynamic leadership—more sophistication, more knowledge, more ways to serve the people inside the country in the liberated areas.

There is one other minor point I should have made in the beginning. This is about the parallel between the *basmachi* era in the Soviet Union and the Afghan jehad. Many good points were made by Professor Naby. There are other points that one has to keep in mind. Geographically, Afghanistan's position is much different from what had been the position of the Islamic Soviet republics. The openness of Western and Eastern borders of Afghanistan and the free flow of people coming and going from the two sides of the border is another factor that you did not have in the 1920s. Afghanistan has existed throughout these times as an independent state—a member of the international community. None of these Soviet republics, the Islamic republics, existed as an independent international entity. And Afghanistan, historically, has always served as a buffer state between the great powers, while none of those areas inside the Soviet Union ever served as a buffer state. The Afghan resistance movement cannot be described in the same terms.

Louis Dupree: I just would like to share with you some thoughts that I have from having had fairly close contact with a number of *mujahidin* leaders over a number of years. Of course, I will do this from the point of view of an anthropologist. One thing I have observed is the psychocultural pattern. In the latter part of the century, Afghan young men are trying to achieve the ideal personality type of the Afghan male—the warrior-poet. This has been the ideal through Afghan society as far back as we can trace in their folk tales, and in all their historical writings as well. We see many young men attempting to become the warrior, and Dr. Majrooh told me this past summer that he receives more Persian and Pashtu poetry than he has ever seen before in his life. These are sent to him for publication; he publishes what he can. This is the time for the Afghan to be what he is supposed to be, a warrior-poet. And that should be fed into our discussions of the guerrillas and the freedom fighters.

Another thing is the seasonal aspects of preindustrial warfare. From the time of the coup d'état in April 1978 until the early fall of 1978 very little happened in the countryside. Those in power in Kabul, the Khalqi-Parchamis, soon to become Khalqis alone, looked around and said: "Everyone is supporting us. Nothing is happening in the countryside." They made the same mistake the British often made in the nineteenth century. In the spring and summer we find that the people are farming and herding. It is the maximum time of economic activity and a person cannot farm and fight at the same time. Come late August, and the first major revolts began to take place. Beginning in Nuristan, spreading to Pakhtia and so forth, as the farming season was finished and large bodies of men could be brought together to attack the Khalqi regime's outposts. In my opinion, from talking to a number of the leaders who participated in these first revolts, the idea was not really to overthrow that regime in Kabul. It was simply expressing an opinion. This is what many groups have done throughout the Iranian plateau and Central Asian history whenever the king has been a bad king—remember, in Islamic political theory a bad king is better than anarchy. Of course, President Da'ud was called Da'ud Shah while he was running the country for the last time. Even the leftist Tariki was looked on as a "Ghilzai king." "We will come in now and we will make our protest and then a *loya jirgah,"* as we heard Reshtia describe eloquently, "would be held and everyone would gather and argue"—this was their train of thought. Afghans always have had "freedom of the mouth," if nothing else, and that is what the Communists tried to stop. The people, however, felt that they would gather together in *jirgah,* they would argue out their points, and everyone would go back farming in the spring and live happily ever after. That did not happen. The regime began to use its sophisticated aircraft and Soviet military equipment, and too much blood was shed by spring. When spring comes the tribal feuds usually end in Afghanistan. There is a custom called "placing the stone on the mountain." The local groups would place a stone on a nearby mountain and would stop fighting. They would go back to farming. The spring of 1979 no one placed stones on the mountains; the fighting continued. This was another signal to the regime in Kabul: "We now are serious. We want to overthrow you." It was obvious to me that, ultimately, the freedom fighters would have overthrown the regime in Kabul unless the Soviets directly intervened, and of course they did.

Another cultural response took place. There are about thirty major tribes along the Durand Line. They have paired off over the years fighting each other. They have traditionally fought neighbors; they do not run down the line 500 miles to fight someone else. This is caused by this segmentary kinship lineage, a vertical structure in which you have the family, the extended family, the subtribe, and the tribe. At each of these levels you have rights and obligations that are reciprocal, and they are social, economic, and political. But when an external horizontal force threatens this vertical structure, these structures come together to try to expel that horizontal force. This is what happened when the British invaded Afghanistan in the nineteenth century. Various groups that had been fighting each other for generations came together to fight against the British. And that is what happened when the Soviets invaded Afghanistan in December 1979. Groups, even enemies, came together to fight on the local scene.

We have seen an increase in the past year of urban guerrilla warfare inside Kabul. We should take a very close look at this, because, after all, Algeria received its independence not from the fighting in the *bled* (countryside), but in the battle for Algiers. It will be interesting to see the end result of this intensified urban guerrilla warfare.

Mr. Kushkaki has mentioned something extremely important—the educational aspects of the freedom fighters in particular. The Afghans already have lost one generation of education for their children. And inside Afghanistan the guerrillas are usually fairly young. Many of them are illiterate, having never been to school. Yet, they spend only five to ten percent of their time fighting. The rest of their time they sleep, they play cards, they play games. In many areas they have volleyball nets set up under trees so they cannot be seen from the air. But an opportunity is being missed to teach literacy to all these young men. They will need that tool of literacy if Afghanistan ever becomes a free country again. I would suggest that some modernist or revolutionary mullahs be brought into this. I suggest that they follow what other classical guerrilla leaders have done. Tito and his guerrilla groups had political commissars, teachers, who taught people to read and write as well as teaching them the joys of their brand of communism. Chairman Mao always had political commissars with his groups as they were moving from place to place and even when they settled down. I was told by the mullahs: "We can't take anything from the communists. After all we are fighting the communists." I said, "You don't know your Holy Qur'an or Hadiths. You may remember that the Prophet Muhammad, peace be upon him, has said, 'Seek ye knowledge, even if you have to go to China.'" I think that something should be done about this educational problem of the young men across the border.

Concerning unity, we will find no unity among the Peshawar "merry-go-round," as I call it, just as we will not find the Soviets leaving Afghanistan easily. The unity which is taking place is occurring inside Afghanistan on a regional basis. If, all of a sudden, these groups in Peshawar really got effectively organized and announced a unity I would get worried. This is not the Afghan way. Their ethnolinguistic groups are the most important aspect of their society. Nation-states come into being when you have an overwhelming literate population and you find reciprocal functioning sets of economic, social, and political rights and obligations between the government and the governed. Where do you find this in Afghan society? You find it at the regional level—the tribal and the ethnolinguistic level. This is where these rights or obligations are; that is why we find unity occurring between ethnolinguistic neighboring groups inside Afghanistan. That is the really healthy thing that has been occurring in the past eighteen months in some areas.

Ambassador Hyder mentioned the movement of the Pushtun groups to the north under the reign of Amir Abdur Rahman Khan. Something that has surprised me is that a number of Pushtun groups that were sent to the north have been coming back south, especially in the Kandahar area. They have taken their families across the border to safe haven in Pakistan, and have returned back to the Kandahar or Pakhtia areas. There they are now fighting with their cousins whom their grandfathers had left a generation or so ago. You may be seeing here a regrouping of the ethnolinguistic groups inside Afghanistan as a result of the war.

I am convinced that what is occurring in Afghanistan is much closer to the Yugoslav partisan analogy than anything else. When the Germans and Italians first attacked Yugoslavia in World War II, the seven major ethnolinguistic groups of Yugoslavia responded immediately within their own area. As the war developed we found two political-military groups developing—Tito and Michailovich. The groups which joined these, however, did not give up their ethnolinguistic and cultural identities. After the war a Federation of Yugoslavia was created, and it was so successful that Marshal Tito could tell Stalin to leave Yugoslavia alone—and he took off on his own communist bent. Of course, you have problems with a federation like this, but Yugoslavia has survived reasonably successfully. I see this type of military-political organization evolving more slowly in Afghanistan, because of the lack of literacy and so forth, as time goes on.

Claude Malhuret: I am the director of a Paris-based group of doctors which goes to war-stricken areas not always with the authorization of those countries. We have been maintaining several hospitals in the liberated areas of Afghanistan since the Soviet invasion in 1979. The remarks I would like to make are related to both the morning and afternoon sessions. The strategy of the Afghan resistance is closely related to the Soviet's antiguerrilla strategy. Many observers consider this strategy from a classical point of view; I think that it is not classical antiguerrilla strategy. The best example I saw this morning was the argument between Miss Leighton and Mr. Carrel. Miss Leighton said that it was a tactical success and Mr. Carrel said it was a tactical failure. I think both of them are right, or both wrong, as you like, because the problem is not the classical antiguerrilla strategy. An example I would like to take to illustrate this is the latest report of the UN High Commissioner for Refugees. If you read the report for the last two or three years you discover that the first six countries producing refugees in great numbers are, first, of course, Afghanistan with the numbers that you know, then Ethiopia with more than 1 million people, then Cambodia, Vietnam, Angola, and Laos. If you consider those figures one thing is striking: those six countries are of the Soviet bloc. Most of them are occupied by Soviet forces or by Vietnamese or Cuban forces. This is not a coincidence. It comes from a very specific antiguerrilla warfare strategy held by the Soviets and their allies. The Soviets know very well what guerrilla warfare is, because they have been sustaining so many guerrilla wars, and they know very well the phrase of Mao Tse-tung: "The guerrilla moves through the population like a fish through water." They have understood one thing, that all the Western antiguerrilla warfare failed because they were trying to separate the guerrilla from the population. They were tryng "to conquer hearts and minds," as Americans say. The Soviets have understood that if they wanted to get rid of the guerrilla they had to empty the ponds, so that there is no more water for the fish to swim. This is what they have been doing in all these countries. This is what the Vietnamese have been doing in Cambodia since 1979; this is what the Ethiopians have been doing in Ogaden or in Eritrea; and this is what the Russians are trying to do right now in Afghanistan.

It is not necessary to elaborate on the details: the bombings of many valleys, the destruction of big parts of Kandahar and Herat, the mines, the antipersonnel mines that are dropped everywhere, the toys designed to maim children, the crops that are burned, and so on. The result, as all of you know, is the millions of refugees in Pakistan and Iran. There are also refugees inside Afghanistan. For instance, the population of Kabul rose from 700,000 or 800,000 before the war to more than 1,300,000 now, which means that there are many more refugees than those which are generally counted by the official bodies. And this number has to be related not to the entire Afghan population, but to the population in the areas held by the resistance. If you consider those figures you discover that it is not one-third or one-quarter which has left Afghanistan, but more than one-half of the population of the areas held by the resistance.

In some ways this strategy is a real success; there is not much water left for the fish in the resistance-held area. But this strategy has succeeded in only one country during this century—the Soviet Union itself. The first time it was employed was in Ukraine during the genocide of 1933. It has been used against the *basmachis* and against other populations like Tartars, for instance. The way they were doing it, apart from massive reprisals against the population, was through the deportation of entire populations to Siberia, tens of millions of people, as everybody knows. Today they are trying to use the neighboring countries, for example Thailand for Cambodia or Pakistan for Afghanistan, as they used Siberia for the Soviet Union. But then they have a problem. The population of the Soviet Union remains there in the Gulag area or in other parts for the Tartars, for instance. They are still under their control. The main problem for the Soviets in Afghanistan and these other countries is that these refugees are in the neighboring countries—they are not under Soviet control any more. This leads to major problems for the Soviet Union. This strategy seems to be successful in appearance. For instance, you could say that in Cambodia, Laos, Ethiopia, Mongolia, Mozambique, and Nicaragua this strategy has been successful and the invader got rid of the resistance. But we would be forgetting that in all those places the resistance still exists. It is at the border: it has a base in the neighboring country and it is still attacking. For example, in Eritrea the war of the resistance has been in effect for twenty years. Since the pro-Soviet regime took power in 1974 the guerrilla movement has not weakened. In Angola I would not be sure at all that Savimbi (Jonas Savimbi, leader of the antiregime guerrilla movement UNITA—National Union for the Total Independence of Angola) will not be in power in Luanda, either through negotiations or because he will gain power by force after some years. These are some places where we are working.

In Afghanistan, the situation is still worse for them because, not only does the resistance have a real base in neighboring countries—Pakistan and Iran—but contrary to those countries I have just mentioned they control the rural countryside within Afghanistan itself, some 90 percent of the country. This means they can circulate and go to and from Pakistan and Iran, which is much more difficult for the other resistance movements in other countries in the world.

The brutality of the means which are used and the number of countries that have been invaded in the last decade have brought a moral and military rearmament of the West. You in America are in the best place to witness it, of course. And this rearmament is much more costly to the Soviet Union than the real cost of the war in Afghanistan. When people estimate the cost of the war in Afghanistan they say they have to send in 100,000 men, they have so many tanks and so on, but in fact, the Afghanistan issue is the one that brought about the rearmament of the West and of America. This means that it is much more costly than the simple cost of the war in Afghanistan.

For the first time there has been condemnation of Soviet actions by numerous countries in the Third World in the United Nations, but also in other forums. For example, even in the Nonaligned Nations' conferences, a speech like the one by the delegate of Singapore would have been unimaginable a few years ago. Now this speech is accepted. I would not say applauded by all the delegations, but accepted by most of them. Another thing is that the strategy the Soviet Union employs toward Third World countries plays upon the theory that Western colonialism is losing ground. More and more this is not so, because for the first time most liberation movements in Third World countries are pro-Western and anti-Soviet. I can quote again—Cambodia, Vietnam, Laos, Angola, Eritrea, the Ogaden, Nicaragua, and so on. This is a very new thing and is probably very damaging for the propaganda of the Soviet Union in the Third World.

This has done grave damage to the myth of the invincibility of the Soviet Union. There is Afghanistan, which is the best example. There has been Syria, Soviet-supported last year, and Grenada, not long ago. These might well have the same effects among the friends of the Soviet Union that affected the friends of America during the recent years when America was considered weaker. The best example of this is the fact that the government of Surinam sent back the Cuban ambassador and part of the embassy the morning following the invasion of Grenada by American forces. I think this is an important sign.

All those remarks were intended to show the importance of the international environment for the resistance. We are working inside the country and maybe some of you were waiting for me to describe what is happening inside the country. I think the way the war is waged is known, but the international environment is a much more important issue. The Afghan resistance has shown that they are going to resist with weapons on the battlefield—on this there is no question. Every time we go to Afghanistan we see that the resistance is stronger. I do not know whether it will last, I am nearly sure it will, but for the past four years the resistance has gained momentum inside Afghanistan, this is for sure. In the beginning we had two or three doctors there; now we have twenty-two permanently in provinces we could not get to before. People think that we go there at night. In fact, we are traveling in Afghanistan by car, by jeep, or by truck, and we are doing this by daylight. We are going everywhere we want, provided we are with the resistance organizations. So in that respect I do not agree with many people who say that time plays in favor of the Soviet Union. The problem is to see the tendency, and the tendency is in favor of the West. Some of you may disagree, but I believe the tendency in the West is for increased resistance to Soviet totalitarianism, at least it is in France, and I believe in America. The tendency in the Soviet Union is the weakening of the economy, because of all those wars and because of the rearmament of the West. We are working in all those places that I mentioned, for example with the Angolan resistance, the Mesquito Indians, the Eritrean resistance, the Afghans, and on the Cambodian border. Each time I visit one of those places one thing strikes me, the fact that the Soviet empire is stretched to such an extent right now that it might well go the same way as did the Roman Empire at the end. Everything is more and more costly for them.

Many people lament the divisions of the Afghan resistance, but I would like to say two things about this. First, in this type of terror war which is unlike all the antiguerrilla warfare we have seen before, tribal solidarities are probably much stronger than political solidarities. That may be one of the explanations of why the Afghan resistance and the Afghan population have been able to resist in the conditions caused by the Soviet invasion, which might not have been the case if they were only obeying political motives. Second, I would like to ask: "Does anyone of you know of a resistance that has been united since the beginning, or even after four years?" The Angolan resistance against the Portuguese was divided into at least three movements, the Eritrean was divided into four movements, the Palestinean resistance, even now, is as divided as is the Afghan resistance. Nobody asks why they are divided, or says that it is the cause of their weakness. So I think it might take ten or twenty years. Then we come to what Ambassador

Hyder said about Pakistan. I would like to remind him that in those cases, for example in the case of Eritrea, those refugees have been in Sudan for more than twenty years. In Thailand, the Cambodian refugees have been there for more than eight years. In other countries it has been the same, not to speak of Lebanon, Syria, and Jordan. Which means that time passes quite quickly and years accumulate before one realizes. It will take some time, it always takes time for a resistance to unify. I do not think we have to keep those same myths that the Soviets have understood; I think that between the guerrilla and an antiguerrilla—the one who wins is not the one who conquers hearts and minds but the one who makes terror reign. Another myth is that guerrillas do not unite, but one group becomes stronger than the other and then the other ones have to rally. I think this will be the way. I know much less than you about the different movements of the resistance, and I cannot tell which one will be the strongest, but I think this will be the way after some years. We just have to allow them enough time to unite or rally in this way. I would like to conclude with a remark about this new Soviet antiguerrilla warfare. The Afghan resistance, first, is fighting for the independence of their country, but second, they are teaching us for the first time how to resist this new type of antiguerrilla warfare.

4

The International Community and Afghanistan: Responses and Options

Marvin G. Weinbaum

The Soviets' December 1979 invasion of Afghanistan that so badly miscalculated the determination of an Afghan resistance also underestimated international reactions. Political and military planners in Moscow apparently concluded that most countries would be either too preoccupied, disinterested, or intimidated to raise strenuous, sustained objections to the armed intervention. By the same token, the United States and others who led the condemnation of the Soviet Union and sought to punish it for its actions overestimated the depth and consequences of the broad international censure. The policy responses of countries, regionally and globally, have not over time produced the moral, material, and political/diplomatic support that the Afghan resistance and its friends had anticipated. Plainly, the direct pressures on the Soviets and assistance to those combating them have fallen far short of what is necessary to help dissuade (or defeat) Moscow in its decision to shoulder a discredited communist regime and destroy its opponents.

Western policymakers and scholars have been prompted to speculate about Soviet geopolitical designs and to assess the impact of Soviet actions on the deterioration of East-West relations. The prolonged hostilities focus attention on the possible fallout effects on the Soviet Union's control over its own Muslim minorities. Differing views are heard on the most appropriate kinds of aid for the resistance forces and, most recently, the possible terms for a compromise settlement. Western observers agree that the chances for Afghanistan to regain its sovereignty, in whatever form, will be determined primarily by events on the ground in the embattled country and by decisions reached in Moscow and perhaps Washington. Yet it is also apparent that the character of the ongoing conflict together with the conditions for a peace may be significantly influenced by broad international developments and the continuing reactions of governments to this Soviet/Afghan war.

This paper first identifies the alignments that states have formed in reaction to the Soviet invasion and major parameters within which national policies are decided. The character of international and especially regional reactions prompts a series of observations and propositions, some fairly self-evident, other perhaps less obvious, about the nature of international reactive behavior in the Afghan case. A subsequent section speculates about possible political changes, mostly of a regional kind, that may bear directly on the course of the conflict and support for an Afghan resistance. In a final section, six alternative political futures are considered, with particular reference to the contribution of countries external to the conflict. Throughout, the discussions attempt to place the Afghan struggle in its larger regional and global context.

Parameters for Policy

The explanations for short-term and sustained national responses to the invasion and occupation are varied and numerous. Many considerations overlap and at least some are contradictory. A number of states have obviously been cross-pressured. The priorities assigned by policymakers to the same factors have of course differed and, in some cases, the national ordering of these has changed over time.

Several motivating and constraining factors lie behind national response to Soviet actions in Afghanistan. These reactions have ranged from approving, though ambiguous, to highly critical. Predictably, it is membership in an alliance system that most determines a country's response to the invasion and subsequent events in Afghanistan. The obligations of alliance, buttressed by economic and political ties, and ultimately coercion, ensure support for the Soviet Union from the Eastern bloc. UN General Assembly votes since January 1980 demonstrate the solid backing of Warsaw Pact countries, excepting only renegade Romania which repeatedly fails to vote on resolutions. While denying that the Soviet intervention is anything more than fraternal assistance to a socialist state, these governments have accepted military actions as an exercise of Moscow's judgment on matters involving its own security and, implicitly, accede to a Soviet sphere of influence that extends to Eastern Europe as well as Afghanistan.

Among Western countries, public condemnation of the Soviets has been unwavering. None has failed to vote for resolutions calling for Soviet withdrawal, and most would have supported more strongly worded resolutions. This censure by Western governments is typically couched in the terms of international law, specifically the Soviets' poorly disguised violation of Afghan sovereignty through armed aggression. But Western governments, especially NATO members, have also asked the international community to share with them an interpretation of the Soviet invasion as strategic rather than defensive in origin, aimed at penetrating the oil fields of the Middle East and realizing historic ambitions for access to the Persian Gulf and Indian Ocean. At a minimum, the Soviets are perceived as having enhanced their ability to project military power regionally with bombers based in Afghanistan. Humanitarian issues are no less stressed by Western governments. Concern for meeting the medical and other basic needs of external refugees and peasants in combat zones dominates the policies of several European countries. The suffering associated with the Soviet "scorched earth" campaigns in the countryside and the Red army's use of poison gas on villagers ensure a continuing Western consensus on Afghanistan just as they also provide grist for effective anti-Soviet propaganda.

The international community's Nonaligned states and other Third World countries have, not surprisingly, been more divided. In the January 1980 UN vote, the nonaligned countries voted 56 to 9 for the resolution against the Soviet Union's actions, with 26 countries abstaining or absent. Taken together, all Third World countries voted 78 in favor, 9 against, with 28 abstaining or absent. Consistent support for Moscow has come only from the Marxist regimes of Angola, Cuba, Ethiopia, Grenada, Mozambique, South Yemen, and Vietnam. They were joined beginning in 1981 by Libya, Madagascar, and Syria which, like the others, have been dependent on the Soviets for economic, political, and military aid.

The far greater number of Third World countries critical of the Soviets in the UN General Assembly and at other international gatherings has endorsed the applicability of the principles of noninterference in a country's domestic affairs and rejection of the use of armed force to settle disputes. The reactions of those states in close geographic proximity to the conflict have been based on more tangible, direct concerns over the altered regional balance of forces and perceived threats to national security. Predictably, Pakistan has led Third World states in trying to mobilize international pressures on the Soviet Union to withdrdaw; but the sometimes sharp attacks on Soviet policies by non-Western-oriented Iran and Iraq reflect a similar anxiety over the exercise of Soviet military power and its possible use to intimidate if not to invade countries in the Gulf region. For the eighteen Muslim states that have regularly opposed the Soviets on Afghanistan, the invasion is also seen as manifesting a concerted effort to stifle an Islamic resurgence outside as well as within Soviet borders.

The roughly two dozen countries in the Third World that have over time retained an ambiguous or aloof stance on Afghanistan come largely from the Nonaligned movement. In a number of cases, the abstentions or failures to vote on UN resolutions and other policies indicating neither approval nor disapproval of the invasion are doubtless influenced by strong, continuing aid and trade relations with the Soviet Union. These attempts at neutrality and avoidance of the issue apparently reflect an uneasiness in breaking ranks with the Soviets, accustomed partners in an antiimperialist front, ironically, despite these countries' continued expressions of commitment to the principle of noninterference.

Relatively few countries have altered their public position on Afghanistan. The stustained efforts of Moscow to win legitimacy for both its intervention and the puppet government in Kabul have never succeeded in obtaining more than 23 votes (in 1981), and support dropped to 21 the following year. The number of UN members willing to demand the Soviets' withdrawal and champion the rights of the Afghan people increased from 104 in 1980 to 116 in 1981, though it too fell back (to 114) in 1982. This consistently broad international sentiment favoring political condemnation has not, just the same, been transformed into a reliable constituency for material aid to the Afghan resistance.

A Propositional Inventory

The motives and rationales for national policies observed above help to generate the following tentative propositions and conclusions about international responses to the occupation and resistance:

International reactions, even if more predictable, would probably not have deterred the thrust of Soviet power into Afghanistan. The political costs of invasion were not then and are not now inconsequential to the Soviets but, in light of the perceived stakes, have been acceptable . In any case, the heavy price in diplomatic terms was paid largely during the first year, assuming no further, sharp escalations in the Soviet military effort.

Notwithstanding feelings of sympathy out of identification with a

Muslim people, coherent, consistent popular pressures on Islamic governments to support the Afghan resistance have failed to emerge. Elite calculations of national interests and obligations have far more determined the degree and kind of support given, whether in distant Egypt or nearby Pakistan and Iran. Predictably, supportive policies will vary with a country's domestic power configurations.

The alignment of support for either the Soviets or their Afghan opponents can only be understood in the context of regional alignments in the Arab and Muslim world and relations with the Soviet Union independent of the Afghan conflict. It is in this way that the uncritical attitude of South Yemen, the clandestine role of Egypt, adoption of pro-Soviet Syrian and Libyan policies, and the variability in Iran's rhetoric and aid to the resistance can be interpreted.

The level of material aid for the resistance has not as a rule been commensurate with the degree of diplomatic support. Nor has it been a function of the resource capacity of the assisting countries. Thus a great deal more assistance from wealthier Arab states could have been expected given their public positions and ability to channel funds. For that matter, the level of aid from U.S. sources is strikingly low in view of the propaganda dividends from the Soviet involvement.

In the competitions for (and receipt of) foreign material support, splits in the resistance forces have been exacerbated, not just between Islamic fundamentalism and Westernized Afghans but also within these elements. Even if the differences among local commanders within Afghanistan are exaggerated, factionalism and corruption among the resistance groups based in Pakistan pose serious obstacles to material and political support and undermine moral support. The lack of unity among groups is also frequently used as an excuse for not giving aid.

Military successes and failures of the resisstance forces have not to date determined the level of external assistance and have had only limited effect on the nature of assistance. Constraints on the delivery of material support have more influence over the quality than the quantity of arms. In general, humanitarian aid is the most easily attracted form, and informal aid is more readily available than formal, governmental assistance. At current levels, international aid to the resistance serves the Soviets more as a justification for staying in Afghanistan than as an impelling reason for withdrawing.

Among states that have refrained from directly criticizing Soviet actions, a greater sensitivity of the geopolitical dangers has emerged along with increased suspicion of Soviet intent. Even so, this has not to date outweighed the mutual advantages of strong commercial and political links to Moscow. In this sense, India holds the most leverage in the Third World in seeking a Soviet withdrawal; yet it has played this strong card weakly at best.

U.S. military actions taken in pursuit of its role as superpower and perceived regional security interests can serve to compromise the moral and political force of criticism against the Soviets in world forums. Despite the important differences between the U.S. invasion of Grenada and the Soviets' extended and brutal warfare in Afghanistan, the comparisons drawn by many states, including the British Commonwealth countries and Pakistan, may have undermined efforts, especially when U.S.-led, to portray Soviet actions as simple, unwarranted aggression.

International Developments

Political change on the global and especially regional scene can have an impact on future international responses and, most directly, on the level and kind of support for the Afghan resistance. Among the most plausible and consequential developments are:

Intensification of East/West tensions. Soviet as well as U.S. politics regarding Afghanistan occur within the context of their global objectives and the state of superpower relations. With a continuing deterioration of these relations, Afghanistan could come back into the limelight as a point of probing and confrontation between the two powers. The Soviets may use Afghanistan as a diversion or way of testing American resolve and capacity in the region, as well as for introducing new weapons. For its part, the United States may become more inclined to see Afghanistan as an open wound for the Soviets, to be bled both for strategic reasons and to satisfy heightened anti-Communist opinion at home. It remains to be seen whether poorer relations will help lift the restraints on more sophisticated weapons from the United States to the Afghan resistance. The willingness of the Reagan administration to employ United States military force in Central America and Lebanon, whatever the diplomatic drawbacks for the United States, probably improves United States credibility in the eyes of Afghan fighters and Pakistan's military. It also perhaps leaves the door open for Afghanistan to become part of an implicit sphere-of-interest superpower tradeoff involving Nicaragua and El Salvador.

Increased turmoil in the Arab Middle East. Material and political support for the Afghan resistance can be expected to decline as sympathetic Arab states become increasingly absorbed by events closer to home. These states do not perceive, as do Americans and the

Afghan resistance, that the Soviet Union is the principal adversary and most immediate threat to their security. Hostilities between the United States and Syria, and greater U.S.-Israeli strategic cooperation in Lebanon could also deter them from acting as surrogates for the United States in aiding Afghanistan's *mujahidin*.

Political instability in Pakistan. A Pakistan embroiled in internal political strife and especially interprovincial clashes will have conceivably less resolve to stand up to Soviet pressures or play a constructive role in a search for peace. A troubled Pakistan will no doubt lead opposition parties to try to capitalize on resentments that exist against the refugees in the Frontier Province and indirectly, against the war. Reversals in the political fortunes of the Jamiyat-i-Islami, tacitly in alliance with the government, could withdraw valued support for fundamentalist resistance fighters. Sensing difficulties in the country, the Soviets might be tempted to stir up troubles for the Pakistani regime through arms assistance to Baluchistan's insurgents and to otherwise instigate opposition among non-Punjabi elements. With officials in Islamabad already anxious to relieve the economic burdens posed by the refugees and avoid further entanglement with the "weapons trail" into Afghanistan, a fading Zia regime may become impatient to settle the conflict—on any terms. Zia's enemies view U.S. military and economic aid as having extended the regime's lease on life. As such, the opposition's success in forcing the military government from power is likely to jeopardize U.S.-Pakistani cooperation on many issues, most notably Afghanistan. A policy of Finlandization for Pakistan, recognizing Soviet hegemony in the region, a view already advocated in some circles, might become an attractive option in a destablized Pakistan.

An end to the Iran/Iraq war. The war that has polarized Arab countries along alliance and ideological lines has not only denied Afghanistan expected sources of support but has also assured Moscow at the most the muted criticism for its actions from its several Arab client states. The prolonged, costly conflict precludes any possibility that Iran may increase substantially its assistance to resistance groups throughout Afghanistan. But relieved of the drain of the war with Iraq, Iran may feel fewer constraints and greater motive to act vigorously to assist fellow Muslims in Afghanistan. It remains to be seen, however, whether the Islamic revolutionaries in Iran will be inclined to aid more than Shiite elements in Afghanistan, and if they would be satisfied with *any* Islamic regime in Kabul. Relations with Moscow might improve and the current rhetoric attacking the Soviets' presence in Afghanistan diminish once Moscow is no longer obliged to try to play its unappreciated evenhanded role. Iran is almost certain to be pushed quickly toward a Soviet embrace if, as a result of Iraq's escalation to end the war, the United States intervenes militarily to rescue the world's oil shipping in the Straits of Hormuz.

The course of the Islamic revolution in Iran. Future developments in the struggle for power within Iran will undoubtedly shape policies toward the Afghan conflict. A period of instability following the death of Khomeini will leave little energy for a more active anti-Soviet campaign on behalf of an Islamic state in Afghanistan. The possibility also exists that elements within the ulama, those less antagonistic toward Moscow, may reemerge as influential if not necessarily dominant figures. More remotely, a leftist *mujahidin* government that came to power or conceivably, in an overdue Thermidorian reaction, a right-wing government (even a liberal nationalist one) would have little interest in saving Afghanistan for Islam. Long-term contention within the ruling party or a full-scale civil war with the Kurds or others could induce Iran's leaders to create a national unity with foreign adventures (e.g. in the Gulf) on behalf of the Islamic revolution. Alternatively, a smooth transition to new leadership and a strong central government might free Iran to renew threats to carry its "message" to the more moderate Arab states. In either case, the willingness of Arab governments, or Western opinion for that matter, to continue support for an Afghan resistance in which fundamentalist Islam is strongly represented might diminish sharply.

Improvement in Indo-Pakistani relations. If the process of normalization favored by President Zia and, for the present, detoured by Mrs. Gandhi, gets back on track, Pakistan may conclude that it has less to fear from a Soviet-dominated Afghanistan. As such, the Islamabad government might be more willing to settle for a compromise that leaves a Communist regime in power in Kabul and provides for an only gradual withdrawal of Soviet ground forces. (Some might argue that a settlement of major differences would instead free Pakistan's military to pursue a more aggressive role in assisting the *mujahidin*.) The constraints posed on policy by Zia's American connection and the informal commitment to a strategic consensus would probably weaken even if they did not disappear entirely. A rapprochement with Pakistan could reduce the anxieties of leaders in New Delhi over the rearming of Pakistan or the possibilities of a 2-front war the includes the Chinese. If, in turn, this lessens India's feelings of dependence on the Soviet Union, it might also strengthen India's resolve to press the Soviets for a compromise solution on Afghanistan. India's long-term interests are not served by a Pakistan intimidated by a Soviet army perched in

Afghanistan, possibly agreeing to have the Soviets underwrite Pakistan's security vis-à-vis India in exchange for refraining to support antigovernment forces seeking to dismember the country.

Six Options vis-à-vis the International Environment

We finally examine the range of possible options or scenerios for the future of Afghanistan and explore how external support may influence the choice of alternatives. Many countries have a strong stake in the direction Afghanistan takes. Obviously, none of the possible outcomes is likely to satisfy all of them, though some options can be expected to have a larger supportive constituency than others.

1. The institution of *an anti-Soviet, Islamic fundamentalist government* is of course the objective of a number of resistance groups, most notably those based in Pakistan. If, as is probable, this government is inspired by the Iranian example, it will be suspicious and critical of both the East and West. Statements by several Islamic resistance groups that they would not permit an Afghanistan under their control to become a base for the West and their willingness to negotiate neighborly relations with the Soviet Union are hardly likely to satisfy Moscow. Signs of Islamic pragmatism notwithstanding, these groups leave little doubt that an Islamic Afghanistan would reject any Soviet presence or influence within the country and would eliminate Afghan elements that had collaborated with the invaders. The Soviets apparently perceive Islamic fundamentalism in the region as no less a threat than Western influence. For that matter, a fundamentalist government in Kabul that pays homage to Khomeini or his successors would be unwelcome by those Arab states that fear Iranian ambitions. And unless a future Islamic government in Afghanistan gave special recognition to Shiite concerns in the country, it might not even be acceptable to the revolutionaries in Tehran. Realistically, for a staunchly anti-Communist government to come to power in Afghanistan requires the virtual defeat of the Soviets and their friends in Kabul, a feat inconceivable without a massive commitment of aid from outside sources, most of all the United States. The Islamic groups insist that they are not anti-American or anti-Western, only that they reject many of the values that Western societies impose. But at least for the present, even seemingly benign Islamic fundamentalism is not likely to be welcomed in Washington.

2. *An anti-Soviet, liberal democratic government* that allots a role for Islamic, tribal, and secular nationalists would be viewed favorably by most states supporting the resistance. It is difficult to imagine such a

broad non-Communist alliance being able to coalesce, much less gain a Soviet agreement to withdraw. The ascendant Islamic components in the resistance have pledged to cooperate with forces that have helped them but are likely to create obstacles to an early institution of democratic elections or even its Afghan equivalent in a convened *loya jirgha*. An Afghanistan left to its many resistance groups might well polarize ideologically and be ripe for civil war. To have any chance for unity, outside pressures by those who aided the anti-Communist forces would have to be impelling. Yet it is doubtful that Iran would accept liberal nationalist accord and might work actively to undermine it.

3. *A nonaligned government* in Kabul that, as in the pre-1973 period, tilted toward the Soviets but avoided outright dependence is a compromise solution that is thought to be negotiable, at least by outside governments. The presence of Soviet civilian advisors, continued cooperation between the Afghan and Soviet military, as well as close alignment of their economies would not be all that different from what prevailed during the monarchy and Da'ud's republic. Most of all, Soviet security concerns would be met without infringing on Afghan sovereignty or isolating the country from the West. This so-called Finland model would predictably be opposed by many resistance groups (based in and outside Afghanistan) that cannot countenance a continued Soviet presence in any form. Because the scenario might leave a role for the exiled Zahir Shah, other objections are raised. But it is an outcome that Pakistan, India, and presumably China would find attractive and that the rest could cautiously accept.

4. *A Soviet-oriented client state* would represent more than the historical tilt and still less than full dependence. The degree of economic, political, and military integration would be more extensive than under pre-1978 regimes. The composition of the government could presumably include communists as participants but not as the dominant element. Some signals point to Moscow's readiness to consider such a formula for a future Afghanistan, at least following a transitional stage. The option would probably satisfy India and conceivably Pakistan, if hard pressed for an early end to the conflict. Its only strong appeal to the West, the Arabs, and Iran would be the removal of Soviet armed forces from Afghanistan and out of their strategically forward air fields. In any case, it is difficult to imagine agreement by any resistance groups to a peace that leaves those viewed as traitors, the Parchamis and Khalqis, with a political role to play, even a temporary or secondary one.

5. *A dependent Communist government,* on the order of regimes in Cuba or South Yemen, probably remains the optimal outcome for the

Soviets. The preferred Kabul government could contain non-Communist and progressive political elements, participating as minor partners, and permit special areas of autonomy for tribal and ethnic minorities. For cosmetic reasons, a new team of Afghan Communists might be installed in power. In theory, the country will remain an independent sovereign state and may continue to claim Nonaligned status. In fact, the country's political and economic links with the Soviet Union and East Bloc would be intimate and largely exclusive, and the Soviet military would either have permanent bases in the country or be just over the horizon. Envisioned is a Soviet-propped Afghanistan, penetrated in nearly every sector of the society and at every administrative level. A fully dependent, pro-Moscow regime would of course have no legitimacy for the greater majority of Afghans. The option promises, then, a continuing armed struggle of indefinite length and with perhaps a greater commitment of Soviet forces. It presupposes, probably realistically, the Soviets' patience and willingness to pay almost any price "to protect the revolution" rather than create a dangerous example by failing to meet their international socialist obligations. At the very most, the West and others could hope for a strengthening over time of nationalist aspirations in ruling circles and the "Romanianization" of Afghan foreign policy.

6. A final scenario foresees over a period of time *the absorption of Afghanistan into the Soviet Union* on the model of a Southwest Asian Mongolia. The process would necessarily be accompanied by policies of reeducation of new generations of Afghans, settlement of ethnic Russians from the Soviet Union, and attempts to destroy the indigenous culture. This option could be implemented partially as the northern tier areas of Afghanistan, above the Hindu Kush, are ceded to the Soviet Union, and what remains is left as an occupied or dominated socialist state, with an Afghan identity. To what extent the Soviets have planned for this alternative remains uncertain, though some current policies suggest its consideration, and the Wakhan corridor appears to have already been incorporated. In a protracted conflict leading to a weakened resistance, it is likely that the disapproval of the international community would carry about the same weight in Soviet policy as it presently has over any "autonomous" Soviet republic.

At least for the present, however, the policies of the international "relevant others" can be consequential. So much obviously turns on regime changes in neighboring countries and other political developments beyond the control of the Afghans. Just to sustain the current standoff probably requires strengthened commitments to the resistance in the form of material and moral backing. Plainly, no political outcomes favorable to the Afghans are possible without external support. Outsiders cannot of course expect to force a solution that most elements opposing the Soviets find objectionable. Yet with the resistance in and outside the country unable to agree on a basis for cooperating or a common formula for governing a future Afghanistan, external influences can help determine which groups dominate and which options are pursued. A very real concern among Afghans and others is that those countries critical to the resistance effort may place their own objectives and priorities ahead of the Afghans, either in seeking a peace that ignores justice for the Afghans or by posing obstacles to practical solutions. Some compromises that promise to reduce the Soviet military threat and provide greater regional stability may come at Afghanistan's expense. Similarly, the strategic gains others might seek by having the Soviets bogged down, diverting resources and attention to the struggle, can only prolong Afghanistan's tragedy.

Commentaries on Professor Weinbaum's Paper

Katarina Engberg

I would like to address the question raised by Dr. Malhuret and Ambassador Carter about the situation of the civilian population in Afghanistan. The balance of the summer campaign in Afghanistan shows that a military stalemate prevails; neither the Soviets nor the *mujahidin* are able to carry out any attack that could decide the war in their favor. But in this situation of military stalemate, political and economic factors become increasingly important for the outcome of the war. In this context I would like to highlight the reports of food shortages that we have received from Afghanistan during the last two years. Jiri Valenta quoted Dostoevski, but there is another great Russian author that I would like to quote. Tolstoy has described the Russian military campaign in the Caucasus in the middle and end of the nineteenth century. Tolstoy himself participated as an officer in this campaign and wrote about his experiences with a lot of sympathy for the Caucasians. In his novel *Hadji Murat* he describes the type of warfare the Russians used to break the population's resistance to the pacification campaigns. The Russians burned crops and tried to destroy the economic base for human life in the Caucasus. This kind of warfare was not invented by the Russians nor is it unique to the Caucasus. Dr. Malhuret mentioned the Ukraine, and there are other examples in modern history. In the present situation in Afghanistan, this kind or warfare gains renewed importance. And the Soviets themselves tend to rely on their experiences acquired during earlier wars against the peoples of the Caucasus and Central Asia.

It is clear that the Soviets are deliberately destroying agriculture in Afghanistan: bombing the irrigation systems, burning crops, dropping antipersonnel "butterfly mines" over the fields, shooting cattle, etc., thus trying to destroy the basis for human life and inhibit popular, civilian support for the *mujahidin*. There is no clear dividing line, as it might appear in the Western media, between the *mujahidin* and the peasant population. There are few regular bands of *mujahidin,* the great majority being peasants who must try to carry out their agricultural work under the present conditions of war. When they are unable to do so, when agricultural structures are destroyed by military actions, it undermines the capability of the Afghan people to resist. This is a factor that must be taken into serious consideration when we try to evaluate the possible outcome of the war in Afghanistan.

I would like to make a Swedish remark on this question. The German magazine *Der Spiegel* (no. 17, 1983) published an interesting interview with Yuri Andropov, in which he makes a statement on Afghanistan: "It is not a matter of indifference to the Soviet Union what kind of Afghanistan is on the other side of the border. In order to make this clearer I would like to make a comparison. The United States could not be indifferent to what is happening in Nicaragua. And Nicaragua lies far away from the United States, while Afghanistan shares a long common border with us. We defend our national interests when we defend Afghanistan."

Andropov's statement shows two things: first, to Andropov there is no such thing as an absolute type of Afghan nation. There can be different kinds of Afghanistan, depending on what kind of regime there is in Kabul. The characteristics of that regime will determine the Soviets' decision whether to respect the national sovereignty of Afghanistan. At first sight this "Andropov Doctrine" for Afghanistan looks like an extension of the Brezhnev Doctrine of the limited sovereignty of the Eastern European countries to Central Asia. But there is a new element in theis Andropov Doctrine. The Brezhnev Doctrine tries to give Soviet intervention policy in Eastern Europe some "legality," alleging that the defense of the "existing socialist system" gives the Soviet Union the right and duty to intervene when the socialist system is considered to be in danger. But in Afghanistan there was no such thing as a socialist system before the invasion. The social system there was described by the Soviets in vague terms of a "popular revolutionary development." So no "socialist legality" could be referred to in order to justify the invasion. Andropov's claim of Afghanistan's limited sovereignty is made out of pure superpower "right," based on the Soviet Union's strategic nuclear parity with the United States.

Second, the statement shows that the Soviet Union is trying to offer the United States a kind of tradeoff between Central America and Afghanistan, offering to respect the American sphere of influence in Central America if the Americans respect the Soviet sphere of influence in Central Asia. He puts it quite bluntly, and the offer is still open for the United States to accept or reject.

Andropov's statement on Afghanistan is a disturbing lesson for the Swedes, or anybody coming from a small, Nonaligned nation, especially if it lies within, or close to, the "spheres of influence" of the superpowers. The Swedes are especially sensitive to the fate of the Afghan nation. Sweden has, for over one and a half centuries, been able to preserve its independence and stay out of wars. Sweden did not participate, directly at least, in the European colonial system. These historical acts have created a special sensitivity in Sweden for the fate of small nations, and a special feeling of solidarity for the Afghan people and its struggle for independence and even national survival.

The invasion of Afghanistan has not, however, produced the same strong public response as did the war in Indochina. There was a strong solidarity movement in the Scandanavian countries with the Vietnamese people. There is in Sweden a frustration over the fact that it is so difficult, if not impossible, to influence Soviet behavior in Afghanistan, while it was possible to influence American public opinion, and through it, American leadership during the Vietnam War. But a fairly strong solidarity movement with Afghanistan is now gaining momentum in Sweden. Many of the activists are veterans from the solidarity movement with Vietnam. We find the same type of local committees collecting money in the streets, publishing information about the war in Afghanistan, and trying to provide humanitarian aid to the people of Afghanistan—not only for the refugees in Pakistan but for these 10 million, more or less, that have stayed in Afghanistan. There has also been a concern among senior Swedish aid workers with long experience in Afghanistan to try to help the civilian population inside Afghanistan. This Swedish concern materialized into a humanitarian aid project of medical aid to Afghanistan. It is only a symbolic kind of help, but it is at least an expression of Swedish concern about the future of the Afghan people and their nation.

I had an opportunity to visit the Kunar province in Afghanistan this year and was able to verify that Swedish medical aid was reaching the population for which it was meant. It has provided some 10,000 Afghans with elementary medical help. The help has functioned also as moral support for the civilian population, an aspect that should not be forgotten. I gained the impression that the Afghans, even the simple peasants, felt that the world had forgotten them, and that Afghanistan is exploited for propaganda or political purposes. Concern for the fate of Afghanistan as such is almost nonexistent. It was encouraging to see, nevertheless, that this symbolic medical help has fulfilled its aim to give humanitarian, nonpolitical aid in the interest of the Afghan people and not in the interest of any alien political force.

The humanitarian needs are tremendous in Afghanistan. The major concern of the population is not medical help, although they are very thankful for it, but the need for food. There is a severe food shortage in Afghanistan. I did not raise this matter so much with the Afghans, but I was constantly confronted by the civilian population about the pressing food shortage, which I could clearly see. Traveling with a group of *mujahidin,* we were always well received by the peasants and they provided us with food, as they do for the *mujahidin.* But they could only give us some bread, milk, yogurt, tea, and nothing else—not even rice was available. Women were complaining that they could not get wheat; they had made bread out of corn. And when they sometimes found wheat the prices were three times higher than before the war. Cattle are extremely important for the rural economy of Kunar province, as indeed for all of Afghanistan. As the peasants lacked wheat for their bread, they had to slaughter their cattle in order to buy wheat or corn, and the Soviet and Afghan government troops kill cattle, shooting them from helicopter gunships.

The peasants pointed out another important factor in the economic situation; they were now cut off from the possibility of doing construction work on the road between Jalalabad and Assadabad, or in the industries of the cities. These supplementary earnings seem to have been an important complement to the peasant economy before the war. The Afghan society is not the kind of archaic society we often imagine. They also mentioned that the sensitive irrigation systems had been bombarded by the Soviets, and crops had been burned as well. The peasants described their situation in the following terms: "We have now come to the bottom of our resources. We have no more goats or cows. We have no more money to buy wheat. We are facing starvation for the coming winter." They believed that this was the effect of a deliberate economic siege by the Soviets. They said: "In order not to risk Russian lives, they are trying to starve us to death."

During the time I was in the area, Soviet MIG jets carried out constant bombings for five days on the villages. I was impressed by the fact that, although the bombings inflicted casualties among the civilians, the peasants nevertheless told me: "We have learned to live with the bombings; we can go up to the mountains during the day and come down to the villages at night, but we cannot learn to live with starvation."

It is essential to understand the situation of the civilian population of Afghanistan. If nothing is done to relieve it, we may face a new exodus of refugees to Pakistan, and that would not be in the interest of either Pakistan or Afghanistan.

Sajjad Hyder

I would like to comment on two points you raised about the political instability in Pakistan and about the absorption of Afghanistan with the Soviet Union on the pattern of Mongolia. Since I was also ambassador to Mongolia for four years, I have some acquaintance with that country. I well remember that in December 1978 when I took leave of the president of Mongolia he said: "Tell your government that I am moving my ambassador to Pakistan from Peking to Kabul." I said, "Your Excellency, when did you have an embassy in Kabul?" "We don't as yet, but I'm going to put one there." I remarked, "It's time the government of Afghanistan learned something from the model of Mongolia."

The two questions I promised to answer yesterday are whether Pakistan can afford to continue to support the resistance movements and whether it can afford not to. Before I answer these very provocative questions proposed yesterday by Dr. Naby, I must make it quite clear that what I am about to say is my own personal view and that I represent *nobody* in Pakistan. That these views also happen to be those of some other Pakistanis is a pure coincidence. I write for Pakistani newspapers now and then, and the response to these few articles leads me to believe that I am not out of step with our realities.

The central determinants of Pakistan's foreign policy since independence have been to safeguard its territorial integrity and political independence for being weakened by the remorseless pull of centrifugal forces generated by India and, second, to get Afghanistan to drop its irredentist claim by recognizing the validity of the Pakistani-Afghan border demarcated in 1893 and reaffirmed no less than four times since. Every other factor in our foreign policy has flowed from these two basic needs, coupled with the recognition that without socioeconomic development there could be nothing to defend—and nothing to defend it with. We turned first to the United States in the 1950s, and then to China in the early 1960s, hoping to achieve a sufficient counterbalance to India and unblock the Kashmir issue. The 1965 war and the dismemberment of Pakistan in 1971 forced us to recognize certain basic empirical realities: (1) China, which we had hoped would become the cornerstone of our security, lacked the necessary force to balance the Indo-Soviet alliance; (2) the United States lacks—even when it has the will—for its own internal reasons, the ability to offer us credible guarantees for our security where India is concerned; and (3) the Soviet Union has the greatest ability to harm Pakistan as it has shown in 1971. Whatever other mistakes we may have made, it was recognized that primacy had to be given to the first determinant of our foreign policy, namely, safeguarding Pakistan from India. Flowing from this supreme national objective was our central assumption that we could never get ourselves in such a position that we might be faced with a 2-front war. All our endeavors in this regard were set at naught with the fall of the Da'ud regime in Afghanistan in April 1978. Earlier, the pressure from Afghanistan was no less remorseless than from India, insofar as Pakistan's territorial integrity was concerned. My friend and compatriot Mr. Ansari spoke yesterday of Afghanistan being the only country to oppose Pakistan's admission to the United Nations in 1947. I do not know how many of you have paid attention to that statement, but I assure you, as a Pakistani, that this has gone deeply into the psyche of each and every Pakistani—the fact that it was a fellow-Muslim country that opposed our admission to the United Nations. Another reality for us was Afghanistan's relentless propaganda campaign against Pakistan for three decades or more, demanding two of our remaining four provinces. Notwithstanding this long, unremitting hostility from Kabul, we have received the Afghan refugees with open arms and clear eyes. We have been conscious of the geopolitical realities of our region and our indissoluble ties with our Muslim brethren from across the border, despite the short shrift we received from them as recently as 1920. No other option was open than to receive and hold close to our breast the refugees. This is the truth. The people of Pakistan would not have allowed the government to adopt any other course. Nevertheless, the pressure of these refugees poses problems. Professor Weinbaum has mentioned the political problem, but there are others—social, economic, etc., of which I spoke yesterday. Every visitor to Pakistan knows that.

Now I come to the essential part of my answer to Dr. Naby and to Professor Weinbaum. Of late, official statements and media reaction from Moscow, Kabul, and New Delhi leave us in no doubt that a concerted, strident international campaign has been started against Pakistan, unprecedented in its intensity and virulence. It is no longer a question of what this formidably hostile combination might do to us at some future date; we are face to face with the danger right now. We know only too well what the Soviet-Indian combination in 1971 meant to us. The difference now is that to this hostile array the government of Afghanistan has been added, 3 million of whose deprived nationals have been given refuge in our country at great risk to our own territorial integrity and political independence. Can anyone around this table tell me which Afghan resistance leader has reaffirmed the sanctity of Afghanistan's border with Pakistan? This is not a demand for a quid pro quo, but an expression of serious concern on the part of a handful of my fellow Pathan countrymen whom I visited earlier this month in Peshawar. With grave concern, they told me that the Kabul irredentist claim against Pakistan has been revived. One of them told me that a map has been put out in Kabul showing the new Afghan border lying on the Indus river. I cannot vouch for this; nobody showed me the map. Somebody in Peshawar spoke to me about this. I was very shocked and disturbed; I refused to believe it. But if there is even a grain of truth in it, it would exercise the minds of the people of Pakistan very much in the present situation.

I study the radio monitoring reports concerning Pakistan every day—from radio Kabul, radio Moscow, and radio Delhi. I am appalled by the abuse heaped upon Pakistan and Pakistani leaders day in and day out. It is no less virulent than it used to be in the 1950s and 1960s from Kabul. The "concern" for the "toiling masses and workers" of the Frontier Province and Baluchistan is the recurrent refrain of these broadcasts. Radio Kabul constantly broadcasts about the "bloodthirsty" regime of Pakistan and the "bloodthirsty" generals of Pakistan. They tell how they are "murdering" the people in the Frontier Province and Baluchistan. It is all very well to ask what Dr. Naby has asked, but let us not close our eyes to the reality of the situation as it exists on the ground today. Four million Afghan refugees outside of their country with noble motives and their glorious struggle do not, I must submit, constitute the nation-state of Afghanistan. The nation-state of Afghanistan is across our border, and we have lived with it for thirty-six years. We hope to live peacefully and in amity with it for thirty-six, a hundred years, or more. That is the reality of the situation.

Hence my belief that the key to the present situation lies in Kabul. Pakistan must, apart from fashioning a reinvigorated relationship with the United States, try to forestall the complete hostility of the Soviets by offering India a no-war pact and also enter into indirect talks with Afghanistan under the aegis of the United Nations. Our offer of a no-war pact was motivated by our policy of support and sympathy to the Afghan cause and that of the Afghan *mujahidin,* which we rightly feared might lead to the potential activation of that front. Because it was feared that Pakistan was exploiting the Afghan crisis for rearming, India turned down our offer of a no-war pact. It was unrealistic of us to expect India to agree when we were in a position of weakness, and a no-war pact would have left us a free hand over Afghanistan against the interests of India's ally, the Soviet Union. This, Professor Weinbaum, will give some answer to your question of India holding, perhaps, the strongest diplomatic cards.

I feel that a far more practical method for reaching a modus vivendi with India would not have been to agree to a goal, a common approach, on Afghanistan. It would not only help forge a concrete step toward South Asian security, but provide a means, perhaps the only means, for getting the Soviets out of Afghanistan, which happens to be now our main national objective. As for the UN initiative, the story of Mr. Cordoves's endeavor in Geneva is well known to us all. The substantial progress made at Geneva in the spring of this year was vitiated at the June conference because of certain doubts and uncertainties in Washington. Mr. Kirby's speech last night, especially his claim that he is in a position to know what has come to pass, must have come as a comfort to those of us who have followed the course of these talks very closely. These talks are about to be resumed in New York next week. I hope and pray that they will cease to remain stalled and progress will be forthcoming, leading to an agreement between the two sides necessitating certain other formal steps. Let us not close our eyes to the realities of the situation. There are constraints and compulsions on both sides and neither can insist on this or that condition as a prerequisite. Speaking once again for myself, I can say that Pakistan has put great store on these talks and their success. I hope Pakistan is not frustrated and disappointed in this regard. If it is, Miss Naby, we may be forced to seek a regional solution of which I have spoken already. In that case, it would not be inconceivable that the answers to your two questions may be "no" and "yes" in that order.

DISCUSSION

Jiri Valenta: The national interest is an important factor in the policymaking of any country, and sometimes there are circumstances which force policymakers to take actions they would have preferred to avoid. Before we discuss the feasibility and equitableness of a tradeoff, we have to carefully examine the outcomes of invasions or military interventions. For example, although the initial justification of the U.S. invasion of Grenada sounded a little like the Brezhnev doctrine, the outcome was quite the contrary. During a visit to Grenada and discussions with many Grenadians, it was amply clear to me that the U.S.

and East Caribbean forces' intervention brought about a better situation in Grenada than did the Soviet invasion of Afghanistan. One must evaluate what an invasion accomplishes in terms of the national interest of the superpowers, but also in terms of the "host" country and its people. In this context one might also mention Vietnam, whose story has yet to be understood in many European countries. We have now in Vietnam, and in Southeast Asia in general, a much more inhumane situation than we had under the American-backed South Vietnamese regime. We have to compare the consequences of seemingly like actions before equating the Soviet Union and the United States.

Regarding Andropov's interview in *Der Spiegel,* we do not know what he implied. He mentioned Nicaragua in what I think was more or less a propaganda statement. He really did not say he would trade Nicaragua for Afghanistan, although this might have been inferred by some. There is much uncertainty now in Moscow, a great stir of clandestine activity. We are facing an unstable leadership and what Andropov said yesterday, Chernenko might refute tomorrow. In other words, I do not detect the kind of implication being suggested here, that the Soviets will relinquish their "holdings" in the Caribbean for our abandoning the cause of Afghanistan. I do not think this is the case.

Katarina Engberg: As to Andropov's statement of a trade-off, I also believe it is a question of propaganda. It is for public consumption and there is not much substance to it. We should be very careful in drawing any conclusion from the Andropov statement. Hopefully, there is no "Yalta agreement" taking shape in the shadow of secret diplomacy. But it is interesting to observe how the question is put by the Soviets. It shows once more that the only thing that really interests the Soviet leaders is to deal directly with the United States and its leadership. Medium-size or small nations just do not count for the Soviet leaders in this respect.

Selig S. Harrison: Professor Weinbaum's "six options" provide a very useful framework for discussion. In connection with his third option on the nonaligned model, he equates this with the "so-called Finland model." This raises an important point. The most meaningful way to bring Finland into the picture in talking about Afghanistan, where there are so many differences in the historical and other factors involved, is with respect to the security relationship that has existed between Finland and the Soviet Union—the treaty relationship in which the Soviet Union, with consultation, has certain reentry rights in the event of aggression being directed at the Soviet Union through Finland. Therefore, I do not think that the equation you make, Marvin, should be made. I think that the Finland model, with respect to the Finnish-style security relationship, really belongs in what I would categorize as a kind of "3a" option, which I would call a *dependent, Soviet-oriented client government*. This differs from options three and four, which you have as a dependent communist government, in two respects. One is that it does, to the Soviets, involve a Finnish-style security relationship, which certainly did not obtain in the case of the Da'ud regime—that is a continuation of the 1978 treaty between the Soviet Union and the Taraki-Amin regime, or some modification of it, giving a reentry right comparable to that in the Finnish relationship. Second, you say that the preferred Kabul government could contain non-Communist political elements participating as minor partners. But it seems to me that the name of the game at the present time is whether the Soviet Union is prepared to consider a modification of the present regime in which non-Communist elements become major partners or dominant partners, without necessarily removing the symbols of continuity of the "revolution" and placing them in the position of defeat. There is reason to raise this question, because the present line that I am getting both from Karmal Afghans and from the Soviet sources I talk to reflects a great change with respect to the possible role of non-Communist elements in the Kabul regime. Until now, the posture has been that "you should be a patriotic Afghan, join the National Fatherland Front, and come into the regime." They got a few people like former defense minister Khan Muhammad to join the National Fatherland Front, but it has not represented any real concession to non-Communist elements. Now they are saying that if King Zahir Shah is able to create an Afghan national united front, a dialogue, a *loya jirgha* could be jointly convened by that organization, embodying as it does significant elements of the resistance and the Kabul regime—more specifically, as the Karmal government puts it, with the National Fatherland Front. The National Fatherland Front and the projected national united front could convene—it was said one week ago by very authoritative Karmal people—a *loya jirgha* in Paris to talk about the composition of the government.

The question of whether this is just a disinformation posture or whether there is reality to this kind of scenario, which would have to come after the initiation of withdrawals under the UN scenario, is really the essence of the kind of issues we will be discussing this afternoon. The continuation of a Communist-dominated government in Kabul would not be viable, not only internationally but also in terms of the Afghan resistance. But whether there is something between options three and four is the real name of the game.

Marvin G. Weinbaum: There are new nuances here; I think they are important and I will try to incorporate them.

Sabahuddin Kushkaki: I would like also to discuss option three of Marvin's paper. Here you suggest a kind of *bitarafi* (Dari expression meaning "without sides," used to describe Afghanistan's traditional Nonaligned policy between the Soviet and Western blocs from the 1950s to the Communist coup), or nonaligned Afghanistan government. I have done a lot of research when I was in Pakistan on how we could organize a coalition among the various groups and parties of the resistance. We were trying to get some kind of consensus among the various groups on what kind of platform they could adopt to establish a coalition. In the end, we did not succeed in gaining the results we were aiming at. But it was very interesting to find out that, especially among the people forming the backbone or the main strata of the Afghan jehad, there is a kind of consensus about what kind of solution they seek. They should not be portrayed as the people who will only continue to fight and resist the Soviet Union, and will not coexist with the Soviet Union as a neighbor. Some fear that if they come to power they will create a hostile base against the Soviet Union. This is completely incorrect. I can say this from talking with the majority of what we decided to call the progressive or revolutionary Islamic elements. They are in agreement with a kind of formula which more or less coincides with this option three of Marvin's paper.

But there are a number of things that they will not be able to accept, at least in the beginning. In the future, when a free Afghanistan is established, maybe we can talk about those things. The thing that they are particularly sensitive about is the presence of Soviet civilian advisors, continued cooperation between the Afghans and Soviet military, as well as the close alignment of their economies. The experiences Afghanistan has had in the past—close cooperation in the military and economic fields—are considered among the reasons for Afghanistan's becoming prey to communism. To immediately restore the same kind of status, which to the Afghans was one of the causes of the Communist takeover of Afghanistan, would mean just begging the question. We had worked out in Pakistan, I think, seven points on which the moderate Islamic groups, who are doing the real fighting in Afghanistan, could agree. The first point is that there has to be a withdrawal of Soviet forces from Afghanistan. The second point is that there has to be a joint action by all those forces in the resistance who are committed to Islamic principles on the one hand, and are also working against the occupation of Afghanistan by the Soviet forces and against an atheist regime. Third—and this comes to the second part of option three of Marvin's paper about King Zahir Shah—these progressive elements say they would resist the emergence in the ranks of Afghan jehad of those groups directly responsible for the present tragedy of Afghanistan. In their opinion, communism did not come to Afghanistan out of the blue. The infrastructure and conditions were laid for a Communist takeover of Afghanistan as a result of apathy, indifference, and failure of our own leadership in the past. They are responsible for the present tragedy and should not be allowed to infiltrate the ranks of the *mujahidin*. The fourth thing they will agree on is to hold neighborly relations with all countries, including the Soviet Union, on the basis of mutual respect for their sovereignty and territorial integrity. The fifth item is that they will cooperate with all those forces which have committed themselves to help Afghanistan against Soviet invasion. There is talk that the Islamic fundamentalists are not keen on Western assistance, because they are at the same time anti-Western. But I would say that the majority and mainstream of the young generation of Afghan *mujahidin* would welcome this help, and also cooperation with international organizations seeking a political solution to the Afghan problem. And then there is talk as to whether they are anxious or willing to resort to some kind of public opinion and public will in forming an Afghan state. At the right stage, they are willing to do that also, to create a kind of administration in Afghanistan based on the will of the people. They would not like to see this in the form of *loya jirghas,* these grand national assemblies which have been historical phenomena in Afghanistan, but they would like to see some kind of mechanism through which the national will is expressed. At the same time, they would like to see an infrastructure being laid for the Afghan government of the future.

Marvin G. Weinbaum: It is very interesting to have these comments; I appreciate them. We should keep in mind that what you consider not to be anti-Soviet, the Soviets may, nevertheless, view as anti-Soviet. I tried to say earlier that indeed, they necessarily must have good neighborly relations. But unwillingness to accept the Soviet presence in any form is naturally to to taken as unfriendly by the Soviets, and would rule out *bitarafi*.

Sabahuddin Kushkaki: I would only say that they would guarantee, for example, that there will not be a hostile state created in Afghanistan. If the Soviet Union came into Afghanistan under the justification that its security was being violated by a foreign threat, they were ready to provide the guarantee that Soviet security not be threatened.

Louis Dupree: The problem of the Durand Line is still a major regional problem; it is one of those legacies of European imperialism left on the landscape. When the British left, they left boundaries on the landscape which cut through linguistic units, geographic realities, ecological entities. I have done a lot of research on this myself. I was among those who were in Pakistan and Afghanistan almost immediately after partition in 1947; I looked into what was happening in Kabul. There was a group of Indians there controlling Kabul radio, and they are the ones who even invented the term *Pushtunistan*. My friend Tom Gouttierre knows who some of them are. They began to push this in the hope that Pakistan would actually disappear.

In researching in the secret and political letters of the India Office Library from the late 1890s up to 1947, I found a paragraph in every one of the secret and political letters sent annually to Whitehall. The line was not described as the boundary of India, but as "the eastern and southern frontier of the Amir's dominion, and as the limit and the respective spheres of influence of the two governments and not that of the Indian frontier." (Published in the classified *Military Report on Afghanistan,* General Staff, India, Government of India Press, 1925, p. 69.) That is a straightforward statement, published year after year in the British documents. Now, who told the Indians, the Pakistanis, and the Afghans that the Durand Line was an international boundary in 1947? Lord Louis Mountbatten. I have been trying to find the orders from Whitehall which gave him the authority to make this announcement. I have not found them yet, but messages were sent to all three governments stating that the Durand Line was to be considered an "international boundary" and that the government of Pakistan would inherit all responsibilities and obligations relating to that boundary.

Quickly, I would like to clarify something I said yesterday. To protect the territoriality of Pakistan does not mean to protect a government in power in Pakistan. This has been the American mistake since World War II. Look at our track record: all the leaders we have supported around the world have resulted in total failure. If another general were to save Pakistan from itself, let that happen. If Pakistan wants to hold democratic elections, let that happen. The only guarantee would be to those international boundaries as we perceive them to be, and as the U.S. allies and the Pakistanis themselves perceive them. This would guarantee this territoriality, and I hope it happens. The guarantor would not only be the United States, but the NATO allies, the Muslim world, and Japan—and I speak ideally.

I will borrow a phrase from my friend Mr. Kushkaki: The people who are partly responsible for the success of the Communist ideology in Afghanistan are the same groups that we find worldwide. They are the comfortable middle class, like most of us, who do nothing if we can possibly help it. I would like to see another term, not *Finlandization* or *Mongolization,* used when we refer to Afghanistan. I would like to have *Afghanization* referred to. I would like to use that term when we use the UN four points, which have been discussed several times during these meetings, and I would like to see Afghanization discussed, not Finlandization, Mongolization, or anything else.

Sajjad Hyder: I cannot allow Mr. Dupree's observation to pass unchallenged. I do not think that we are concerned with what the explanatory letters from the Ministry of External Affairs in New Delhi said about this line. This is the line which has been agreed upon, part of the treaty between the British government of India and the government of Afghanistan. This line has been reaffirmed right up to 1931. This is the line that, as you said, through our status as a successor government, by international law has indeed devolved upon us, as our right. We are going to hold on to that right whatever happens. We are not going to say that some other line along the settled districts, or some other line, would do. You have no idea how disturbed I have been since yesterday when Professor Naby, in her paper, talked about Hindu Kush absorption. I said something yesterday on the subject which a very friendly participant told me I had not explained too well. What I said was that if the Soviets say that the Afghan border should lie on the Hindu Kush, it really coincides with Jawaharlal Nehru's 1946 telegram to Sir Giles Squire in Kabul, asking him to go and tell Sardar Hashem Khan that if you talk about a referendum also having accession to Afghanistan as one of the conditions, then tell him that the natural boundary of India lies on the Hindu Kush. Now, if both India and the Soviets come to convergence on Hindu Kush, where are our two provinces? Gone to Afghanistan?

Louis Dupree: Certainly, I was not trying to justify the Afghan position, the Indian position, or a Pakistani position. I was simply stating what is in the British document, that is all. Several have used the Durand Line to their advantage at different times, and this is what the Indians were doing at that time. Also, the first boundary treaty signed by Abdur Rahman is very carefully wishy-washy. It is one of the "Charlie Brown" treaties of all the Indian subcontinent. It does not really establish the Durand Line as an international boundary, and subsequent treaties referred back to this first treaty. International law is only meaningful if someone has the power to enforce it. Pakistan had the power to maintain the Durand Line and it has. To me, that is justification enough. Also, Bhutto and Da'ud, in their meetings just before both were overthrown, totally agreed that the Durand Line could be the international boundary between the two countries with certain modifications. And those modifications were necessary. I have been up and down the Durand Line myself, and there are some places where a town or village is on one side and the fields are on the other.

Sajjad Hyder: There was also a boundary on the other side, along the Amu Darya, between Afghanistan and the Soviet Union. That boundary was demarcated during the past century probably also by Sir Mortimer Durand. And that boundary later on had to be precisely determined. They never said what part of the Amu Darya would be the boundary. By a subsequent treaty they agreed that the middle of the river of Amu Darya would be the boundary between Afghanistan and the Soviet Union.

Louis Dupree: It is all academic, because the boundary of the Soviet Union is now on Pakistan. They have the Durand Line.

Reinhardt Rummell: I want to address two remarks to Professor Weinbaum's paper and one to Ambassador Hyder. The paper states that international responses, even if predictable before, would not have deterred the thrust of Soviet power into Afghanistan. The experience in Poland is relevant in this context. The United States and the West Europeans had prepared for what was threatened—an invasion. Western preparation for this event shows that one learned a little from the Afghan case. So I would not really agree with what you are saying about the future. Rather, if there is a better preparation than there was for Afghanistan, the Soviets may be deterred, and in the future the Soviets will have learned their lesson too. With respect to risk taking, they are much more cautious.

The second aspect I wanted to bring up is your statement that the international costs of the Soviet invasion were substantially paid during the first year. I would agree to the extent you are talking about political costs caused among the Islamic conference, the Nonaligned countries, the UN, and so on. Although I would say one has to ask why was that the case. It very much depends on the degree to which the West takes movements like the Nonaligned countries, the Islamic conference, or the United Nations for that matter, seriously. UN resolutions could be a more helpful policy if you did not have the president of the United States saying that the UN resolution that was passed on Grenada did not even upset his breakfast. What is done on the one hand should not undercut the other. Still, beyond the diplomatic costs, one has to refer to other costs that have been very substantial for Moscow and will continue to be. It started with the lessons President Carter learned in a very few days, and continued with the Reagan administration. Afghanistan really demonstrated the aggressiveness of the USSR. That was not only helpful to the U.S.

side, but also for a number of other countries including the European, even though they had been very reluctant in supporting the United States at the time. The fact that there is Afghanistan and that it is kept up as a living example of Soviet behavior bears very much on our own behavior toward the Soviet Union, or the question of how to cope with it, whether to cooperate or not and how to pass certain rearmament measures through Congress and other bodies. In that respect Afghanistan is not dead by far; it is rather working as a very substantial instrument.

I had the impression from Ambassador Hyder that he was saying that Pakistan is taking over quite a heavy burden in the course of the ongoing Afghan tragedy. We were referring to it yesterday with the term *arms trail*. And today we mentioned the question of the refugees, of encirclement, and so on. One has to take this seriously, but one has also to look at the whole situation in broader terms. Although I know it is not comparable, I would like just for a while to compare Pakistan's situation to that in Central Europe. We have had the Soviets there for almost forty years now since the war, and we have coped with it. I can say from the German point of view that we faced a particular kind of Soviet Union—one that asks for peaceful coexistence but means the projection of power. We are going through a difficult phase right now with the INF deployment and the talks about it. It shows quite well what "Soviet neighborhood" means. My country has felt that we are at a borderline, and that we have to cope with that geographic and geopolitical situation. We have a responsibility to do so. Not only for ourselves or for the Central European region, but far beyond. This approach bears on the degree of responsibility we have accepted. What is safe for Pakistan is that kind of overall view that goes beyond the question of the temporary, local feelings that might be threatening Pakistan. I do not underestimate that these threats are there, and that they are perceived, but one has to add another dimension.

Sajjad Hyder: This is the whole point. I see the validity of your advice. But then I would say, you have been able to survive this division because you still have the hope to unite sometime in the future. I am afraid we have lost it forever.

Seyed Qassem Reshtia: First of all I would like to express our deep gratitude to our friends from Pakistan for the help and support they have offered the refugees from Afghanistan as well as the *mujahidin*. This is very important and we will never forget it. Future generations will always remember this act of generosity which reflects the true meaning of Muslim brotherhood. On the international scene, also, they have offered their unshakable support to the cause of Afghanistan in the face of the very serious threat from the Soviet Union. They are continuing it until now. As far as past relationships are concerned, I prefer and I beg my senior brother Ambassador Hyder to leave it to history to pass the final verdict. But for the sake of the records I must clarify one point: The negative vote cast by the Afghan representative in the United Nations in 1947 was later *withdrawn* after clarification of the vote.

Robert G. Neumann: Whatever the foreign office or Indian office records may reveal, I went to Afghanistan in 1966 with the guidance and instructions of my government that we had recognized (I forget the year, I think 1959 or thereabouts) the Durand Line as the international border. Since I was in Afghanistan a long time, during certain times of the year there was an increase in the decibel count of the Pushtunistan propaganda on radio Kabul. I was usually called in to the foreign office, the prime minister's office, or sometimes by the king. I never took that very seriously; I do not think they did either—it was a ritual we went through. They reminded me of their position and I reminded them of ours, and we had this behind us for another six months. I never could discover the slightest indication of any great sympathy for Pushtunistan joining Afghanistan on the other side of the border. I do agree that if Afghanistan is to emerge under new leadership, as an act of gratitude as well as to clean up certain historical garbage, it would be nice to put this ridiculous problem behind us. But since neither gratitude nor mercy are part of the vocabulary of either the Middle East or the subcontinent, I have no faith in it.

The second point is in the interesting paper by our main speaker. What bothered me a little is that the different options are lined up, almost like some policy papers I have seen and which I have heavily criticized, as if they were equally obtainable. In an operational sense, and after all the purpose of diplomacy is not to win debates but to obtain results, the question really is whether the Soviets are ready to have a change in the situation. And as a corollary, do they wish a diplomatic fig leaf, which diplomats are professionally trained to advocate? If that fig leaf is to cover their desire to remain, I do not see the slightest interest in our doing it, but if it is to cover their desire to withdraw, it is very interesting. It is to explore this latter possibility that I see the main, in fact the only purpose of the UN Mission. I do not think the UN Mission means anything else but talks with the Soviets, from time to time, about this possibility to see whether they are interested. I do not see in it, as yet, and I do not know if we will ever see, the possibility of serious negotiations coming from it. The operational question is not which of the formulas may work—that is way down the line if anywhere. The operational question is: Are the Soviets, for reason of their regional or global perspectives, ready to contemplate a change involving their withdrawal? Then, further diplomatic steps can take place. Otherwise, this is a signaling operation which is significant; I do not diminish it. But to somehow fantasize that serious negotiation will come from it is beyond my poor capacity to comprehend diplomacy.

Marvin G. Weinbaum: That is well taken. Is it not, though, unimportant to consider what kind of a fig leaf we will give them? And, in that sense, we do get into certain options. Assuming that they are willing to accept one, we can say: "What kind of fig leaf can we offer?"—both in terms of what the Afghan groups are prepared to give and what we feel, in a larger strategic way, we are in a position to give.

Zia-ul-Islam Ansari: First of all, I would like to point out that whatever observation I may make should not be taken as representative of Pakistan. I would like to comment as a friend of the Afghan resistance and the freedom fighters of Afghanistan.

A question has been raised as to the acceptability of this fundamentalist government. If we judged a certain type of government and its acceptability to this or that group, this would run against item two of the UN principles about the solution of this problem. When we talk of the right of self-determination of the people and their right to choose their form of government, to lay down preconditions that this type of government will be acceptable to us or to them, we support the position of the Soviets that they want a particular government in Afghanistan. Let us be objective when we talk on this subject—whether such a government can be formed or can be practically functional. I want to express my appreciation of Dr. Naby for suggesting the discarding of the word *fundamentalist*. I would suggest that we use *pragmatic, realistic* Islamic forces. This would be a better, more acceptable form of government for the people, as well as for the East and West.

Again, it is a matter for the people of Pakistan what type of government they have and whether it is stable, whether the Jamiyat-i-Islami comes to power, or whether they have closer relationships with the Afghan *mujahidin*. These are questions to be answered by Pakistanis and by the Afghan *mujahidin,* or by those 3 million refugees living in Pakistan. So let us discuss whether this alternative is workable or practical.

Briefly, I would like to suggest another alternative which has not been mentioned. The two options being ruled out are (1) the defeat of the Soviet armies by the *mujahidin* and (2) a negotiated settlement.

Both are improbable. But there is a third alternative, based on the claim the Russians used for going into Afghanistan: that they wanted to safeguard the integrity of the motherland from some things happening in Central Asia. We shall, for discussion's sake, accept this claim that they went there for this purpose only, and that other things are byproducts. So let us work on that alternative as well. This will be to support the sort of arrangements around Central Asia which would attract the Muslims living there as a sense of inspiration. For that we will have a long wait, but no longer than for the defeat of the Red army by the *mujahidin*—and not longer than for a negotiated settlement. In all three cases the time frame will be the same—ten, fifteen, or maybe twenty years.

We must allow the establishment of free and pragmatic Islamic societies without interference. And then to have these countries flourish and have stable economic conditions. Finally, we must release the pressure on the Muslim countries elsewhere in the Middle East, so that they may align themselves with a brotherhood living under better conditions than obtain in Central Asia.

One more point. The Indian stand is referred to here and again. I would like to pose a question to all the scholars here. Although India seems to be a big democracy in the world today, and although it is a big power and a regional one as well, let us realize that, gradually, it is becoming a Soviet proxy state and all the talks of seeking its support for a resolution of Afghanistan are vain hopes. We do not realize that the Indian bureaucracy is increasingly becoming dependent on the Soviet connection. There is a public opinion in India realizing the dangers of the Soviet invasion of Afghanistan, but India's bureaucracy is increasingly becoming dependent on Soviet support and the Soviet connection. If it is allowed to go on like this, India will also become a Soviet satellite or a communist state, and will pose, without any invasion or occupation by the Soviet Union, a serious problem for the rest of the world.

Laurent Carrel: On the subject of international responsibilities, I would like to briefly look at one option for the European countries. Looking at the six options Mr. Weinbaum presented to us, it seems that Afghanistan needs in each case external support, also from Europe, to achieve a preferable or good solution for its future. I would like to point out a remark Miss Engberg made when she tried to explain the Swedish policy toward the war in Vietnam. She said the Swedish opposition may have been so strong against the war because there were high hopes to influence the U.S. leadership in decision making. On the other hand, the absence of a strong opposition in Sweden against the war in

Afghanistan seems to stem from the realization that one has very little influence on Soviet decision making. I would like to ask the following question: How much influence can we have on Soviet decision making by informing the Western public about what is going on in Afghanistan? I am not sure that one can just claim to have no influence at all. I think Afghanistan creates an embarrassment for Soviet relations with most of the world. It is an obstacle to more friendly dealings with China. The Soviet Union is to a certain degree sensitive to political pressure, especially that coming from the Third World, because they would like to be the leader of the Nonaligned states. The Soviet Union is also susceptible to pressure coming from neutral countries, and I think we should not overestimate the influence we could have. On the other hand we should not underestimate it either. If Marxism-Leninism makes the distinction between just and unjust wars, we can make today the distinction between wars *with* television and *without* television. In wars *with* television (Israel or Vietnam are good examples), front line reports can have a tremendous impact on the public. Afghanistan would be certainly considered a war without television. We in the free West have a responsibility toward Afghanistan. One of the reasons for the lack of interest in Europe, is that so little is reported about the war in Afghanistan. One important option for building up pressure on the Soviets is providing more information about the war in Afghanistan. This seems to be one of the primary European responsibilities. Since there is more information coming out lately, interest in the Afghan war has been on the rise. I have experienced that myself, by publishing regularly military assessments of the situation in Afghanistan. The responses I get from all over Switzerland tell me that if you inform the public, the latter is more aware and talks more about it. I am not so sure that the Soviet Union is not susceptible to that kind of negative public opinion about its behavior in Afghanistan.

Marvin G. Weinbaum: That is well taken, but certainly you would want to consider too that not all information is necessarily helpful. The media may very well focus on aspects which would not necessarily reflect well on the resistance. Of course, if they choose to focus on brutality, it can only win sympathy for the Afghan cause. But they go where it is easiest. It may very well be to those places in Peshawar where people are arguing amongst themselves. We are getting some coverage from Afghanistan which suggests groups fighting one another within the country. This is bad. But on the whole, I think you are right. As time goes on and the resistance becomes more frustrated, the dangers from the kind of reporting that we would not see as helpful increases.

Katarina Engberg: Western media have contributed to the lack of sensitivity in the West toward the situation in Afghanistan. Some journalists going into Afghanistan are more concerned with the militaristic and adventuristic aspects of their journey than with the pressing situation of the civilian population. I think that Soviet leaders are sensitive to the reaction of public opinion in Western Europe because they want to be considered as Europeans and not Asians. There is no unanimous acceptance within the Soviet Union, not even within its leadership, of Soviet policy in Afghanistan. I doubt, however, that it is possible to influence Soviet leaders in any real way.

Eden Naby: It is important to use positive rather than negative terminology. If we are trying to describe something that is new and ought to be explored, giving it a name such as "revolutionary" pidgeonholes it immediately in people's minds. What we want to do is explore what is there rather than shut the door on what we may find. This is one reason why I would prefer to use a term like *progressive,* which sparks the imagination, even though it may be a socialist, Third World term. We use *freedom fighter,* which is also a Third World term. This is the reason why many of us have insisted on using the term *resistance* from the very beginning rather than *rebels*. This is the sort of thing I am talking about—being positive rather than negative and defeatist.

Going back to the question of the Hindu Kush that was raised so briefly and fleetingly yesterday: I did not mean to suggest the Hindu Kush as a boundary in terms of known present Soviet policy but merely as an option. I was suggesting that if we are going to talk about any form of annexation of Afghanistan, we may also discuss dismemberment.

In discussing the options for a future Kabul government, we would want to pay some attention to what would be acceptable to the Soviets. The question seems to be: Would the Soviets negotiate a compromise with progressive Islamic forces if the latter were willing? I think there are certain conditions under which they would. Mr. Kushkaki has referred to some of these; Ambassador Neumann has talked about the operational aspects. I think the gist of what you were saying, Ambassador Hyder, at least in connection to my presentation yesterday, lies in the need for Pakistan to deal with a stable Kabul government. As I understand it, your objection to considering only the 3 million refugees in Pakistan as a basis for negotiations for a future Afghan government is that these, perhaps, do not represent the possibility for a stable government. I agree with you, but I would also say that we must keep in mind what Dr. Engberg has been telling us. Although these groups in

Peshawar, either the 3 million refugees or the *mujahidin* groups in Peshawar, do not represent a future stable government in their present form, nevertheless the 10 million people in Afghanistan are in sympathy—in one respect or another—with the groups outside. If we are talking about dealing with Kabul, we cannot speak simply about dealing with a small group of elites in Kabul. We have to consider the whole matter of an awakened politicized countryside. This is why Mr. Kushkaki mentioned some sort of a consensus, possibly a plebiscite, as important in talking about a future settlement.

Sajjad Hyder: It is very difficult for us in Pakistan to know who is behind what they are saying in these daily radio broadcasts. They are beamed into Pakistan, particularly in the Frontier Province, in Pashtu language, and the language they use is abusive. We cannot but be exercised by the use of this language; we cannot but be concerned about this attack on our territorial integrity. Especially so, when we find it echoed in the broadcasts from Moscow and Dehli. We cannot but be saddened. I hope you have noticed that in these past two days I have not presumed to speak about anything which is in the province of the government of Afghanistan or its people. But I feel entitled to talk about my own country and people. And we are very disturbed at this onslaught on us from Kabul, Moscow, and Delhi.

Noor A. Husain: Permit me to go back to a point raised by my very good friend, Louis Dupree, and by Ambassador Hyder, concerning the Durand Line. I do not have the expertise of Louis, who has walked on both sides of the Durand Line, nor the ambassador, who is evidently aware of this letter, but let me tell you that the Durand Line has been demarcated as an international border on the ground. If it was not meant to be an international border, why was it demarcated? The only places where it has not been physically marked are perhaps Bajur and Chitral, and that is because the demarcating party could not climb up those difficult mountains. There they have what they call the watershed agreement—the international frontier runs clearly along the top of the watershed. I also want to clarify what Ambassador Sajjad Hyder said in referring to a letter of 1946. I would like to remind this gathering about the pronouncement by the Indian foreign minister, Swaran Singh, the day after King Zahir Shah was overthrown. In the Indian Lok Soba he made a statement to the following effect: "The historical security frontiers of India lie on the Hindu Kush." This was in July 1973. When the Soviets moved in, this statement was ignored. During my visit to India two years ago after a lapse of thirty-five years, I found indicators—in official, academic, and research establishments—that some Indians had either an inkling or at some level they had given a tacit understanding to the Soviet move into Afghanistan. I have not been able to establish it with certainty, but there were strong indicators to this effect.

Sabahuddin Kushkaki: Just a brief comment for Ambassador Hyder. As far as I have studied the Pushtunistan issue in Pakistan, among my brother refugees, this is a dead issue. I think any intelligent, any proven Afghan leadership to emerge among the resistance would agree that this is a dead issue. We have brotherly relations with Pakistan. I do not know why this question bothers you so much, because it should be very clear to you by now that the Afghans are no longer insisting on this. We are not talking on behalf of the Kabul government here; we are talking on behalf of the resistance. This Afghan resistance will seek a solution to the Afghan problem and will not pursue the Pushtunistan problem.

5

U.S. Policy on Afghanistan

Harmon E. Kirby

It is critically important that the brutal, dirty war in Afghanistan, which has gone on for nearly four years since the Soviet invasion on December 27, 1979, not be forgotten. International attention to the conflict encourages the *mujahidin* to stand fast and keeps pressure on the Soviets to withdraw and leave Afghanistan to its people. Conferences like this, attended by knowledgeable people from around the globe, help keep the spotlight of international attention on the war.

In attempting to lay out U.S. government views on the Afghan situation and our policies toward that conflict, I hope that I shall be stating nothing that most of you have not heard before. Our policies have been consistent, and I like to think they are reasonably well known and understood. Still, it seems useful to review and restate those policies to this audience for several reasons: (1) We live in a busy world with all too many crises that tend to crowd in, blotting out of public consciousness such long-festering, long-running sores as the obscenity of Afghanistan; (2) it would be understandable if some of you who have come to this conference from distant lands were not as familiar with our policies as those among us who have heard them stated frequently; and (3) tonight's session should serve as a useful framework for our half-day discussion of alternatives to U.S. policy scheduled for tomorrow.

First, I would like to give an overview of U.S. policy by summarizing at some length the main themes of that policy. Then I will go on to pick up each of these themes and elaborate them in somewhat greater detail.

Major themes of U.S. Policy toward Afghanistan

The United States strongly opposes the Soviet occupation of Afghanistan and seeks an end to the terrible agony it has brought to the

Afghan people. Apart from our very real concern about the Afghans themselves, we view the Soviet invasion and continuing occupation in a broad strategic context, as an example of Soviet willingness to use its ever-growing military might beyond its borders in ways that not only threaten American interests but peace, stability, and freedom in the Central-South Asian region and throughout the world. For this reason we believe it is essential that Soviet aggression in Afghanistan be checked and not succeed.

The United States is committed to seeking a political settlement for Afghanistan. This settlement must be based on the principles already spelled out in four UN General Assembly resolutions on Afghanistan, with a fifth resolution along these lines scheduled for adoption by the General Assembly next week (this resolution was adopted on November 23, 1983 by a vote of 116-20 with 16 abstentions): complete withdrawal of Soviet forces; self-determination of the Afghan people; independent and Nonaligned status of Afghanistan; return of the refugees with safety and honor. These resolutions also call upon the secretary-general of the United Nations to use his best efforts to find a solution, which would include appropriate international guarantees.

The United States believes that every avenue leading to a peaceful settlement must be explored. This is why we have supported the efforts of the UN secretary-general's personal representative, Diego Cordovez, as he tries to determine the possibilities for a negotiated settlement under UN auspices. We will support these efforts as long as they are consistent with UNGA resolutions on Afghanistan.

The United States has worked closely with Pakistan in the search for an acceptable political settlement for Afghanistan. We think the newly reinvigorated U.S. security relationship with Pakistan, reaffirmed during President Zia's December 1982 state visit to the United States, strengthens these complementary efforts. Both the United States and Pakistan have resisted any moves that would tend to legitimize the Babrak regime.

The United States, like Pakistan and others in the international community, has pursued a multitrack approach to try to bring the Soviets to negotiate a political settlement. This has included international pressure through various organizations such as the UN, the Nonaligned movement, the Islamic Conference, and the EC, and efforts through bilateral contacts with the Soviets. It has also included media and other public diplomacy efforts. The struggle of the *mujahidin* on the ground in Afghanistan, where the freedom fighters have prevented the Soviets and their puppet Babrak Karmal regime from solidifying their control of the country, is central to this multifaceted approach. The spirit of the *mujahidin* in fighting for their freedom is indeed an inspiration to the rest of the world.

While the search for a political settlement continues, the United States has not forgotten the humanitarian problem of caring for the world's largest refugee population—the nearly 2.7 million Afghan refugees who have been given shelter and care by the government of Pakistan, assisted by international organizations led by the UNHCR and private groups. This has been an impressive act of hospitality by Pakistan and we have been pleased to contribute over $300 million to Afghan refugee relief through 1983.

Strategic Setting

Now I would like to pick up and expand on some of the themes included in the foregoing summary. First, I want to discuss the strategic setting since, as I have said, the United States views the Afghan turmoil in its broad strategic context. After almost four years of Soviet occupation, Afghanistan remains an important unresolved issue in world affairs.

The Soviet Union has been unable to accomplish what it set out to do—strengthen the Communist government in Kabul, gain international acceptance of the Karmal regime, create an effective Afghan army, and eliminate the resistance.

Soviet control of Afghanistan has not been accepted, either by the vast majority of Afghans or the majority of the community of nations, and certainly not by the United States. Two successive U.S. administrations have made it clear that the unconscionable Soviet action must be reversed. Afghanistan has been a priority agenda item for the Reagan administration since it came to office in January 1981.

On the other hand, the Afghan resistance, while increasingly effective and demonstrating the ability to inflict steady losses on the Soviets, has not been capable of militarily ousting the Soviets, and diplomatic and public pressure has not yet been able to bring the Soviets to a negotiated political settlement.

We continue to believe that the presence of over 100,000 Soviet troops in Afghanistan is a cause of instability in the region and in the world, creating a great threat to an area of vital concern to our national interests—the Persian Gulf and the Straits of Hormuz. It brings special pressures on important friends of the United States like Pakistan in the South Asian region.

Our strategic goal remains the same. We want to get the Soviet troops out of Afghanistan; we want to remove this cause of instability in the region and in the world. Soviet withdrawal would suit the best interests of the Afghan people and the strategic interests of the United States and of the countries of South and Southwest Asia.

Situation on the Ground

During the past year the military struggle for Afghanistan has continued unabated. If anything, it has intensified in recent months. The *mujahidin* have done very well during 1983. Their morale is high. Despite significant casualties, they appear stronger, better armed, and somewhat more cohesive than at the end of 1982. They have demonstrated remarkable resiliency.

The *mujahidin* have inflicted a number of serious defeats on the Afghan army (and on the Soviets) during the past year, and we heard something about that in passing at our conference earlier today. In May, they decimated an elite Soviet-trained commando brigade, the 38th, which had been moved to Paktia Province from the Panjsher Valley. The *mujahidin* surrounded the brigade, killing over half of them and their Soviet advisors, while the other half of the unit defected to the resistance. Some have said it was the worst military defeat of the war. During June, July, and particularly in August, the *mujahidin* staged several impressive raids on Kabul, with heavy damage to the Soviet-manned Bala Hisar Fortress on August 13.

While the Soviets have from time to time inflicted serious losses on them, the *mujahidin* have generally been successful in avoiding major set-piece engagements, and usually have reoccupied the areas where they had been attacked, including positions close to Kabul, immediately after the Soviets' departure. They have also been particularly effective against Soviet/DRA supply convoys during the course of the summer.

During much of the summer there was heavy *mujahidin* activity in the Herat and Kandahar areas, two of Afghanistan's major cities. Despite repeated, heavy Soviet bombing attacks, the *mujahidin* stood their ground. For regime forces, Herat presents a hostile environment. Civilian officials and the military keep close to their installations in the city and move about only in force. In Kandahar, Afghanistan's second largest city, there is similar lack of full regime control.

In late summer, the *mujahidin* against stepped up pressure in Paktia and Paktika provinces, which lie astride major supply lines from Pakistan. During August and September many isolated government outposts in these provinces were overrun or simply deserted. Major cantonments were brought under siege. Although no major towns fell to the *mujahidin* during the September attacks, the fighting highlighted the growing strength of the resistance in that region and reflected increasing tactical coordination between *mujahidin* bands inside Afghanistan. The resistance efforts in Paktia and Paktika provinces were significantly boosted by the interdiction of Soviet and regime resupply convoys traveling through the Logar Valley.

Although still suffering from factionalism and rivalries, the *mujahidin* have generally achieved more unity and cooperation in the past year. There is evidence that, with certain noteworthy exceptions, *mujahidin* leaders both in Afghanistan and elsewhere have a greater realization of the importance of cooperation, if not outright unity, and that this is being reflected increasingly in their military operations.

Soviet military efforts have been concentrated on building up key logistical bases, on improving security for lines of communication, and interdicting *mujahidin* infiltration from Pakistan and Iran. However, the road links remain insecure and efforts to choke off infiltration routes have not been successful.

The Soviets have also signally failed to achieve their political objective of building up a stable Communist government. The Babrak Karmal regime remains badly split by factional strife and almost totally isolated from the people. The Afghan army is barely maintaining its depressed strength levels of 50,000 men compared with 100,000 in 1978, and the regime has had to resort to press gang-type conscription and the retention of reservists beyond the expiration of their legal two-year military obligations.

As a consequence of the continued serious losses inflicted on the Soviets and DRA forces by the resistance, the level of bombardment and violence against the civilian population by Soviet firepower appears to have reached new heights in 1983. The Soviets appear to believe that by such actions they can wear down civilian support for the resistance and wait the resistance out. The stepped-up brutal reprisal policy by Soviet forces also appears to reflect frustration that the war is going far from well from Moscow's, and Kabul's, viewpoint.

Reprisals against villages located near the sites of *mujahidin* activity have long been standard practice by Soviet and Afghan regime military forces. Soviet frustration has, however, grown as they have proved unable to interdict resistance activity despite intense efforts, including bribes and truce offers, as well as direct military action. During recent weeks we have seen the evolution of an apparently deliberate policy of increased terror and brutality against civilians and their homes. Acts of extreme cruelty and destruction are obviously intended both as a vent for the fear and anger of Soviet troops and as an attempt to drive a wedge between the Afghan people and resistance forces. Let me give some examples.

A French journalist who visited Afghanistan reported the June 30 summary execution of twenty-four persons in the village of Rauzda near Ghazni on the Kabul-Herat highway. The attack came in retaliation for the killing of a Soviet officer during a search of the village.

In mid-October the villages of Moshkizai and Kolchabad near Kandahar were assaulted in reprisal for a resistance attack on a passing Soviet convoy the day before. Approximately 130 villagers died in a ground assault by Soviet troops, which included bayonetting women and children and shooting old men. The day after the massacre, the lesson was driven home by a heavy aerial bombardment of the village. This incident, first reported in the *New York Times,* has since been confirmed by independent sources.

I want to say a special word about recent Soviet reprisal activity which has not yet been mentioned much publicly. In late October credible reports from several sources substantiated rumors of a Soviet operation against the historic village of Istalef in the Shomali region north of Kabul—again in retaliation for resistance activity in the area. Citizens of Istalef, known for the brilliant blues of its fine pottery, were murdered in a days-long orgy of death as resistance forces sought to protect the village from overwhelming force. It was reliably reported that Soviet soldiers bayonetted and slit the throats of children found in the houses of suspected *mujahidin.* We have no exact casualty figures, but losses were high on both sides, with perhaps as many as 400-500 deaths. About 40 percent of Istalef has been leveled.

Despite this increased savagery against civilians by Soviet troops—and we believe there have been many unreported incidents—there is no indication that the people of Afghanistan have reduced their support for the resistance movement. Instead, they continue to provide the *mujahidin* with food, information, shelter, and recruits.

Diplomatic Moves, Including the Status of UN Negotiations

Although there were mixed signals from Moscow at the end of 1982 that under Andropov there might be some changes in Soviet policy toward Afghanistan, there have been no real signs of Soviet flexibility or willingness to negotiate meaningfully on the withdrawal of Soviet troops, the key to a negotiated political settlement for Afghanistan. Today, because of Andropov's uncertain health, we face new uncertainties about whether the Soviets, even if so inclined, could undertake initiatives designed to end the Afghanistan conflict.

The UN negotiating process of indirect talks between the governments of Afghanistan, Pakistan, and Iran, has provided some hope that a political settlement might be possible. Hope was especially evident after last April's session in Geneva.

The indirect talks ran up against hard reality in the later June session in Geneva, however, when the Soviets were unwilling to give a definite date for withdrawal of their troops. Although a certain amount of modest progress was announced on other issues, such as the question of a possible role for external guarantors and a mechanism for consulting the refugees, the UN talks appeared virtually stalled during the past summer. We understand, however, that Mr. Cordovez will be exploring with the parties in New York this week and next, on the margins of the UN General Assembly, prospects for resuming more active negotiations in the weeks and months ahead. We hope he will succeed in that effort.

The Soviets have tried to blame the Pakistanis (and the United States) for the lack of progress at the June session, saying that Pakistan had pulled back from earlier agreed positions because of "U.S. pressure." This is flatly untrue. I am in a position to know.

The United States has consistently supported the UN negotiations as a means of achieving a settlement for Afghanistan, and Secretary Shultz wrote to Foreign Minister Gromyko in late May to reiterate the U.S. desire to achieve a negotiated political settlement for Afghanistan and our support for the UN process. The Soviet reply was not encouraging.

Secretary Shultz had intended to probe Soviet intentions toward the UN indirect talks during his meeting with Gromyko in Madrid in September, but the agenda for this meeting was obviously changed following the Soviet shooting of the Korean airliner.

In all high-level contacts with the Soviets over the past two years, U.S. officials have emphasized the importance of the Afghan issue and our conviction that U.S.-Soviet relations will not improve appreciably so long as the Soviets are in Afghanistan. As opportunities arise, we shall continue to make these points to the Soviets, but the Washington-Moscow dialogue is presently not promising.

Although we must continue to make these efforts and remain optimistic, Soviet willingness to withdraw from Afghanistan remains problematical. Current Soviet policy toward Afghanistan makes it appear that the Soviets intend to stay for a long time. They are maintaining current troop levels, improving the military infrastructure, continuing the Sovietization of Afghan society, and attempting to wear down civilian support for the resistance.

U.S. Policies Restated

As I said at the outset, the United States does not accept Soviet control of Afghanistan. Our policy goal remains to get the Soviet troops out because we believe it suits our own and our friends' strategic interests.

We are committed to maintaining a multiplicity of pressures on the Soviets—through bilateral, multilateral, and public diplomacy—to bring them to the negotiating table.

Bilaterally, the Soviets know—and we have reiterated this to them—that their occupation of Afghanistan remains a serious impediment to the improvement of relations with us, and with many other countries as well.

Multilaterally, we are again supporting Pakistani efforts at the UNGA to obtain next week the overwhelming passage of yet another (fifth) resolution on Afghanistan, calling for the withdrawal of Soviet troops, the independent and Nonaligned status of Afghanistan, self-determination for its people, and the return of the refugees with safety and honor. As regards self-determination, we have not said how this must come about, but simply that Afghan people must be allowed to determine the type of government they wish to have in Kabul.

In the field of public diplomacy, we will use every available opportunity to keep Afghanistan and the human costs of the Soviet occupation before world public opinion. The Soviets have paid, and will continue to pay, a significant price in the arena of international public opinion, just as they have paid a price over Afghanistan in other arenas. Top U.S. officials will continue to issue clear public statements on Afghanistan, just as the president and others have done on the anniversary of the Soviet invasion last December, and again on Afghanistan Day in March. Senior officials will also continue to receive visiting Afghan leaders bearing witness to Soviet atrocities and *mujahidin* hardihood. The State Department, in cooperation with the University of Nebraska and USIA, is planning a major international public conference on Afghanistan in December, on the eve of the fourth anniversary of the Soviet occupation. Your own efforts here highlight the importance of the Afghanistan issue and play a valuable role in this overall objective of keeping Afghanistan's heroic story alive before the world.

As Secretary Shultz said on July 2—when he visited the refugee camp in Peshawar—and I considered it a great privilege to be there with him at that time: "We are with you . . . you fight valiantly and your spirit inspires the world . . . the United States has, does, and will continue to stand with you." You can be sure—and I wish to state this with the greatest emphasis—that how best we can bring home to the Soviets the cost of their invasion of Afghanistan, will remain a top priority item for the U.S. government.

6

The Role of Perceptions Concerning U.S. Interests in the Afghanistan Resistance

Thomas E. Gouttierre

The last half of 1983 saw six conferences held around the United States which were in whole or in significant part devoted to the topic of Afghanistan. This seemingly burgeoning interest in Afghanistan is not coincidental. I believe it is a demonstration by the U.S. government, American scholars, and private citizens of concern for Afghanistan and a desire for a resolution of this particular crisis.

Unlike the situation pertaining to U.S. official involvement with the opposition forces in Nicaragua or the government in El Salvador, as examples, information concerning U.S. involvement in support of the Afghanistan resistance is sketchy. There is substantial information concerning the efforts of the U.S. government and American humanitarian organizations on behalf of Afghan refugees in Pakistan. What we know about U.S. assistance to Afghan freedom fighters is based on rumors, leaks, and speculation. Officially, the United States is providing no assistance to the resistance.

At conferences such as this and at other gatherings where the matter of Afghanistan is discussed or presented, perceptions of the U.S. role relating to the Afghanistan resistance remain varied, but seem to be consolidating along certain lines. This same development seems to be occurring in international circles where Afghanistan is a matter of concern. In this paper I am going to present the more salient of these perceptions and then examine them as they might affect American interest related to the war in Afghanistan.

Background

In the past several years there have been a number of articles that have analyzed America's historical involvement with Afghanistan. Of these, perhaps the most cogent has been the article by Leon Poullada in the *Middle East Journal* titled "Afghanistan and the United States: the Crucial Years" (vol. 35 [Spring 1981]: 178-190). In this provocative and interesting account of American diplomatic involvement in Afghanistan, Poullada cites studies made by the U.S. Joint Chiefs of Staff and the National Security Council which seem to indicate that, in the period shortly after World War II, Afghanistan was regarded as being of little or no strategic importance to the United States. This was predicated on the National Security Council's assessment in 1953 that the USSR did not consider Afghanistan's meager resources to be worthy of any serious attention, but that, if it believed its objectives could be served, the USSR was of the mind it could take Afghanistan regardless of the Afghans' will to resist.

A reversal of this thinking appeared to take place in the mid-1950s when U.S. development activities increased and when, in 1957, the National Security Council stated that it felt Afghanistan should be encouraged to look to America and other free-world sources for military training and assistance.

In spite of this seeming reversal, and indications that most personnel at the American Embassy in Kabul felt strongly about the need for the American presence in Afghanistan, American foreign assistance declined in every year of the important "democratic experiment in Afghanistan" of the 1960s and early 1970s. Throughout this period, American intelligence interest in Afghanistan focused on the proximity of that country to the Soviet Union. Most of the specialists assigned to the embassy in Kabul were Soviet-oriented.

U.S. Reaction to the Soviet Invasion

Against this background of inconsistency in American interest in Afghanistan, we are presented with the Carter administration reaction to the Soviet Union's invasion of 1979. More than any other single international event, including the embassy occupation in Iran, the invasion of Afghanistan by the Soviet Union caused the Carter administration to adopt a "born-again" foreign policy. The Carter administration clearly demonstrated that it felt that its adherence to U.S.-Soviet détente had been betrayed by this action. Officials of the administraton reiterated time and again verbally that there had been agreement between the United States and the Soviet Union that Afghanistan, as an independent and Nonaligned country, was within the sphere of influence of neither.

The Carter administration, through the advice of individuals like

Marshal Shulman, sought to avoid every possible confrontation that might in any way upset the objective of maintaining an undisturbed détente. This was most evident throughout 1979 in the lack of attention the Carter foreign policy gave to very clear signs that the Soviet Union was prepared to intervene in massive manner in Afghanistan.

Once the Soviets had moved to occupy Afghanistan, the Carter administration was faced with two alternatives: to regard the invasion as a matter between the USSR and Afghanistan, or to regard it as an event with regional and global implications that had an impact on U.S. interests. Having decided on the latter, the next step was to determine the manner of response. Direct military response was ruled out. No military counterpressure was initiated. (Although a rapid deployment force was later announced for the region, no insertion of U.S. forces in the area was made.) Regional response which may have included India and Iran was rendered impossible due to the current state of U.S.-Iranian relationships and the impending Indian elections.

Aside from the public steps of announcing the U.S. boycott of the Olympic Games in Moscow and an embargo on American wheat shipments to the Soviet Union, the Carter administration apparently decided to seek some way to assist an insurgency which had already been in place against the Marxist government of Hafizullah Amin which had been displaced by the Soviet invasion. This insurgency had now, of course, become a resistance movement against a foreign occupying force. It was further decided that the U.S. government would couple this objective with applying strong political pressure through condemnation of the Soviet action wherever possible. Repeated assurances of support were pledged to Pakistan, which no longer enjoyed a buffer between itself and the Soviet Union.

While U.S. government officials will admit to no overt military support for the Afghan resistance, there have been numerous suggestions that the United States was involved in providing covert support. The most dramtic of these was the statement by Anwar Sadat shortly before his assassination. While one has to question whether any support which is *publicly* labeled as covert retains that definition, it does indeed appear that the United States has involved itself with other nations in an effort to assist the freedom fighters of Afghanistan.

Some have maintained, including Selig Harrison in numerous articles and statements, Sajjad Hyder, who was Pakistan's ambassador to the Soviet Union at the time of the invasion, and Indira Gandhi, that the manner of response to the Soviet occupation of Afghanistan precluded any possibility of a negotiated statement at that time. This assessment ignores the situation inside Afghanistan. The Soviets had committed 85,000 troops for the purpose of occupation. The resistance, which had been an insurgency against the Amin regime, had been gaining in strength and experience. The Soviet invasion intensified the determination of all those previously in opposition to the Marxist turn in Afghanistan. It introduced into the situation, at least on an emotional level, most of the remaining population of Afghanistan. The fighting which had been going on in Afghanistan throughout 1979 was increasing under a new set of circumstances. The Afghans were determined to oppose this occupation of their country with or without outside support.

U.S. Objectives

In a statement made before this conference, Harmon E. Kirby reiterated the U.S. government position concerning America's role relating to the crisis in Afghanistan. He stated that it is America's position that Soviet aggression in Afghanistan must be checked and should not succeed. While this statement is not as unrelenting and uncompromising as another statement made for this conference, that the only way to stop aggression is to drive it back from whence it came, it is a clearly emphatic statement. At the same time, Mr. Kirby also indicated that it was U.S. government policy to seek a political solution. He rejected any implication that the United States was or would be party to fighting the Soviet Union to the last Afghan in Afghanistan. He indicated that in seeking a political solution, terms that must be included are: (1) a complete withdrawal of Soviet troops from Afghanistan; (2) the right of the Afghan people to self-determination of their future political life; (3) nonintervention in the affairs of Afghanistan; and (4) the opportunity for repatriation for all Afghan refugees in safety and honor. He further indicated that these events should take place in this order.

Perceptions Relating to the U.S. Involvement in the Afghan Resistance

Current alternatives for the United States relating to the future of the crisis in Afghanistan are governed as much by perception as by reality. While these perceptions may differ somewhat in various regions or international organizations as well as with individuals within the United States, they currently are more a part of the public consciousness relating to the U.S. relationship with the Afghan resistance than is actual knowledge.

In discussions with scholars and others interested in and concerned about the situation in Afghanistan, whether they come from North America, Europe, Islamic countries, or from other countries in the Third World, a number of perceptions dominate. The most prominent are these:

1. The Carter and Reagan administrations have made a commitment to assist the Afghan resistance.
2. This U.S. commitment is insufficient to the food, medical, educational, and military needs of the resistance.
3. The United States and the USSR have an understanding that constitutes a tradeoff regarding the numbers and kinds of weaponry which either would introduce into the other's areas of concern (for example U.S. involvement in Afghanistan vs. Soviet involvement in Central America). This particular perception has been in the fore of arguments that have supported the Tsongas-Ritter amendment before Congress concerning American assistance to the Afghan resistance.
4. The United States is fighting the Soviets to the last Afghan in Afghanistan. This particular perception was expressed most vehemently by an Indian diplomat at the South Asian Regional Conference at Madison, Wisconsin, in November of 1983.
5. The U.S. role relating to the Afghan resistance is predicated very much on the delicate position of Pakistan. Relating to this, there is concern that Pakistan does not encourage unity in the resistance and does not want to permit the arming of the Afghans to the degree that its own interests would be in any way endangered.

In this media-conscious world, it is not difficult to surmise, based on the degree to which one hears the above perceptions expressed, that representation of U.S. policy toward the resistance may be limited to a significant degree to confirming or refuting these perceptions. If it is perceived that the United States has made a commitment to assist the resistance in Afghanistan (and the visits of Secretary of State Shultz and Secretary of Defense Weinberger to refugee camps in Pakistan certainly support the development of such perception)—what impact does this perception have on U.S. foreign policy? One can take the position that, relating to the Afghan resistance, U.S. consistency in foreign policy and its steadfastness in maintaining commitments are again under scrutiny and testing. The most common question one hears from Afghan freedom fighters and from individuals in the Islamic world who profess their interest in Afghanistan, relates to how long the United States might persist in its support of the Afghanistan resistance.

Perceptions among foreign scholars and public officials are that the United States is shackled by its own democratic process from embarking on consistent application of foreign policy. The statements by King Hussein of Jordan in March 1984 are perhaps the most dramatic representation of this perception.

U.S. Interests Relating to the Afghan Resistance Based on Perceptions

It would seem in the best interests of the United States to find ways to demonstrate to other countries that our democratic institutions are not necessarily impediments to the maintenance of our foreign policy. U.S. policy relating to Afghanistan seems to enjoy more bipartisan support than any other foreign policy issue. The degree to which this fact can be represented and demonstrated would be most beneficial in reversing negative perceptions.

Apart from the strategic and political considerations and advantages the removal of Soviet troops from Afghanistan would have for the United States, there are other areas in which the interests of the United States and the resistance are parallel.

The Afghan freedom fighters probably constitute the best rapid deployment force U.S. Central Command will likely have in the immediate future in Southwest Asia. One might speculate that U.S. interest in the resistance has increased in direct proportion to a demonstrated capacity on its part to sustain its struggle.

The United States tends to underestimate the degree of concern with which Third World countries perceive the U.S. role in situations like that in Afghanistan. Oftentimes the public and private opinions of Third World leaders are divergent. The overwhelming vote at each year's UN General Assembly is a good indicator of the concern and direction of Third World countries relating to Afghanistan. More importantly, Third World countries are apprehensive about what appears to be an increasing reluctance on the part of the United States in situations that require a balance to Soviet expansionism.

The war in Afghanistan provides the United States with a political advantage in dealing with most of the Islamic world. While it is true that the degree of support and public expression of interest relating to Afghanistan on the part of Islamic countries has been disappointing, both from an Afghan and American point of view, most Islamic countries are vehemently opposed to the Soviet occupation of Afghanistan. Muslims see this as a struggle betwen atheism and Islam. At a time when U.S. interests in the Middle East are under fire, perception that the United States is supporting the Afghan resistance is bound to have some positive implications.

Questions Relating to U.S. Support for the Resistance

If one accepts the fact that the American role relating to the Afghanistan resistance is affected more by perceptions than by knowledge of that role, it might be well to examine some of the questions these perceptions provoke.

How are U.S. interests served by an approach to provide military assistance that is described as covert? While there has been no admission by the U.S. government to any such form of assistance, the perception is that the United States is providing covert military assistance to the resistance. Is the primary reason for this related to the delicate position of Pakistan in the Afghan question? Or is it more dependent on U.S.-Soviet relations? In this context it is interesting to recall that the warmest years of détente were those during which the Soviet Union was providing very overt assistance to the Vietcong and North Vietnamese.

Do the amount and the kinds of weaponry to which the Afghan resistance has access serve our interests as well as those of the Afghans? It can be reasonably argued that the current levels of military supply may be a source of division among the Afghan freedom fighters. Often, when there is competition for resources in a dependent society, confrontation is inevitable. One can readily remember how much the unity of the PLO was enhanced by what became a surfeit of weaponry. The perception is that the United States is assisting the Afghan resistance. Is it not in the American interest to address the matter of the levels of weaponry so that we are not continuously saddled with the claim by people both at home and abroad that it is our policy to fight the Soviets to the last Afghan?

Does using the lack of unity in the resistance as an excuse for not providing certain forms of assistance serve U.S. interests? The track record is that as regional and local groups get more assistance they cooperate more. Within the context of this topic, might not the best policy be to seek to improve assistance to the various active groups in their own regions?

Has the United States been sufficiently active and imaginative in putting the Soviets on the spot concerning their brutality in Afghanistan? Can U.S. policy involve the Third World more actively in this question, other than just at the UN General Assembly? The kinds of embarrassment that should be coming to light concerning the Soviet war crimes in Afghanistan are important to the USSR and its relationship with the Third World. The United States has not really pressed the Soviets on this particular matter to the same degree that the Soviets pursued during the Vietnamese conflict.

Has the United States, in cooperation with Pakistan, done enough toward supporting an initiative by various Afghans in Pakistan designed to permit the continuing development of Afghan cultural and philosophical thinking? Such an initiative could strengthen the resolve and depth of the Afghan resistance. It would also provide an outlet and sense of purpose for many Afghans idle in Pakistan who are unable to fight.

Are U.S. objectives in Afghanistan too dependent on Pakistan logistically? This question does not necessarily advocate working independently of Pakistan. However, one must wonder if all avenues relating to the Iranian role in providing assistance have been explored. Other alternatives might include some that may be more direct.

Does current U.S. policy provide any obstacles to any of the initiatives which seek to promote a united voice in presenting the Afghan resistance to the outside world? This is a delicate matter that demands constant sensitivity. The U.S. approach to date has been correct. One concern that is related to this question is what would be the U.S. policy if some manner of government-in-exile would emerge that enjoyed resistance support. With an embassy still in Kabul, what would U.S. policy be?

The Geneva Talks

The Soviet Union has been utilizing the Geneva talks for its own propoganda purposes relating to Afghanistan. These talks are used by the USSR as a distraction as it goes about its business of bombing and intimidating Afghan civilians who are able to provide any source of refuge or support to the freedom fighters. These talks help focus the attention of the world and the media relating to the question of Afghanistan on Switzerland rather than Afghanistan where the battles are being waged. Even more important, the Soviets have sought to utilize the Geneva talks to transfer the blame for the failure of these talks to the United States. Selig S. Harrison suggests that it should be U.S. policy to put the onus on the USSR and Kabul for any setback in these negotiations. At the same time, his statements raise the question of whether U.S. objectives in Afghanistan are to keep Soviet forces tied down for reasons of global strategy or to truly seek a Soviet military withdrawal. Mr. Harrison suggests that what appears to be a calibrated U.S. approach to assisting the Afghanistan resistance seems to substantiate the impression that the U.S. objectives are to keep Soviet forces pinned down.

In discussions with officials of the State Department it is not possible to obtain any indications that U.S. objectives in Afghanistan are anything but to seek the withdrawal of Soviet troops. At the same time, there is a little indication on the part of the Soviets, that they have ever been serious about establishing a true timetable for withdrawal, despite their protestations to the contrary.

The United States should publicly and frequently give full support to pursuing a political solution acceptable to all parties. The State Department needs to be more attentive than it was in the winter of 1982-83 so that the cause-and-effect sequence not get turned around through Soviet utilization of the Geneva talks. For a time, by suggesting that they would pull out of Afghanistan once the freedom fighters had been prevented from crossing back and forth over the Afghan-Pakistani border, the Soviets were able in part to transfer the blame for the failure of the Geneva talks on the United States. In so doing, the Soviets were suggesting that the United States was being unrealistic in first demanding a withdrawal of the Soviet troops. Statements made by Secretary of State Shultz during his visit in 1983 to Pakistan and other statements made by the State Department in the spring of 1983 restored the cause-and-effect sequence to its proper perspective. The war of resistance in Afghanistan was created by the occupation of that country by the Soviet Union. In order for the war to be brought to an end, Soviet troops must first be withdrawn.

The United States also needs to be careful that whatever policy it pursues or options it supports at Geneva, there must not appear to be a deal arranged over the heads of the Afghans. In such a situation, the United States would not have gained much more regard among Afghans than have the Soviets. Again, our credibility in the Third World would suffer and the respect for our ability to maintain commitments would once more be found lacking.

Summary

The United States, in addressing its interests relating to the resistance in Afghanistan, needs to be more sensitive to the perceptions shared around the world, including those at home. Due to what is perceived as a covert approach in U.S. assistance to the Afghan resistance, perception is what has become the dominating factor relating to the U.S. involvement with the resistance.

In this context I feel the United States needs to state in some creative ways its objectives relating to the war of resistance in Afghanistan and to what degree it is committed to maintaining these objectives. At the same time, the United States should be very visible and serious in supporting the pursuit of a negotiated settlement acceptable to all parties.

Finally, the Reagan administration should continue what I consider an enlightened and admirable policy on the part of the Department of State, the Department of Defense, the USIA, and others, to seek input from academic and humanitarian sources concerning Afghanistan. The individuals within the NEA/PAB Bureau of the Department of State have never been more actively involved in seeking the participation of others outside the Department of State in the Afghanistan question than in recent times. Conferences such as this are excellent examples of this kind of cooperation.

Commentaries on Professor Kirby's and Professor Gouttierre's Papers

Robert G. Neumann

The discussion is on a subject that I am sure is of great interest to everybody—the interests of and alternatives for the United States. Policies exist in the Department of State on almost every country. They have to be cleared, unless the higher authorities consider them too unimportant to pay any attention to, and are generally a list of objectives which the U.S. government wishes or hopes to achieve. They do not normally contain a section on strategy, if such exists, for that would be signaling ahead of time, especially as policy statements are often drafted quite some time in the past, and the tactical and strategic situation may well have changed. Therefore, the speaker last night (Mr. Kirby) ought not to be blamed for having stayed very ably within his mandate. Those who criticize, and of course there is every freedom to do so, any policy have a moral obligation to show how their alternative suggestions can be implemented. U.S. policy toward Afghanistan—with which I went to Afghanistan in 1966—was set in 1955, when the then secretary of state Dulles decided not to grant, and I think on very sound grounds, military assistance to Afghanistan. From that a number of things followed, including the fact that the U.S. place was not identical with the place Britain had occupied. Nor did we have the obligation of India, which Britain had exercised until India's and Pakistan's independence. As a "superpower," we must be concerned with the other superpower and see things not only in a regional but also in a global context. Here lie some differences, not only in Afghanistan but in many other regions as well. I have heard some criticism, not of anything I have said but of others, that perhaps our policy, or the statement thereof, seems unfeeling. That was not my reaction, but I am reminded of the statement of a former British prime minister, Stanley Baldwin, who said: "I have heard many a moving speech in the House of Commons, but never one which changed a single vote."

Selig S. Harrison

American interests in Afghanistan can be defined in terms of five objectives. All five would be undermined by an escalation and polarization of the Afghan conflict in which the Soviets are increasingly dependent on this narrow Communist group with which they are now working. Objective number one is military—getting the Soviet forces out and limiting or eliminating their base presence as part of a political solution. Number two is the stability of Pakistan. This would obviously be undermined in a steadily escalating situation in which the Soviets supported Baluch and other elements in Pakistan that they are not now actively supporting. Number three is the stability of the South Asian region, which would be greatly affected in a chain reaction if the stability of Pakistan were to be undermined. Fourth is a healthy American relationship with Pakistan—a country of nearly 100 million people in which we have important interests—and our Afghan policy has to reflect that priority. Finally our objective is the promotion of our own values in the future Afghanistan, through the creation of conditions in which non-Communist evolution and progressively increasing independence of action in foreign policy become possible over time. We must recognize that escalation is possible, even likely, and that the continuation of the status quo is unlikely. To talk of a stalemate is misleading. Charles Dunbar (former American chargé d'affaires in Kabul) has properly introduced the term *standoff,* which implies that the Soviets are in a position to apply much more damaging pressure if they so chose. That is where we stand now; we are at a turning point. Obviously, they are keeping the option of greater economic and political integration open. At the same time they are keeping a diplomatic option open. They have not yet gone to a strategic base capability. They want to see if what they consider a favorable political solution is possible.

The continuity of the "revolution" of 1978 is not something they are prepared to surrender. They want a transformation, not a replacement, of the present regime. They are not prepared to entertain any scenario which would involve a replacement of the present government with a new one, a transitional or interim government. They are talking increasingly about some form of institutionalized dialogue with resistance elements represented through whatever bodies are created. This might result from the king's efforts, or as a result of other efforts that may follow the king's efforts, in which the coequal status of the projected national united front of the king or other groups with the

National Fatherland Front (an organization established by the Kabul regime in an attempt to secure a broader, non-Communist party backing), and possibly with the regime, could be recognized—thus facilitating some kind of reshaping of the existing government with the flag of the revolution still there. This seems impossible for many to entertain. Under present circumstances, many assume that no Afghan would be willing to participate in such a dialogue. However, the fact is that the Soviets are talking in terms of the need to deal with the resistance, within a framework of national reconciliation, as against the terms that we put forward, which is a position for the resistance at the international bargaining table. It is an important new development. It defines the limits of what they are pursuing. Militarily, they are seeking a Finish-style security relationship in which they have the formal right of reentry and a continued presence of military advisors. I am not advocating anything in this analysis, I am trying to define what I think they are prepared to do. We do not know they are prepared to do these things, but we have enough signs to make it the basis for testing this through the UN process.

What is the UN scenario all about? Section one is a text, now of some twenty very detailed pages; this is not just a series of aimless discussions leading nowhere. Serious progress has been achieved and there are some serious obstacles that have not yet been overcome. But there is a piece of paper which represents a clear scenario: "The gradual withdrawal of the foreign troops will begin within 30 days of the announcement by the Secretary-General of the settlement and shall be completed within ———." As you all know, the "blank" is the time frame. That is very important, because coincident with the beginning of the withdrawal would begin the operation of pledges by both Afghanistan and Pakistan of "noninterference and nonintervention." These pledges are very detailed. Since the resistance would not be getting assistance if these pledges were observed beginning with the settlement going into effect, it has to be a short time frame. This is what the negotiations are really about—Pakistan attempting to get the time frame specified by the Soviets. Section three covers endorsements by the major powers. Section four deals with the refugees.

I cannot in the time available go into this very much, but I want to make one basic point. The political dimension of what kind of regime is to be in Kabul is simply not addressed in this scenario. It reflects the Soviet objectives I have just described and the UN's and Pakistan's judgement of the political realities. The change in the regime in Kabul that would obviously have to take place to make this viable settlement in which the Soviets could withdraw is left to parallel processes.

Pakistan and the UN people involved envisage a parallel process, not something that anyone is comitted to in any legal sense, but something which would have to take place, and it is understood would have to take place, if the Soviets were going to be able to implement their commitment to withdraw. This lack of a formal political scenario is something that the United States has disliked about this settlement from the beginning. Many officials who are senior colleagues of Harmon Kirby and others are very frank. They have been very frank with some Americans, Pakistanis, and others about the workability of this scenario. Apart from whether we want to believe the Russians were really prepared to have this whole thing at all, the stated position of the United States is that we are prepared to have it. But we find it an unworkable scenario. It is this issue of tying down the political dimension that has prompted American questioning of Pakistani goals. I would not challenge Harmon's statement that pressure has not been exerted. I think Pakistan is pursuing its own interests, trying to balance its interests in Washington with those on its border, and the way Ambassador Hyder put it is very correct. Doubts and uncertainties in Washington, as Pakistan became aware of these between the April and June (1983) rounds, caused it to modify its position. It trimmed its sails and made some tactical adjustments. In the April round, it said: "We will agree to the language of noninterference that we have negotiated, four pages worth, if the Russians come forward with an acceptable time frame." By the June round, that willingness to make this contingent commitment had somehow faded away. All parties in any negotiation tend to engage in a lot of equivocation and the Russians are doing it too. Another question is at what stage would Pakistan have to recognize the regime in Kabul. The *loya jirgah* scenario I spoke of would become operative only after the withdrawal starts. Withdrawals would start and, say at six or eight months, the king's council or some other resistance council and the National Fatherland Front would begin a dialogue, possibly a *loya jirgah*. But this would be after the withdrawal starts. So you have Pakistan willing to pursue a recognition of this regime, with Barbrak Karmal himself removed and another figure replacing him within the same regime, and then to embark on this scenario of a 6–8-month withdrawal. During that period, it would accept the risks of the type of *loya jirgah* dialogue I have talked about. The United States is not willing to accept that at this stage, and if Harmon is willing to say that we are, I would be very happy to hear it. The name of the game here is the question of whether a political evolution in Kabul must take place before the settlement can be concluded and before the United States can say that it will endorse the settlement that has been already drafted.

The Iran factor has been mentioned by Harmon; I agree it is very important and I am also hearing a lot more of this from the Soviets and Afghans. However, at this stage, you cannot say that it is necessarily going to obstruct the conclusion of this testing process. The Soviets may not step over the brink, but to find out whether they are going to, we are going to have to say that we would accept the text negotiated so far as a basis for concluding this agreement—if an acceptable time-frame can be agreed upon. That is substantially the Pakistani position at this time.

To sum up, Harmon said last night: "We want to get the Soviets out of Afghanistan." That is a very loose way of putting it. "The Soviets," is not the same as Soviet forces. Does it mean we expect to remove Soviet influence as well?

Sabahuddin Kushkaki

I just want to make a brief comment on what you said, Mr. Ambassador. You said, regarding U.S. policy for giving or for not giving arms to Afghanistan, that when the government of Afghanistan asked for U.S. arms, John Foster Dulles, as secretary of state, refused. Tom Gouttierre read a number of reviews and decisions made by the National Security Council which at that time gave little or no strategic importance to Afghanistan as an independent state. If that was, as Ambassador Neumann said, a right decision as far as not giving arms to Afghanistan, maybe that was because of many other reasons, but also because the American government at that time did not attach any strategic importance to Afghanistan. Then why should we regret that today Afghanistan has become prey to communism and Soviet invasion? I would also like to add another phrase to Tom's long list of various kinds of interpretations given to Soviet motives in Afghanistan. Did you use, Tom, "international socialist obligation of the Soviet Union?" You could add it to your list.

Let me talk about covert and overt operations and assistance. These are the things that I have just learned this time around in the United States. They have been used in relation to U.S. policy in the Caribbean area, but it is interesting to see that it is also being used in relation to the Afghan issue. I can honestly say this to all my American friends here—the Afghans do not know whether you are offering us covert or overt cooperation. Maybe that is because of the covert operation, that the Afghans should not know about this, but Afghans really do not know—including myself and the people who head the various resistance groups. We simply do not know whether American arms are given to us, and in what fashion. We are aware of the enormous amount of assistance offered to the refugees and to the humanitarian causes through the government of Pakistan and the United Nations and, of course, the Afghans are very grateful for that.

A very central theme occurred to me while listening to Tom's description of American alternatives and American policy regarding the Afghan issue. We should keep in mind that the Afghan issue should not be used as a tool of policy for others—whether it be Pakistan, Iran, the United States, or the Soviets. We know that the Afghan issue cannot be solved until we meet the requirements of all these countries. With Pakistan we have many fraternal ties, especially after the invasion by the Soviet Union. Pakistani brotherly assistance and open arms have created an enormous positive impact and influence on Afghans. Any future Afghan leadership emerging from the main ranks of the Afghan jehad will never pursue a policy hostile to Pakistan. But to ignore the wishes of the Afghans themselves, ignore them and use them as a tool of policy of others, is something I am very much against. That does not mean that the Afghans are wishing for a solution of the Afghan issue only in their armed struggle, and that the escalation of that armed struggle is top priority. It also embraces a diplomatic and political solution for the Afghan issue. That policy, which I more or less described this morning in seven points, embraces all the other interests as well—including those of the Soviet Union. If the Soviet Union came into Afghanistan under the pretext of the vulnerability of its borders and fear that a hostile regime or atmosphere was being created against Soviet interests, the Afghans are ready to guarantee that no Afghan regime will be established that will be hostile to the Soviet Union. We should always keep in mind that there is a nation, a nation alive, fighting for its independence and survival. All the policies geared toward supporting the Afghan resistance should see that a responsible, coherent, and widely based resistance movement is supported and that it is not used as a tool for others' policies.

Now, how to help this resistance that exists and wants to have its own voice heard in the international community, especially among our friends? They are in dire need of arms. You know that we are very short of arms. To what extent the international community and first of all the Islamic community, is helping the Afghans to receive these arms? I have many doubts. Then, we need many kinds of welfare services, not only for the millions of refugees along the borders of Afghanistan and Pakistan, and Afghanistan and Iran, but also for the internal refugees. This morning there was a discussion about the situation in Kunar—the people who are loosing their crops and their homes. What can we do to help them? There is the intellectual need of creating an infrastructure and ideology for the resistance. There are Afghans who are very concerned with helping the *mujahidin* to have some kind of intellectual infrastructure. That is the kind of help that *mujahidin* would like to receive from the international community, and especially from a government like the United States. We have to see that something concrete is done other than arms. Any alternatives or negotiations aimed at the weakening of the Afghan resistance should be avoided; none of us should subscribe to it.

I want to say a couple of things about Dr. Harrison's remarks. We know about each others' views and I respect his views very much, although I disagree on many points. As an Afghan who has tried to put himself in the shoes of a real *mujahid*—to sit down around the table with people who are the symbol of treason, of gross destruction, of people who have sold their soul and country to an enemy, to sit down with those people around the table, is something no Afghan can stomach. It might be that a number of people or groups from the Afghan ranks will join in such a venture, but eventually, it is the people of the country who are going to carry out a treaty or agreement. You people who are around this table, and I would like to invite comments on this, do you think that the Afghans can bear seeing the Parchamis and the Khalqis, who have been the symbol of treason for their compatriots, tolerated in the government and leadership ranks?

DISCUSSION

Jiri Valenta: The objectives Selig is suggesting that we espouse with respect to Afghanistan would almost surely produce what might appropriately be labeled the "Mongolization" of Afghanistan, a different kind of Leninist regime, one with a Muslim face. We might not like that, but the Soviets believe that the Mongolian People's Republic and the Central Asian republics serve as models for the long-term development of Afghanistan. The kind of thing that Selig is suggesting would not change the basic situation nor would it contribute to the basic objective of the United States; perhaps more important, it would not be accepted by the majority of the Afghan people.

Laurent Carrel: I have a short comment for Mr. Kushkaki. I think what he said was very important. If a friend is in trouble, the friend determines what kind of help he needs, not the donor. The list he has given us is the same list we hear from everybody who comes out of Afghanistan. Every resistance fighter, every freedom fighter or commander, puts weapons first, and specifically, weapons against helicopters, missiles, or antitank weapons. We have seen very clearly during this conference that the Soviet Union deems the consequences of a withdrawal still unacceptable and the cost of the continued military presence tolerable. I see no signs that the Soviet Union is willing to enter into any serious negotiations. On the other hand, there are many facts that show that they want to continue the war at the present level. If these weapons which are requested were given to the Afghan freedom fighters, the human and material losses they could inflict on the Soviet Union would increase Soviet readiness to consider a negotiated settlement to the Afghan crisis. It would dramatically raise the price they would have to pay, not only because the Afghan *mujahidin* fight so fiercely and committedly, but also because the Soviets do so poorly tactically. I agree with Dr. Malhuret that when you look at the counterinsurgency strategy, including all the actions against civilians, that this is another story, but I am talking about their military actions, and there as a whole they still do very poorly.

One last point has to do with the credibility of our own efforts in defending the free Western world. Consider how many millions, how many billions, are spent every year in equipping and training our armies in Western Europe. At the same time we watch this little country, fighting our potential opponent on their own, not being given sufficient military aid: I think it makes everybody who is aware of the situation heartsick sometimes.

Reinhardt Rummel: I have a brief question to Tom. I wonder to what extent your institute looks at the very question that was raised several times—how to get rid of the Soviet Union in Afghanistan. How do you get the Soviet Union to be ready to compromise? I think you are taking the second step before the first. Over the last three or four years one has got used to looking at Afghanistan from two perspectives, one focused on the resistance and how to keep that up, and the second on what were the motivations for the Soviet Union to go in. We could shift now to the other aspect, how to get the Soviet Union out. This is a totally different perspective involving a totally different kind of motivation on the Soviet side. I wonder to what extent your institute has done research on cases where the Soviet Union has given up on any of the requirements it had set. I wonder what the factors should be, or the overall situation should be, to create the climate or the geostrategic situation where you could even think of these kinds of very sophisticated ways of talking about the options you have been talking about. I had the feeling that you were looking at it as if it were a Cuban missile crisis, without taking into account that the overall Moscow-Washington relationship is probably not focused on Afghanistan but on many spots around the world. Maybe much more on Central America. Then again, what is the price the United States would pay for what it might achieve in Afghanistan? Is it really a top priority? Or is it mainly—as described earlier—a tool for achieving other goals? Are you not trying to solve the problem of Afghanistan, not for the sake of that country alone, but rather for an overall strategic objective helping the United States more than it is helping the Afghans? I would suggest you place your institute's approach in a more geostrategic view, and then ask what the stakes are. Probably, then, you can find out what the overall climate has to be in order to think realistically of these kind of options we are dealing with.

Harmon E. Kirby: I consider this to be largely a learning session. It is addressed to alternatives for the U.S. government, and I have been listening with a great deal of interest. I would like to comment on a couple of things Tom Gouttierre has said and then one or two of the points Selig made. First of all, Tom, and I do not mean this with any discourtesy, I did not totally understand the "overt and covert" discussion. Indeed, I heard it very imperfectly through a great deal of background noise. So my silence on that issue implies neither that I heard it or that I have not, or that I agree with it or not.

I would like to recall what I said last night. The United States has a clear, direct involvement in a multiplicity of pressures on the Soviet Union. First of all, there are the diplomatic pressures in terms of our bilateral contact with the Soviets, and then in the context of multilateral diplomacy and in our public affairs efforts. We are very proud of the refugee assistance that Mr. Kushkaki was nice enough to mention. We are involved, and I think we will continue to be directly involved, in all those arenas that I have just referred to. I would like, second, to take up a point that Tom laid out so well—what lies behind U.S. policy. Tom talked about perceptions such as that the United States is willing to fight the Soviet Union in Afghanistan to the last Afghan. The same question was put in a slightly different context: Does Afghanistan matter as such or is it being used for other purposes? Is it a priority or is it a tool? What I tried to say last night was that we, first of all, want the Soviets out of Afghanistan. We want the Soviet army out of Afghanistan. And we think this serves two interests. I used the phrase last night and meant it with the greatest feeling—we simply want to end the agony of Afghanistan. We do not like seeing Afghans killed. That was what I was trying to convey in talking about reprisals. It was not designed primarily to put the Soviets in the dock—while it does that too—but to say, "enough is more than enough." We would like to see a negotiated settlement to get the Soviet army out so that the Afghan people can go back to peaceful pursuits in running their own lives. At the same time, we see Afghanistan in a strategic context. There is a misperception in some quarters both at home and overseas (in some cases it is a genuine misperception; in others it comes about as a result of the disinformation campaign) that perhaps the United States would keep the Soviet army in Afghanistan, that we want to bleed them, that somehow we want to try to turn it into their Vietnam. This has been addressed by the top levels of our government; and the policy decision at senior levels was that U.S. interests are served by getting the Soviet army out. In the first instance, the Afghan people's interests are served; the killing would stop. Beyond that, we have concluded that our strategic interests and those of our friends, the Pakistanis and others, are far better served with the Soviet army back behind its own borders than to let them 400 miles to the south of their borders. You could talk, as I did last night, of the Persian Gulf, the Strait of Hormuz, pressures on Pakistan, and what have you. So we want them out for these twin reasons—the Afghan cause as such, whose importance speaks for itself, and also for strategic considerations. So we do support efforts, all efforts, at a negotiated settlement.

I shall refer to something Selig had to say. There are many points that we agree on. But there are a couple of points I have to address. It is not correct to suggest that somehow we had been acting in the UN negotiations as a restraining influence on the Pakistanis. It simply has not happened. In the discussions we have had with the Pakistanis we have done far more listening than speaking. It is Pakistan that is engaged in these negotiations. It is Pakistan's interests that are most directly affected. We recognized this early on. We said: "You know, the Pakistanis are going to have to conduct the negotiations, obviously, as it suits their interests." We have the impression that they are doing that very well and very capably. We have found, in talking to them—and they always take the lead in explaining to us how they see Afghanistan—what their purposes are. We have found a great compatibility of assessments and instincts. But at no time have we tried to restrict them. We have not said anything privately that we have not said publicly—and not just we, but the international community in the General Assembly resolutions. We have said that there has to be an integrated political settlement that takes into account all the elements in the General Assembly resolutions. There is the question of self-determination. The international community has spoken to that, not just the United States. In private we have said nothing that conflicts with our public statements. I was a little surprised, although I found it interesting and indeed at one point breathtaking, Selig, to hear your recapitulation of the events that transpired between the Geneva rounds of negotiations in April and June. Possibly for lack of time, it seemed to me that you left out the central issue. My understanding, although we are not engaged in negotiations and we only know what people tell us, is the reason there seemed to be cause for optimism at the end of the April round was that the Soviet man behind the scenes in Geneva hinted that in a later round the Soviets might be willing to discuss an explicit timetable for withdrawal. We are told that when the Geneva indirect talks reconvened in June the Soviets stepped back from that and said that they were not prepared to talk about a withdrawal timetable. So we were left with the impression that the reason that not as much progress was made in the June round as some people had hoped was that the Soviets simply did not negotiate on the central issue. I do not pretend to know the Soviet mind and purposes, but it struck me as sobering that one week following the April round in Geneva, where the Soviets had given the signal that maybe they would be willing in the next round to negotiate seriously, some of their seniormost officials were telling third-country diplomats in Moscow: "Don't take that too seriously; we're really not at that stage yet." So I must say that I have always been confused about what the Soviets really intended to see come out of the April round. The signs were equivocal at best. You have heard the eloquence of Ambassador Hyder and Brigadier Husain, so I suspect you all have your own opinion of just how firmly the Pakistanis are pursuing their own interests. Do you really think that we could restrain or pressure them if we wanted to? Fortunately, I think we have had the good sense not to try.

Marvin G. Weinbaum: I want to pick up on something that Reinhardt Rummel mentioned before, since we are talking about alternatives. That is the value of the historical perspective. We are talking about creative alternatives—I do not know whether we have been very creative. I do not know whether there is much room to be creative in this instance. So far, our alternatives have been based on getting the Soviets to do something they obviously find it difficult to do under pressure. We are talking about negative sanctions. But we know something about the Soviets: when it comes to security questions, they have an ability to marshal their resources, to pull in their belts, to do whatever they think they have to do and to accept the consequences. Should we, therefore, perhaps be looking for positive incentives rather than negative sanctions? That may strike some of us as a little distasteful, because it may suggest we are going to reward them for their aggression. On the other hand, if we are interested in ending this horror in Afghanistan, we also would have to consider that maybe we're going to have to make some tradeoff. We could, for example, talk about a reverse sphere of influence. That is, if they do some compromising in Afghanistan then we, perhaps, will pledge things we will not do in Central America. This goes back to the missile crisis, where that was the kind of incentive we had for them to do something difficult. I am not saying that this is the way to go, but it reflects the kind of thing I am thinking of. We must be constructive—not simply add one more alternative. Clearly, there are some ways which would be unacceptable to us, such as offering to try to "Finlandize" Pakistan.

Louis Dupree: I would like to give another scenario which I think is very interesting and would relate to what's been said here. I'd also like to ask a question quickly of the three panel members. Have you reached an *ijma,* a consensus? I think that you possibly have—weapons, food, education for the Afghans inside Afghanistan; food and other supplies needed for the refugees; and continually to seek a political solution.

I would like to take a look at something I'm writing now called "The First Russo-Afghan War, 1919-?." I think somewhere down the line in the next few years the Soviet Union will agree to establish a timetable to leave Afghanistan. It will begin to leave with its troops. At that time the *mujahidin* groups will surround Kabul and continue to fight one another. Whoever is sitting in Kabul will turn and say *"Komak mikonam,"* "I need help." On the basis of the December 1978 treaty, *legally,* the Soviets turn around and come back into Afghanistan. They will have already surrounded the *mujahidin* with an airborne operation the like of we haven't seen since the Second World War. And then we shall see the Afghans continue to be driven out of Afghanistan into Pakistan and Iran and my worst possible scenario will continue.

Zia-ul-Islam Ansari: As my brother Kushkaki said, in referring to one alternative, that any alternative which weakens the resistance would be unacceptable, I wanted to know whether it would be possible for him to spell this out.

Gregory M. Kortanek: I attempted to resist responding to Professor Gouttiere's comment about the resistance being the best RDF that USCENTCOM could have. First of all, I want to restate what should be very obvious: there are no lines of communication from USCENTCOM headquarters to the *mujahidin.*

Having said that, I would like to stress, both in the case of the situation of Afghanistan and regional security in general, that the creation of this new unified command is seen more in the case of deterrence than of compellence. We have a unified command able to consult across a broad spectrum of military matters, not simply on planning the deployment of forces, but on security assistance programs, exercises, and other combined activities with states within the region and also bilaterally with allies in Europe. This would act as a deterrent, so that the "standoff" that Ambassador Dunbar and you referred to could be maintained. This at least might deter the Soviets either from escalation within Afghanistan or from further destabilization throughout the region. Therefore, USCENTCOM aids in the creation of an atmosphere in which the negotiated withdrawal of Soviet forces that we look for can, in fact, take place.

Stephen A. Garrett: My point has already been made by Professor Weinbaum and Dr. Rummel, but I would like to elaborate on it. The extent to which the United States can have an influence on solving this situation is part of the overall context of Soviet-American relations. It strikes one, at least for the present time, that U.S. leverage over Soviet calculations is probably at the lowest point in twenty years. If we are going to do historical research on how to get the Soviets out of a country that they have already occupied, incidentally, we might want to look at the Austrian state treaty in 1955. As far as I know, that is probably the best example where the Soviets voluntarily withdrew from an area they had occupied previously. Again, we must view this as part of the overall framework of Soviet-American relations.

Noor A. Husain: I would just like to pose a question to Mr. Kirby: Supposing one of these days the Soviets turn around in New York and say: "All right, we'll give you a timetable for withdrawal, provided you come to some understanding or sign a treaty of peace, friendship, and cooperation with us." What would be the reaction of the United States government?

Harmon E. Kirby: I have not thought about this at all. In diplomacy there are times when it is best to study a hypothetical question but not offer an answer to it. But it is a good question.

Charles J. Adams: I feel that in our conversation this morning we did not take seriously enough Ambassador Hyder's remarks concerning the predicament of the Pakistanis. We did not face that issue squarely. Nor does it seem that Mr. Gouttierre's remarks this afternoon confronted the issue with the directness and seriousness it demands. When we speak, as we did this morning, about international responsibility, we must consider upon whom it devolves. If one were to divide the responsibilities incurred in giving support to the Afghan resistance into portions and ask on whom most of it falls, I would submit that 95 percent of the interational responsibility for any kind of response to the situation in Afghanistan falls on the poor Pakistanis. To talk about greater publicity for Afghanistan in Europe, where in any case the publicity is far more and better than it is on this continent, or to talk about making the American public more aware of the situation in Afghanistan, is to deal with the fringes, the mere periphery of this issue. The Pakistanis, however, by virtue of their geographic situation, constitute the only possible entry or area from which any kind of aid or influence can be directed toward what happens in Afghanistan. For them this issue poses an enormous threat. There is both the possibility of direct Soviet retaliation against Pakistan as well as enormous internal pressures generated by the Afghan crisis. The Pakistani predicament has to be more clearly recognized. From the standpoint of American policy the United States has at least for once to consent to take a secondary place behind its ally in whose hands the primary initiative must lie. This is true particularly if there is to be any response to the call for supplying always more and better arms to the Afghan resistance. Given the situation in Iran, there is no other possibility for arms assistance in considerable amounts going to Afghanistan. Any attempt by the United States to introduce more arms to the resistance movement without the primary initiative of the Pakistanis would be disaster for everyone, especially for the Pakistanis. As sympathetic as one may be to the desperate straits of the resistance fighters and however admiring of their courage and determination, it would be irresponsible not to recognize the problem posed for Pakistan should it openly permit the free passage of arms through its territory.

Sayed Qassem Reshtia: I would like to say that the Afghans mostly need arms. That is the first priority. In a recent remark regarding the kind of assistance the Afghans are expecting to get from the free world, President Reagan said: "It is not fair to give the Afghans enough arms to fight and die, but enough arms to fight and live." We Afghans, would rather say: "Give us enough arms to fight and win."

Harmon E. Kirby: Professor Adam's remarks were particularly useful. I just want to say that we recognize these points. This is the policy we are trying to follow in every respect. Pakistan has taken the lead in every way—from the care of refugees to efforts in the political and diplomatic arenas. We acknowledge that and are grateful for it. Our attitude all along has been that, as the neighbor most affected in every sense, we should follow their lead. I hope that has been explicit in every thing I have said. That is really what I meant to say by "we've been doing something or other." Perhaps this attitude is not an American characteristic, but on this set of issues we have been doing a lot more listening to the Pakistanis than talking to them. I support entirely what you say and hope that has been clear.

Eden Naby: I would like to pose a question to Tom and perhaps to Mr. Kirby as well. We have said that Pakistan is the only avenue for arms supply. But Tom has referred to Iran, and I wonder if anyone is free or able to comment on that. How able are we to function on the Western side?

Robert G. Neumann: We are free but not able.

Marian K. Leighton: No one has raised the question of the situation within the Communist ranks in Afghanistan. There was a point made that perhaps an alternative leader to Babrak Karmal might be installed as part of a settlement. I wonder to what extent the continued factional fighting and even killing between the Communist factions in Afghanistan is a real constraint on the Soviets, aside from what the resistance might accept; and what kind of external guarantees could be set up in the context of a settlement. I just wonder whether the Soviet could possibly afford a settlement at this stage of fragility of their own base in the country.

Laurent Carrel: After so many compliments have been made to the Pakistanis, I would dare to ask whether it is true that from the arms going through Pakistan to Afghanistan, the Pakistanis always cream off the best weapons for themselves.

Sajjad Hyder: We will tell you when you send us some weapons. We will take the cream and then tell you what we have kept.

Robert G. Neumann: I once asked a gentleman in a part of the world which I will not identify whether he was as corrupt as the rumor had it. He said that he never took more than what was expected of him. Does that answer your question?

Laurent Carrel: Well yes, I phrased it as a rhetorical question knowing well the answer.

Sajjad Hyder: I gave you a rhetorical answer.

Jiri Valenta: In observing the linkages between what the Soviet Union is doing in Central America and in other parts of the Third world such as Afghanistan, it is important that we pose the question in a way that would not prevent us from dealing with a particular region as we see fit in exchange for the Soviets' agreeing to curb their behavior elsewhere. A more positive goal would be to try to restrain and freeze behavior elsewhere. A more positive goal would be to try to restrain and freeze Soviet involvement on a global scale. It is important to conceive the situation as the Soviets do. They do not look just at Afghanistan; they also covet other strategic areas of the Third World, including the Caribbean basin. (It would be interesting to have some of the practitioners of international politics, such as Bob Neumann, comment on this.) I think that if you look at the Soviet economic and military commitment to Cuba, which amounts to $3 billion a year (exceeding U.S. assistance to all of Latin America), and if you compound this with their expenditures in support of other client states such as Angola, Ethiopia, and Nicaragua, plus the costs of maintaining the Soviet empire in Eastern Europe, you cannot help but ask to what degree and for how long the Soviets can maintain this empire by military, political, and economic means. In global politics, Afghanistan plays an important role. It is not only bleeding the Russians physically; it is also costing them in an economic, psychological, and political way. If these costs continue to rise, they might have a restraining impact on future Soviet policies.

In this important juncture, it is not just what we do for the Afghans on a moral level that counts, although this is very important; it is also what we do for ourselves in the United States. The situation we have been facing since the early 1970s has been the Soviet attempt to create a pax Sovietica, but in the 1970s there were several interventions which suggest to me that the Soviet Union, although perhaps not expanding, is becoming very assertive. This began in 1978-79 with the work of the Cubans and other Soviet proxies in Africa and continued with the Soviet breach of the informal understanding with the United States regarding Afghanistan. It is in the interest of the United States but also, as pointed out by Major Carrel, of other small independent and neutral countries (Switzerland) to contain the Soviet Union within its strategic perimeter. The British understood this in the nineteenth century and that is why they accorded Afghanistan its deserved importance. I believe that some Pakistanis who do not understand this now, might come to understand it later. It is important to assist the Afghans even more than we are now doing, for if we do not, one among us could be next. It is in the global interest of the world community of nations to reinstitute and maintain the balance of power disturbed in the 1970s. If we help the Afghan *mujahidin,* if we rescue Grenada, all these actions are linked and aimed at containing the Soviet Union. So we should not ignore these linkages. Ultimately we help ourselves.

Claude Malhuret: Though I am not a political analyst, I would have to remark on some of the comments that have been made. Some of them frightened me quite a bit, such as supporting the Geneva Conference or trying to find a solution in which we accept a cosmetic change of the government of Afghanistan by replacing Babrak Karmal by another communist leader. I am afraid these two things are exactly the aims of the USSR's policy in Afghanistan. Looking at their policy during the last thirty years, you discover that what they want is to be legitimized. Once they have invaded a country or installed a communist party, they ask for legitimacy. After this nobody will ask them anything. This is our interpretation of the Helsinki conference, which was the consequence of thirty-five years of efforts by the Soviet Union to make the status quo in Eastern Europe recognized by the West. This is how I interpret the efforts by the Cambodian government of Heng Samrin to have negotiations with Thailand. They have nothing to negotiate with Thailand—they just want to be recognized. This is how I interpret their efforts to be recognized at the United Nations. They have nothing to gain except recognition and legitimacy. This is exactly what they are looking for in Afghanistan. And this is why they have been trying to have discussions in Geneva directly with Pakistan and Iran, and not through the UN commissioner. This is also why they do not want to negotiate with the resistance, because they want to be legitimized and not have the resistance as an interlocutor. The conclusion is that the only way to assist the Afghan resistance is to help; help it until it is united enough and can be a valid interlocutor. Anything done within these other plans would be behind the back of and against the Afghan resistance.

I would like to speak of three different kinds of help. The first is humanitarian aid. Everybody has stressed this fact. I would like to make suggestions for this. The United States would be in a very good position to suggest this, because it contributes most of the UNHCR budget—it might suggest that the UNHCR set up a special body, like UNRWA for Palestine or UNRBRO on the Cambodian border. Right now the Afghan refugees are supported by UNHCR, as are all refugees in the world, but once you create a special budget like UNRWA, it provides a strong political support. It brings this as a special cost, and I think this would be feasible for the Afghan refugees, and it would be of political help to them. It could be supported by the fact that it is the biggest refugee problem in the world.

The second thing is military aid. I agree with Mr. Carrel. But I am not as pessimistic as are many. Right now the Afghan resistance has individual weapons in large quantities, they have launchers and mortars in quite a quantity, and the only thing they are lacking is ground-to-air arms. But on the whole, as I said yesterday, they are gaining momentum. This is the only course to continue to supply at least what has been supplied up to now.

Third is the diplomatic situation. I think what should be done is exactly the contrary to what was proposed here a few moments ago.

One should not support the Geneva conference and try to find too hasty a compromise. We should not enter into discussions about replacing Babrak Karmal with another Communist. As far as Pakistan is concerned, the problem is not to guarantee its borders. Pakistan and everybody knows that this is impossible. The problem is to sustain them diplomatically and financially long enough for them to support the Afghan resistance. And I am not pessimistic on that, contrary to Ambassador Hyder, because, if you look at Pakistan's history, it is a country that has been created and populated by refugees. Among the 100 million people in Pakistan a lot of them are refugees. The 3 million Afghans are new refugees who are not in any way asking to be integrated. Pakistan knows how to handle the problem of refugees because it was created with refugees. I do not think it is an impossible task.

Then the last thing that has to be provided would be from a diplomatic point of view as well. For example, when the French doctor, Phillipe Augoyard, was captured by the Soviets, he was jailed for several months. Negotiations between the French and the Soviets were in a stalemate because the French had just expelled forty-seven Soviet spies in May. So we went to see the French government and asked them to call back their chargé d'affaires in Afghanistan for consultations. There was a threat that he might be called back forever, and this might have been the beginning for other countries to do the same—just like in Cambodia where there are no ambassadors of Western countries. Ten days after the French government told us they were in favor of this and they were going to recall their chargé, Dr. Augoyard was freed. I do not know what was the relationship of these events, but I conclude that the problem is not to legitimize by one means or another because we want a rapid solution. It is always a problem of time between the Soviets and the Westerners. The problem is not to legitimize them—on the contrary, it is to try all the means to delegitimize the Afghan government.

Sajjad Hyder: I only want to make one comment in reply to my colleague's remarks: Would he be so kind as to do Pakistan the honor of being capable of knowing its own interests and furthering them as best it thinks. This observation made by the last speaker—that Pakistan should not do this, Pakistan should not do that—Pakistan is constituted of 100 million refugees and they could easily look after another 3 million—this lesson has been read to Pakistan. I thought I should make a very modest and innocuous observation by saying we are quite capable of understanding and furthering our own interests.

Gerald C. Steibel: I would like to elaborate on the point that came up here about studying how the Soviets get out in addition to how they get in. (This came in an informal caucus during lunch, which is one of the good things that usually happen in a conference like this.) There are two models for study in getting the Soviets out of places, and neither is very hopeful to the aims expressed here. The first one is Azerbaijan. Their withdrawal in 1946 was the very simple matter of President Truman shaking the atom bomb at the Soviets and telling them to get out. That, obviously, cannot be repeated. The second is what I would call the Austrian model, which also applies to Berlin and Cuba, the other two major places where we at least stopped the Soviets. As Dr. Malhuret has pointed out, the Soviets will withdraw under the proper conditions, which always include legitimizing something they want. In the Berlin crisis of 1948, which we broke via the airlift, the quid pro quo for the Soviets was the beginning of legitimization of their control over Eastern Europe. For a very brief moment this country played with the idea of using the uprising in East Berlin to spark a revolution throughout Eastern Europe. This had been the assumption of the whole "liberation" policy upon which Radio Free Europe and Radio Liberty were founded. We decided against it, as great policy decisions are generally made, in the heat of crisis. The net effect of the settlement of the Berlin crisis via airlift instead of something stronger was to say to the Soviets: "While we do not acquiesce in your control over Eastern Europe, we are not going to do anything very effective to destroy it." Incidentally, we repeated this assurance in the Hungarian crisis of 1956. In the Cuban case of course, we know that the quid pro quo to the Soviets in return for taking out the missiles which, incidentally, they followed by putting even more and worse stuff into Cuba, was that we would refrain from attacking their man Fidel Castro. This is a commitment to which we have faithfully adhered, at least up to the present. This may be changing—I hope. The Austrian case gave the Soviets what they wanted in terms of the then growing Western European Defense Union which they did not want to see. We agreed to stifle it, so they got out of Austria. In all these cases the only way in which they withdrew voluntarily, which I think has to be the operational model if there is to be any for an Afghanistan withdrawal, is that they got out only in return for receiving something. Past models, of course, do not bind us for the future. It may well be that the resolution of the Afghan situation will create a third model. Where we are at this point, realistically, is that the first option, which is to simply frighten them out of there, is not going to work. The second one is going to have to involve something that will be an incentive for them to move out along with, perhaps, the implied threat that if they do not, things will get worse. But we can not simply legitimize any position they have in Afghanistan in terms of realpolitik, which is what we are facing now. You have to settle for what you can obtain and not continue to deal in the realm of ideal solutions.

Katarina Engberg: I want to address this to Mr. Kirby. Has the Afghan crisis had any consequences on U.S. policy toward India?

Harmon E. Kirby: I do not think it has had any major consequences, but there is a relationship. We have been trying, with some success over the last eighteen to twenty-four months, to improve relations with New Delhi while simultaneously restoring this broader and deeper relationship with Pakistan. There is evidence that there has been some success. I think there has been a desire on both sides to improve relations somewhat. Whether that will continue I do not know. To date this has been more in tone—in rhetoric and so on—than in substance, although there has been an attempt to nibble at substance as well. On Afghanistan, we have said to the Indians from the beginning that we hoped they would use their special friendship and special relationship with the Soviet Union to try to nudge the Soviets toward constructive, productive negotiations. As we discussed Afghanistan with the Indians our advice to them has been that the problem of Afghanistan is as relevant for India, if once removed, as it is for Pakistan. Therefore it would be in their interest, and that of us all, for them to urge the Soviets toward negotiation. The Indians claim that they have privately done some of that—that they have expressed displeasure at the Soviet presence in Afghanistan and have tried to nudge them. Whether they have done it in fact and to what extent I do not know.

Robert G. Neumann: I promised the panelists time to respond and the time has come. First, however, I want to answer for the record this question raised by Mr. Kushkaki: "Why did Secretary Dulles make the decision?" Judging from the record, which I studied before I went to Afghanistan and in conversations with some of Mr. Dulles's associates, it was based on the consideration that to have a large arms program to Afghanistan a base or near-base would have to be established by the United States on the border of the Soviet Union in a position of maximum vulnerability for the United States and maximum strength for the Soviet Union. It would be 2,000 miles or more from the nearest American logistics base and at the mercy of a transit country. It simply did not come out. And it was on these purely physical but very compelling considerations that the decision by Secretary Dulles was taken. This was by a man not known for being particularly backward in facing up to the Soviet Union. This is merely what I learned, not my own opinion.

Several remarks illustrated the fact that decisions by countries are not made abstractly but under the pressure of events. The question, as Professor Naby raised, whether to consider Iran as a supply route, would have to be decided after having clarified our relation with Iran on many other points of greater importance—effect on the Gulf, or Iraq, on Saudi Arabia, and so forth. It would not be taken solely, or even primarily, in an Afghan context. Again, I take no position on whether this is realistic.

Sabahuddin Kushkaki: First of all, I would like to respond to your answer. What I was aiming at was at that time the U.S. policy, which gave very little strategic importance to Afghanistan. It had been written off, because the United States thought then that Afghanistan could at any time come under the Soviets' domination.

Robert G. Neumann: But that is nothing of the kind, Mr. Kushkaki. It was a technical decision or something that we felt we were unable to do. That is all. No judgment of the importance or unimportance was involved.

Sabahuddin Kushkaki: Ambassador Poullada has discussed this in great detail. At that time U.S. policy did not really understand the importance of Afghanistan and that is why I am elaborating on the views of an American expert. (Leon B. Poullada, "Afghanistan and the United States: The Crucial Years," *The Middle East Journal* 35 [Spring 1971]:178-90).

Mr. Ansari asked me a question. I think I did not say, "will not be accepted," but "should not be accepted." The question of arms was raised, whether arms are given to the Afghan freedom fighters, and what is the purpose of giving these to the *mujahidin*. I simply do not know. This is a question that is entirely up to the government of Pakistan to decide, as a sovereign government, what to do and what not to do. I am not in a position to say, and this is a covert operation. We Afghans simply do not know that any arms are given to us or not. I want to emphasize that this is Pakistan's sovereign right, and Pakistan has to decide on the eventual outlay of arms to the Afghan freedom fighters.

Regarding the question of linkage, if you propose: "If you do this in Afghanistan we will do the following in the Caribbean and Central America"—do not make the Afghan request first, ask me about the Caribbean situation first. It would hurt the Afghans very much if you said: "If you stop your infiltration on the Caribbean we will let you do what you are doing in Afghanistan."

The Iranian element is very ticklish. In any settlement we are always thinking of Pakistan. Certainly, Pakistan is in the picture, and this is very obvious and natural. But eventually, any settlement for Afghanistan will have to include the Iranians. You cannot simply ignore that. The Iranians refrain from taking part in any international negotiations and dialogue or actively assisting the Afghan resistance. But if there is any kind of alternative or settlement for the Afghan question, the government of Iran also understands that they, too, have a long open border with Afghanistan. Iran could become a potential dissenter on any kind of agreement; it can create lots of trouble and obstacles in the way of implementation of any kind of accord.

Selig S. Harrison: The underlying issue that involves some of the differences we have heard is whether the application of increased pressure over the years in Afghanistan will improve the bargaining position of non-Communist Afghans. A number of people here who share my feeling of emotional involvement with Afghanistan believe that this pressure will lead to a stronger bargaining position. I regard this as extremely sentimental, naive, soft-headed nonsense. Anyone who looks at the Soviet Union realistically must begin to face the real choices in Afghanistan. The choice boils down to what is now evolving, which is the Mongolian pattern. The curtain is going down very rapidly. We may have another year, perhaps, in the context of the global superpower relationship, to get anything better than that. We are now headed for a greater Soviet involvement militarily, complete with strategic bases and a greater dependence than ever on an expanding body of Communist cadres, and of all the ugly things that go with the kind of commitment they are quite prepared to undertake in Afghanistan. All the evidence that any hard-headed person confronts indicates that this is what they are in the process of doing. That is why I did not gild the lily. I did not try to make a pretty "peacenik" case for what is going on either at the UN negotiations or in the Soviet posture. It is an ugly, painful set of choices that we face. If we are very lucky, and if we show considerably more imagination and flexibility than we are showing, we might be lucky enough to come out with an "option 3a" of the kind I mentioned this morning. I call it a dependent, Soviet-oriented client regime, which would open up the possibility of a long-range evolution or some kind of non-Communist representation within a framework that the Soviets would consider acceptable in security terms. It is not Finlandization because, regrettably, the Afghans are not behaving like the Finns—with the kind of political unity or military discipline the Finns showed to get the position of autonomy they have. This is quite consistent with what Mr. Steibel said. We are facing a question of whether we are going to function in terms of realpolitik intelligently applied in pursuit of the American national interest and that of our non-Communist friends in Afghanistan, Pakistan, and other countries, or whether we are going to let ourselves go into a "feel-good" stage. We feel better and better by casualty counts of Soviet soldiers, forgetting what is happening to the Afghans caught in the middle who do not share some of the political commitments that some of the speakers here have talked about in terms of progressive Islam or other political commitments. Let us not forget what Ambassador Hyder said. There are a lot of people in Afghanistan who are in the middle: they are not activists. Of course, they are fighting against a foreign presence, but what would happen in a situation in which you did get the Soviets out through a withdrawal scenario under the UN model? It is unlikely for some reasons, but desirable for others. Something might loosen up a little in which the Soviets would get involved with somebody other than this miserable little group they are committed to and will stay committed to. They will continue to build up their regime regardless of how many people they must kill; we must get down to reality. It does not necessarily have to be a Leninist regime. It may turn out that is all they are prepared for, so I am not prejudging it. Let us recognize that in policy terms what we will face is a reluctance, a refusal to agree to what we are demanding—that the resistance be given a coequal seat at the bargaining table. I would love to see the resistance get a seat at the bargaining table. Things I wrote about a couple of years ago would have gone much further than that. But if you look at reality in the face you see they are willing to talk to the resistance in other ways that would save face on their terms. I have mentioned this *loya jirgah*. Its purpose would be to create a situation which the king's council, or your council, or anybody's council of non-Communist Afghans would parley with the National Fatherland Front and the government of Kabul over precisely the issue of whether it is going to be a Leninist government. If it is, there is no deal. It is quite clear there is no problem. It will all be sorted out and we will all be behind a considerable escalation of assistance to the resistance in the years ahead. We do not know yet whether that is what they are willing to accept. And they have given us enough reason to test them much more fully.

I think it is very important to face the question of what is going on in the negotiations more candidly. Of course, the Soviets did not come through with a timetable in the June round as they agreed they would do in April. They stepped back from their part of the bargain that was then reached. It was a secret diplomacy bargain. But Pakistan was making a contingent commitment to the language of the noninterference clause of the agreement and to the concept of dealing with a new cosmetic change of the government in Kabul with a leader other than the one who came to power, as President Zia ul-Haq said, "on the top of Soviet tanks." This was as a first step to get the withdrawal started, to set the stage for the *loya jirgha,* a joint one or whatever. In the June round Pakistan, for tactical reasons that I can understand, confronting the kind of understandable reasoning that I hear in Washington quite a lot from colleagues of yours: "How is this going to operate? How is it going to work? How are you going to get the Afghans to agree to this kind of scenario and so forth?" Pakistan said: "Wait, we are going too fast. This thing can't be wrapped up now; nobody's really ready for it." So they backed away from this. They reneged, but so did the Soviets, of course. And the Soviets keep increasing the stakes on this question of a bilateral treaty of the kind that Brigadier Husain referred to. This too is part of the bargain. When it comes and how much broadening of the regime takes place before it comes is what the negotiations are all about. So it is not a question of pointing the finger at the United States or Pakistan or the Soviet Union. There is a mine field of conflicting interests and objectives here, and all I ask is that we do not kid ourselves as to the choices. Can you really tell me when you think we are going to get to one particular better bargaining position by going into Iran, or by air drops, or by whatever we are going to talk about doing? It is a 2-track problem. We have to aid the resistance as long as the Afghans are willing to fight and the Soviets are not willing to get out. But let us make sure they are not willing to get out before we go that route.

Thomas E. Gouttierre: I agree with what Selig said in that there has to be a 2-track approach. The thing that is important to remember is that the Afghans are doing the fighting; we cannot control them either. If they are going to be fighting the Soviets, we have to decide what our role is. Do we help their supply dry up, do we keep it at a level, or do they get to fight the way they want to fight? I do not pretend to have the answers. When I said that it was time for a reexamination of the manner in which we are providing assistance to the Afghans, I did not say, nor was I concluding, that what we are doing now, whatever that may be, is inappropriate. It is important for us to look at that periodically. We ought to remember, during the warmest days of détente, what was going on in North Vietnam, and what the Viet Cong were doing, did not have much of a negative impact on our ability to deal with the Soviets. Why can things not be both ways?

Also, I was thinking of something Dr. Malhuret has said. Maybe in terms of personal weapons the resistance has sufficiency. One of the things I have suggested is whether it is time for us to examine things again, whether we should be more open about it. Harmon, I had "tongue in cheek" when I was talking about "the best RDF," and maybe you did not see my tongue in my cheek when I was talking about all these semantics "overt/overt," "covert/covert," etc. It must be very difficult to manage your policy in any case, if you have to worry about how many times you have to repeat the word *covert* to make it *covert*.

Finally, I want to make a comment on the point Eden raised. When I was suggesting Iran, I was not implying direct bilateral negotiations with Iran. I asked a question, whether all the logistical avenues, other than Pakistan, had been explored. Iran, obviously, was one of those avenues. I feel a little uncomfortable at the logistic dependence we have. As Professor Adams mentioned, I did not really face up to Pakistan's predicament in my presentation. I left that to what I thought was the topic of this morning's session. You get into a certain amount of simplicity because you have twenty minutes to present all the various points.

One last statement relating to the model that you were talking about, Selig. The Finns are a different kind of people. The homogeneity is there. We cannot look at them in the same way we look at the Afghans. But I appreciate your point, you said a "Finnish style," not a "Finlandization." However, I think other kinds of models will have to be constructed. My statements have in some measure been a reflection of my own frustration. I talked of dealing with perceptions when you go out and speak about Afghanistan. And most of these perceptions are based on a lack of information. That is why I feel it's so important to reexamine what we are doing, to restate what we are doing, and to restate once more what we are doing.

7

Alternative Futures for Afghanistan

Noor A. Husain

During the last three days we had very learned and analytical presentations and discussions on Soviet aims, policies, and alternatives on the Afghan resistance movement, international responses and responsibilities, and objectives and alternatives for the United States. I have been asked to attempt a futuristic projection—alternative futures for Afghanistan, which is by no means an easy task since it involves elements of visualising, perceiving, and forecasting both through the mists of strategy and the fog of war. I shall try not to repeat what has been said earlier, except to reinforce a line of thinking or argument, and I am conscious that in this august gathering are sitting many experts and specialists on Afghanistan including our brave Afghan brothers, who have far greater insight into the subject than I. Since the fate and future of neighboring Afghanistan is of vital concern to Pakistan's security, I shall briefly highlight the geostrategic compulsions of the region.

Geostrategic Compulsions

Pakistan shares a 2,100 km international border with Afghanistan, also called the Durand Line, which was demarcated in 1893 and reaffirmed as an international border by successive Afghan regimes in 1893, 1919, 1921, and 1930. Pakistan is situated at the geopolitical crossroads of Central Asia, South Asia, and West Asia in proximity of three nuclear powers, next to the highly inflammable Persian-Arabian Gulf. Across 3,000 kilometers of Pakistan's western borders conflicts have been raging, involving the Soviet Union, Afghanistan, Iran, Iraq, Syria, Lebanon, Israel, the PLO, and now the peace-keeping forces of the United States, Britain, France, and Italy. This is not an ordinary crisis situation but a megacrisis, quite unprecedented in ancient, medieval, or modern history, just as it is the first time since World War II that Soviet Armed Forces are engaged in a ruthless and brutal war in a neighboring country with which it had a Treaty of Peace, Friendship, and Cooperation and which was a member of the Nonaligned Movement, the Organization of Islamic Conference, and the United Nations. Afghanistan has also been traditionally the security zone of South Asia, and to some extent of South West Asia. In the present and the foreseeable future, whichever power wishes to control or influence one-fourth of the world's population of 1 billion in South Asia, or three-fourths of the world's oil resources in the Gulf region and thereby the economies of Japan and Western Europe, that power will control the region around Hindukush—present day Afghanistan. This was the essence of Brezhnev's concept of an Asian collective security system, which imperceptibly and gradually has come into being with India and Afghanistan as the main pillars of the system. India is also the Soviet Union's largest trading partner today, and more than 50 percent of its military hardware is of Soviet origin, while Afghanistan's economy is totally in Soviet hands. Being two-thirds in Asia, the Soviets regard themselves as an Asian power. A significant dimension which has been added to the Soviet perspective since the early 1970s (perhaps after their role in the East Pakistani crisis) is the self-image of their increasing power and a definite "shift of correlation of forces in favour of Socialism."[1] The Soviet Union also perceives that it enjoys superiority of strategic orientation in South and South West Asia which perhaps cannot be easily matched by the United States. So much for the geostrategic factors of the region.

In almost four years of an ongoing conflict, a tribal society armed with their faith and small weapons has exposed to the world that the Soviet soldier is not ten feet tall. *Mujahidin* claim control of almost 82 percent of Afghanistan, and the fight goes on costing the Soviets anything from \$15 to \$20 million a day. Refugees continue to pour into Pakistan while resolutions demanding Soviet withdrawal have been passed by the UN General Assembly, the UN Human Rights Commission, the Organization of Islamic Conference comprising forty-three Islamic states, the Asian and European communities, the Commonwealth, NATO, the Peoples' Permanent Tribunal, the heads of seven major industrialized democracies, the International Confederation of Free Trade Unions, the European Parliament, the Nonaligned Summit, and the Afghanistan Freedom Organization. The indirect UN-sponsored talks have held a few sessions in Geneva and New York on basis of the UN resolutions demanding complete withdrawal of Soviet Forces, independent and Nonaligned status for Afghanistan, self-determination for the Afghan people, and return of the refugees with safety and honor. According to the UN's secretary-general, "the diplomatic process had moved in the right direction," but he "was concerned at the slow pace of talks" and with "the suffering of the Afghan people." It is evident that the Soviets wish to gain time to dig in militarily, politically, and economically, to accelerate and spread the process of Sovietization in all walks of life, investing heavily in the younger generation of Afghanistan, and in the process to flush out of the country all opposing tribes. That explains why they are so reluctant to give a timetable for the withdrawal of their forces, preceding a political settlement, that the international community has been demanding.

We on our part must put all our diplomatic efforts toward an early political solution in which the timetable for withdrawal of forces is the most important element and the most desirable alternative future for Afghanistan.

Alternatives

Let us consider some future alternatives. These can be both short-term (5–10-year period) and long-term (10–30-year period). I shall confine myself to the short-term alternative, since there are a number of variables that could change in the long term but which apparently have been constant in the short term. Even "short term" and "long term" are relative, when we remember the prediction voiced by the humanistic scientist and analyst Charles W. Williams, Jr. that "the change during the next thirty years may be equal in scope to the change of the past two or three centuries."

As at present, future alternative choices will obviously not be made in a vacuum. They will be based on lessons from the past of Central Asia, doctrines and pronouncements of Soviet leaders, superpower globalism, domestic issues of the Soviet economy and leadership, repercussions in Soviet Central Asian republics, events and situations in West Asia, particularly in Iran and Pakistan, and above all the nature and degree of resistance of the *mujahidin*. The most desirable political and military alternative may not necessarily be the most feasible and attainable and would be largely determined both by necessity and opportunity as the overriding factors.

To this date, the Soviet commanders in Afghanistan have not displayed the tactical flexibility, the small-unit combat expertise, or the political finesse and sensitivity required to subdue an armed freedom struggle which combines nationalism with jehad, and which continues to oscillate from time to time and area to area, as all such armed freedom struggles do. So while on the diplomatic front parleys continue under the aegis of the UN, on the military front the Soviets are apparently acting on the doctrine of both czarist chancellor Gorchakov and the czarist general Skobeleff of the last century. The former believed "it is a peculiarity of Asiatics to respect nothing but visible and palpable force,"[2] while the latter observed during his campaign in Central Asia in 1880-81: "I hold it a principle that in Asia the duration of peace is in direct proportion to the slaughter you inflict upon the enemy."[3] Drawing on three and a half centuries of experience of ruthless dealings with Muslim subjects consisting of Tartars, Bashkirs, Kazakhs, Turkmen, Daghestanis, and Cherkess and Abkhazian tribes—genocide, forced exodus, ethnic fragmentation, and extinction and assimilation through economic aid and political ties and treaties appear to be the other most evident emerging alternatives for the Sovietization of Afghanistan. In this process the geographically contiguous Soviet Central Republic of Uzbekistan with all its historical, cultural, intellectual, scientific, religious, and economic façade—showcase and window dressing—may well be the primary model the Soviets wish to impose on Kabul. Uzbeks and Tajiks have been involved in fairly large numbers in the technical and administrative cadres of Afghanistan for some years now, including the deputy ministerial level. The initial invading force consisted of almost 30 percent Central Asian soldiers. An inter-Islamic, interethnic hue has thereby been given to the Soviet intervention, and these interlinkages are likely to form part of the future of Afghanistan. Also Mr. Karmal's month-long visit to Mongolia in July-August this year, and the appointment last year as ambassador to Kabul of the Mongolian minister for farms is significant. Mongolia has been the world's second communist state since 1921, has almost the same number of Soviet troops "on invitation" as has Afghanistan, has similar treaties and some of the same geopolitical problems as landlocked Afghanistan. Religion and size of population are dissimilarities, as is also Mongolia's insularity from direct U.S. regional interests. Together with the Central Asian republics the Mongolian experiment has more relevance to the future alternative of Afghanistan than, say, Poland or Finland.

A combination of both the Delphic method of forecasting and opinion polls was conducted among Pakistani experts to assess the future of Afghanistan, by asking a number of questions. One question was: "What is likely to happen in the coming 5-10 years?" Seventy-eight percent of the experts asked felt that after the USSR devoured Afghanistan at certain losses and costs, it would wait till the world went to sleep. Then one day, with the excuse of having been "invited," it would drive a wedge through Pakistan and Iran, occupying the Baluchistan areas on both sides of the border and reaching out to the Indian Ocean. Only 18 percent felt that Afghanistan would become a Vietnam for the Soviet Union. In five years Muslim areas north of Afghanistan and Iran would rebel. In ten years the USSR might lose areas east of the Ural mountains.[4] This was the forecast over three and a half years ago. One may not totally subscribe to the other part of the forecast regarding the Baluch option to the Soviets, or the uprising in Central Asia and the area east of the Urals, because it may be too premature and only perhaps a long-term alternative.

So on the forecasting principles of both continuity and analogy, but without strict bondage to the past, a combination of the Central Asian and Mongolian models appears as the second most likely alternative emerging for Afghanistan.

There is another school of thought, advocated by my friend Theodore C. Mataxis, which foresees "Polandization" of Afghanistan as another alternative policy option for the Soviets. "Nations tend to replay successful operations and the partition of Poland westward was a highly successful operation which might be repeated in Afghanistan as it is within the capabilities of the Soviets."[5] He feels that the Polandization of Afghanistan could be accomplished because of tribal and ethnic contiguity across the Soviet-Afghan border, with Turkmen, Uzbeks, and Tajiks, and the Afghan-Pakistani border consisting of the Pushtuns. By gradually assimilating or absorbing through economic and cultural ties, areas north of the Hindukush into the three republics of Turkmen, Uzbekistan, and Tajikistan, and incorporating or making claims to Pushtun areas of the tribal belt of Pakistan and Baluchistan, they would be replaying the shifting of Poland's western boundaries to include a slice of East Germany.

In this alternative, just as the "tail" of Czechoslovakia was annexed to uncover Hungary and Czechoslovakia, Wakhan in all likelihood has been annexed to uncover the northern area of Pakistan, giving the Soviets direct border contact and access to Pakistan, and proximity to the Karakoram Highway and to the disputed states of Jammu and Kashmir. Wakhan has already been depopulated and connected to the Soviet Pamir Military District with headquarters at Murghab. Since such a move would not bring Soviet troops directly on the Persian Gulf in the initial move, it is not likely to create a state of military confrontation with either the United States or the West, and even Soviet-allied India may acquiesce. I do not visualize such an alternative in the short term, unless in a leadership reshuffle in the Kremlin the armed forces emerge on top, while the United States and the West become militarily committed in West Asia, Thailand, or Korea. Then it may become a different ball game, and the doctrine of hot pursuit would prevail across vulnerable parts of Pakistan and Iran and a combination of both necessity and opportunity would become compulsions of strategy for the Soviet leadership.

Afghanistan, after a build-up of anything from 200,000 to 300,000 Soviet force level could become a springboard with various strategic options and directions. After all, from time immemorial the Hindu Kush region has witnessed invasions toward South Asia and the Indo-Gangetic plains, especially when the warden of the marches—the area of present-day Pakistan—has been militarily weak, disunited, or unstable. The scores of passes connecting present-day Pakistan with Afghanistan have in the past opened like sluice gates and let in floods of humanity. Today history is being repeated, except that refugees instead of invaders and adventurers continue to pour into Pakistan, which not even a superpower has the capability of stopping or blocking.

One school of thought feels that playing the Baluch card against both Iran and Pakistan is a feasible long-term alternative for the Soviets in Afghanistan. That would be possible depending on how strong and stable both Iran and Pakistan were at that time and how closely Afghanistan and its people get integrated into a Soviet subsystem.

Conclusion

During the last decade there have been about thirty-two cases of coercive Soviet military diplomacy, either directly or through surrogates. Afghanistan with its geostrategic and geopolitical situation offers perhaps the most options and alternatives to the Soviets and the greatest strategic gains in the long term. Which of the many alternative futures the Soviets select will depend largely upon how soon they can be made to accept a political solution in Afghanistan. In the final analysis the policies and strategy of the United States, the West, and the Islamic world and their will and resolve will largely determine the fate of our brave Afghan brothers, now fighting the battle of the free world, in an area which is from here, the other side of the globe.

Notes

1. Ivan Kovalenko, *Soviet Policy for Asian Peace and Security* (Moscow: Progress Publishers, 1979).
2. Prince Gorchakov, the czar's chancellor, in a memorandum in 1864.
3. Olaf Caroe, *The Soviet Empire* (London: Macmillan, 1967), p. 79.
4. M. A. Khan, "The Conflict in Afghanistan: Delphi Forecasting and Pakistan's Options," *Strategic Studies* 3 (Summer 1980): 63-68.
5. Theodore C. Mataxis, "Afghanistan II: Soviet Miscalculation—Drive to Warm Water," *Suburban and Wayne Times* (April 21, 1983).

Commentaries on Brigadier Husain's Paper

Louis Dupree

I cannot do much more than emphasize and reinforce some of the things that Brigadier Husain has said and possibly bring out a few of my own prejudices. Concerning the Durand Line, let us let the poor Durand rest in peace, if he possibly can with the Soviets right across his line.

I would like to emphasize a point that Husain made, and that is that what happens *outside* Afghanistan is equally important, if not more important, as to what the options for the Afghans inside happen to be. What happens around Afghanistan, in the nations friendly to Afghanistan, to those who are lukewarm toward Afghanistan, and what happens in the states of the Islamic brothers of Afghanistan is equally important. I am looking more to the long term now—Husain did it beautifully in the short term. Of course, as he mentioned, a stable Pakistan is definitely needed for the options favorable for the Afghans. Not only must we have a stable Pakistan but also an Indo-Pakistani rapprochement on virtually everything in the region before we can find stability for both India and Pakistan.

Husain emphasized, as did Dr. Malhuret, that terror is a tactic. And this has been very effective in the past for the Soviets in their subjugation of minority peoples. Terror is a tactic not associated with winning the hearts and minds of the people. These terror tactics might not be as effective today, however. We have to remember this is not 1923 but 1983. Communications are much better worldwide than they were during the *basmachi* revolts. If the necessary work is done with the media, probably more and more people will know more and more about Afghanistan. There is one option I wish the Afghans would take now. I wish they would hire a public relations firm with offices in Europe and the United States of America to bring out, at least once a week, a major story on Afghanistan—public relations firms can do this sort of thing. That would be a good way of using some of the money donated to the various Peshawar groups.

Let me discuss very briefly north of the Hindu Kush, the Wakhan and the Pamir. Remember the Wakhan is a corridor. You can drive a jeep in the Wakhan corridor all the way to Qala Panja where the Pamir begins. I have done it. In the dry season you can drive a jeep at 60 kilometers an hour across those little terraces. When you get beyond Qala Panja you are in the mountains. This is the difference between the Wakhan corridor and the mountains. They are actually two geographic zones. The Soviets have occupied Wakhan of course; we know that is a fact. All this terrain in the Wakhan—the corridor area—is excellent for establishing missile bases on the ground. There are nice flat river terraces that could possibly be used to sink in missile sites.

In addition, the non-Pushtun peoples north of the Hindu Kush, the Turkmen, Tajik, Uzbek, and other groups, are refugees themselves that go back to at least two generations and sometimes three or four. We must remember that most of these people of Northern Afghanistan are anti-Russian, from the Czarist period or the *basmachi* period. They have fought against Russian aggression of one sort or another for several generations. The war that is taking place in northern Afghanistan is just as fierce, if not more so, than the one taking place in the south. But very few correspondents can go to the north to find out what's happening there. I can assure you there is quite a bit of fighting going on and the people are definitely, very vehemently, anti-Soviet. It would be difficult to incorporate these people into the Soviet Union. If you bring in immigrants from the outside, you certainly would not want to bring in Muslims from Soviet Central Asia. This would create more problems for the Soviets than it would solve, because this would encourage the potential, but latent, nationalism that still exists within these groups in Soviet Central Asia. I am not predicting a wide revolt in Soviet Central Asia or anything like that, but difficulties would arise if transplantation takes place. We know this from the fact that about 30 percent of the invading force in 1979 were Muslims from Soviet Central Asia. The Soviets sent them in because they thought that these Muslims from Soviet Central Asia, being linguistic and cultural cousins, could get along well with the Afghans in the north. They did. They got along so well that some of them are fighting with the *mujahidin* now, not many, but some. They did mingle with the Afghan population. They integrated with them very well, and they found out that they were there under false pretenses. They were not fighting Americans and Chinese and so forth but simply the Afghans. The Soviets began to send these Muslim troops home in February 1980. The Central Asians combed the bazaars of all the urban areas in Afghanistan where they were stationed and bought up copies of the *Holy Qur'an* and took them back to Soviet Central Asia.

Gerald C. Steibel

Let me give you a layman's observations. Let me also stress that there is nothing critical intended or implied in what I am going to say. But let me give you the outsider's reactions to what I have heard here. I have picked out the three points which seem most pressing. First, let me begin with what appears to be a "nomenclature gap" on who is doing what in Afghanistan. When I hear the term *anti-Western materialism,* which has been used to describe the so-called progressive Muslims, I run for cover. Now maybe this is grossly unfair and if so I want to enter my disclaimer. But I have had personal experiences and my country as a whole has had experiences with those who reject Western values, who are against Western materialism and, rightly or wrongly, this has come to represent to us a code word for something that goes a good deal beyond philosophical or cultural differences. Strategically speaking, I understand the attraction in cooperating with the people who are said to be the most effective enemies of my enemy. I do not want to discourage that kind of reason at all. I simply want to tell you that when I hear that they reject Western materialism, my question is: (1) Can we live with such a regime assuming that it comes to power? and (2) Can we even collaborate with it on its way to power?

Second, I would like to comment to a very limited degree on Professor Valenta's excellent presentation. I join with the rest of you in calling it superb. One of the things which makes it superb is that it is an eminently well-reasoned piece. It represents our Western rationality at its best. He mentions the Soviet sense of threat, and he puts it under external factors. I would put it under internal factors. This placement is critical to the kind of problems we have been discussing. The Soviet sense of threat is part of the residual Marxism-Leninism of the Soviet Union. What has survived of this ideology and what has become deeply ingrained is the sense of threat. This is almost an institutionalized paranoia—if the Soviets did not have a threat they would jolly well have to go out and find one. As we know, their economy is anywhere from half to two-thirds on a war footing now. They have a siege mentality without which they could not survive, at least under their present system of control. The sense of threat is not just an external mechanism at which we in the West look and say, "Well, here is how they see the threat from outside; let us deal with it, perhaps assuage it in some way, and thus we can get along with them." This is a very common mistake made in this country in all dealings with the Soviet Union. Once we understand that this sense is rooted in the dynamics of their own rule, we are looking at a somewhat different problem. I would do one other thing, and that is to link the sense of threat with the sense of history—as the Soviets understand it. History, to them, is what tells them that one way or the other all the forces will come in their direction and they will prevail. With that historical sense, which is linked to the sense of threat, the Soviets take one step backward when they have to. Therefore, if we are going to look for any satisfactory resolution of Afghanistan, or any other crisis, we should keep in mind the deeply ingrained strength of their sense of history. It is that particular approach which enables them, if you will, to resort to their sense of history to take that step backward.

Finally, I have been rebuked privately for bringing this up, but I must bring it up nonetheless. One of the problems that you as a group have is that your war is not salient. It is what *The London Economist* calls "the war that the West has forgotten." This is not good for you. You are absolutely convinced that what the Soviets are doing in Afghanistan is wrong. We are 100 percent emotionally with the Afghans, but how urgent is the issue? What priority does it have in our national thinking? Much as I regret to say this, wars today are not only politics by other means—they are media events. For many years the East European émigrés kept their cause alive not as an appeal to charity, but as a strategic necessity. Here, they said, are 100 million people under the yoke of the Communist oppressors. They would be critical of any war. Therefore, when you contribute to the cause of Radio Free Europe, Radio Liberty, etc., you are contributing to your own safety. There is nowhere in the proceedings of this conference how to make a discussion of the Afghanistan problem more salient, how to get a constituency. If you want support, if you want the backing, if you want the government to put more in—to send more money, to give you the arms of whatever—the Afghan cause has to have somebody who is beating the drums within the country. To have right on your side, to be just, noble, that's all fine—it gets you nowhere. You have to study the dynamics of the problem. For scholars, for professional researchers, this may be anathema, but I close on the note that unless you do it, what you risk is a situation in which everybody has adjusted. Afghanistan is not as threatening as Lebanon, Grenada, or whatever, let it be. That spells stalemate and that spells failure.

DISCUSSION

B. A. Hamzah: I have been keeping quiet for two days. That is not because I do not have any ideas to contribute, but rather, because I have been thinking about what to contribute and to avoid hasty statements. We have discussed many issues. I, too, would like to share some of the sentiments—anxieties, concerns, apprehensions, and hopes—of what is happening and has happened in Afghanistan. We must recognize the fact that Afghanistan is moving quite rapidly into the Soviet orbit. This is a fact we must recognize. The effects are very telling on the Afghan economy as well as the social fabric. Despite encouraging remarks and the positive situational report from Dr. Majrooh two days ago, it will take a lot of courage and effort to free Afghanistan from the clutches of the Soviet Union in a short time. I have the following reasons to support my argument. First, the Soviet Union has made it quite clear that they have geostrategic interests for being in Afghanistan. They will not give up so easily. I do not think it is fair to equate Afghanistan to Egypt, Somalia, or Indonesia—Afghanistan is a different kettle of fish, one the Soviet Union would like to hold for itself. Second, the Soviet Union has the machinery to destroy Afghanistan if it wants to by sheer use of force. It is not quite accurate to describe the situation in Afghanistan as a stalemate; it is rather a standoff. The other reason why I suggest that the Soviet Union is not likely to get out of Afghanistan very quickly is because of the extensive processes of Sovietization in the Afghan economy. About 90 percent of the aid that goes into Afghanistan comes from the Soviet Union. The latter spends more than 50 million a day to manage the economy. In addition, the social fabric of the society has also been transformed, if not completely shattered at a heavy penalty. The loss in economic terms has been estimated by one authority at some $2 billion a year. The Sovietization of the economy has also another ugly face—inflation. Prices of basic commodities have risen very sharply since the invasion: Wheat has gone up by about 400 percent; meat by about 500 percent; cooking oil by 300 percent. Katerina Engberg spoke of the shortage of food in the countryside yesterday. I do not have to elaborate on this issue.

I would like to submit here that the Soviets have a difficult time in quelling the freedom fighters because an insurgency of that nature in an inhospitable terrain is extremely difficult to take care of. I do not think they will be in a position to eliminate every *mujahid*. But a question is: Is this their policy? Is the elimination of the *mujahidin* a Soviet strategy? Cannot the Soviets do some other thing to serve their end? To me, the Soviet military strategy of attrition and scorched earth policy is deliberate and serves their purpose very well. I submit here that the Soviets are not interested in wasting their energies going after every *mujahid,* especially in inhospitable terrain. They are interested, rather, in dominating Afghanistan by controlling the lines of communication, the major arteries and nerve centers. However, I also hazard a guess here, that the resistance will continue for a long time, and I think they will continue to gain some strength. So long as it does not reach a certain point, it will be tolerated; and that point is so long as the *mujahidin* do not pose a real threat to the Soviets' primary interest in Afghanistan, or so long as the Soviet soldiers do not have to do all the fighting on behalf of Babrak Kamal and his people. We can find this parallel already shaping up very well in Vietnam and now in Kampuchea.

While we realize that the *mujahidin* are doing a good job in Afghanistan, we must also recognize limitations and constraints on their capacity to improve their situation without outside help. They are too dependent on external support for their weapons, for their ammunition, and for other logistics. In this respect, the free world nations have a moral responsibility, if not obligation, to come to their aid. I would like to float an idea here. I am making an appeal to rich Muslim countries, rich Muslim philantrophists, and many other peoples in the world. We should start a fund for the *mujahidin*. I would like to appeal to the other rich countries to be more forthcoming with their contributions to this fund. Perhaps, I'm addressing this issues to some of my Muslim colleagues in this hall, that the matter be discussed in the Organization of the Islamic Conference. It may be too late now to place it on the agenda of the next meeting in Dhaka. But together we can influence our own governments or the need to contribute to this fund for humanitarian purposes. I would also like to place on record here that presently there are about seventeen private organizations rendering help to the *mujahidin*. Being private organizations, they are limited in their resources, they are not coordinated in one way or another, and they are very individualistic. These organizations have noble intentions. Perhaps this is one area which the Muslim countries and organizations could emulate. And, finally, the chairman asked me yesterday to say a few words on what I consider to be the Third World attitude toward Soviet agression in Afghanistan. I think the position of the free world nations is well known. My own country has been quite outspoken as far as Soviet actions in Afghanistan are concerned. Singapore has also been vocal at the previous Nonaligned meeting in New

Delhi by actually rebuking the Soviet Union position in Afghanistan. We condemn the Soviet invasion and the injustices that followed. We also demand a Soviet withdrawal. But beyond that, we have very little leverage to bring about a change in Soviet strategy. I am confident that Third World countries, particularly the Muslim countries, would be willing to assist the *mujahidin* by contributing to the proposed fund. I think the Soviet Union has alienated the Third World countries by its ruthless actions in Vietnam and Kampuchea, as well as in Afghanistan. The Soviets did not expect such widespread agitation from Third World countries, nor did they expect the strength of the *mujahidin*. With regard to Soviet policy we must approach the problem from a global perspective and we need global action.

Jiri Valenta: I agree with Gerald Steibel that since 1978 the Soviets have perceived some aspects of the Afghan issue as internal to the Soviet Union. Certainly as soon as the Afghan regime began to adhere more faithfully to the Leninist model, the Soviets responded by linking developments in Afghanistan to Soviet domestic politics. This is a key impediment to a Soviet policy reversal in Afghanistan. A retreat from Afghanistan would not only bear on the Soviets' much improved strategic position vis-à-vis its adversaries. Over the long haul it would have a powerful ideological repercussion at home. I think this is one consideration that is motivating the Soviets to do what they are doing.

Tom Gouttierre asked me a question, and I hope I can answer it now: "How long will the Soviets stay and what is their long-term objective?" Most of us agree that they would like to stay as long as possible. But they are still leaving open an ideological window by not defining the Afghan system as socialist, but rather a "socialist-oriented" regime. Unlike the countries of Eastern Europe, which they categorize as socialist, the Soviets classify Afghanistan, Nicaraqua, Angola, and Ethiopia as "socialist-oriented countries." This is a special category they developed after their bad experiences in Egypt, Somalia, and elsewhere. In other words, it implies that the process of socialization is still reversible. However, lately I have seen evidence of the Soviets' referring to Afghanistan as a kind of popular democracy. This is an ominous sign because popular democracy was the label the Soviets affixed to the countries of Eastern Europe in the late 1940s to designate their having arrived at the second stage in a country's passage to Leninism. The Soviets still have not pledged a total ideological commitment. Nevertheless, any retreat from Afghanistan would be very painful and perhaps detrimental to Soviet domestic interests.

There is some hope that we can change the situation in Afghanistan. However, we should not fall into the trap of supporting the Afghans with military aid in such a way as to push the Soviet Union into a corner. Here I think that some of Harrison's suggestions are well taken. Of course, when we talk about Finlandization of Afghanistan we should remember that the Finns fought bravely to extract Soviet concessions. The latter never would have accepted the modus vivendi they have with the Finns had the Finns not resisted them in the winter war of 1940 when there were enormous Soviet losses.

This same logic applies to the disparate Soviet treatment of the Eastern European countries. Hungary's 1956 revolution was crushed, but many Soviet lives were lost in the process. The kind of liberalization we now see in that country, Hungary's "socialism with a semihuman face," is a better solution than that imposed on Czechoslovakia, which failed to resist the Soviets in 1968. There are other examples in Eastern Europe, but I think these are sufficient to relay an idea of how carefully the Soviets calculate potential costs before opting for a military solution: "How many lives?" they ask. "Of course, we can subdue most of our neighbors, but how much are we going to pay for it in terms of economic adjustments, the lives of our soldiers, and, most important, the political costs in terms of our relations with Third World countries, the international Communist movement and so forth?" For us in the West it is important to provide military aid to the Afghans while also pursuing a diplomatic track. We really cannot know whether the Soviets will respond. I object to Selig's suggestion that we be optimistic simply because I am weighing realistically what is happening in the Kremlin and this is an important variable. There were hopes in the spring of 1983 that the Soviets might try to bargain with us. I for one gave up hoping after Andropov's disappearance in the Kremlin. Without a strong leader in the Kremlin who can consolidate his power and who can sell his strength and policy positions to the military and other elites, there is little hope for compromise. When Khrushchev retreated from the Finnish bases in Pokkala in 1955 and from Austria's occupied western district, he did so after demoting Malenkov and putting Molotov, who was opposed to that arrangment, in a corner. Today we do not have a similar situation. Whoever replaces Andropov will not have enough muscle or influence, I am afraid, to strike a deal. However, we must not cease to hope that the Soviet troops will leave Afghanistan. Meanwhile we have to pursue the two tracks I have suggested and be vigilant and ready should any opportunity arise that would assist us in achieving our objective.

Sabahuddin Kushkaki: This phrase, "anti-Western materialism," I think I was the one who used it. I have an obligation to respond to that. Maybe it is a misnomer. What the Islamic progressives mean by

"Western materialism" are evils which are essentially a byproduct of Western civilization. If that satisfies my friend I will not discuss it further, but I think you should give them the right to oppose anything considered to be an evil byproduct of Western civilization—like alcoholism or the mini-skirt. For example in the early 1970s there was an uprising and turmoil of religious groups in Afghanistan against communism. At the same time they were very disturbed by a number of events and developments that were taking place and which they thought were being brought into Afghanistan from the West—like mini-skirts. There was a Mosque in the center of Kabul and opposite to that there was a nightclub. They were bitterly opposed to things like that.

Let me go a little deeper. Afghanistan and the Muslim countries have their own values and standards. Central to these is the idea of family life and women's sanctity in it, the fact that her freedom and way of life should not be disturbed by Western technological and scientific advances. Why should an Afghan woman be compelled to be visited by a man who is vaccinating? Islam, after all, does not prevent women from being educated to take part in social welfare and other social activities. Why should an Afghan family be compelled that their women be visited by male census takers? They are very much against this, and we should see that the values of Muslims and of the Afghan society are their birthright. They should not be violated. This is what I meant by "anti-Western materialism." If it is misleading, let us define it differently.

Laurent Carrel: I really appreciate the presentation by Brigadier Husain, and I would like him to comment on two short questions. He mentioned that the cost to the Soviet Union amounts to about $15-20 million a day. I would like to ask him whether this figure includes only military costs, or also the costs of the so-called Sovietization program—and also the economic costs? Specifically, I would like him to comment on a statement made by the U.S. Defense Department. Recently they published their second assessment of Soviet military power with a chapter on Afghanistan. The Defense Department claims that by Soviet standards, the war in Afghanistan is a cheap war in terms of casualties and cost.

The second question concerns the assessment of the strategic goals of the Soviet Union in Afghanistan. Recently, there has been some very disturbing news in open military sources that the Soviets have created a new TVD (theater of operations) command in Tashkent under the command of Marshal Sergei Leonidovich Sokolov—commanding not only the 40th Army in Afghanistan, but also the military districts in Turkmen, Central Asia, and the Trans-Caucasus Military District, thus building a framework for an overall military "Southern Command" also covering the Persian Gulf. I would appreciate your comments on these two questions.

Robert G. Neumann: I apologize for always stressing practical points. It is not a disparagement of academic approaches, but I am interested in results. Several speakers have made comments about the Afghan friends needing public relations firms or something like that. I am not going to address that, but rather how some of their activities look to American officials. I fully appreciate the reasons for the divergence and disparity of different Afghan groups. However, I am just saying that for American officials it is a pain in the neck. If they came in one group, one delegation, I could get them to see the president. But when they come in groups all the time I call the desk officer, the lowest level of the bureaucracy. I simply cannot bother people who are very busy to see one group after another. Now, you could tell me that that cannot be changed, well fine, but you pay the price. Second, if a different group comes there is always a question of whom they represent. How do we know that they are as representative as they say? To this comes also the fact that there are in America some private organizations that are very active but whose leaders, who shall remain nameless and happily are not here, clearly have their own game to play, which is part of the dynamics of the situation. But again, this becomes a matter of disparity. They very frequently come with highly picturesque *mujahidin,* with turbans and everything else, but the question arises: "Is it show or is it reality?" I think you are hurting yourselves with this kind of approach. Then, the presentation slides and so forth are interesting but frequently highly repetitive. There is no shortage of drama and tragedy in the world. It is difficult to compete with all of them. This is simply a fact.

Third, there is a peculiar approach which I resent and I think my official colleagues resent. It goes on two tracks. One is, "Please talk to the Pakistanis because they are discouraging Afghan unity." This has come up before. Whether the Pakistanis and General Zia discourage it or not is not what I want to say. All I want to say is it is not for us to talk to the Pakistanis but for the Afghans to talk to them. Unity is *their* job, not ours. The argument which I resent even more is, "If you talk to my group or give financial assistance to my group, the others will rally." That approach is guaranteed to turn the interlocutor against you. I guarantee this does not work. And it should not. The last thing Afghan freedom fighters, who risk their lives, need is an American stamp. This is a foolish approach and it gets even worse when, at the end of the conversation, you get a request for visas for fifteen relatives. I shall be very blunt but this is my chance too, and I understand these problems. My wife and I have sponsored personally Afghan refugees, so we are not insensitive, but to combine the two is the worst possible thing. If you come for a political cause, come for a political cause. If you want a visa or green card, come for *them*—do not combine the two.

With all that, Afghanistan is getting quite a bit of attention from the media. When you consider how much else there is, how much attention you get now of the continuing deaths in Cambodia, the Haitians, or the boat people, and when you consider television time is twenty minutes interrupted by fifteen commercials every two minutes or even in a newspaper where there is more space, there is really quite a bit. I think the accusation is unfair considering what is available. More is desirable, but then there is another newspaper trick—that is a hook. The general history of tragedy is not news, because there is a certain limit to what the individual can take, and then he tunes out because he does not want to hear of more tragedy. This is especially true of people who themselves are not suffering. This is where I think the suggestion of a public relations firm is good; they know what the hook is on which a story is to be hung. All these things do not cost that much. A very interesting suggestion has been made about an Islamic fund. I discussed this, actually, with Mr. Shafiq, the secretary-general of the Organization of the Islamic Conference. I do not think you should expect an excessive degree of dynamism from them. Obviously, you know what I am talking about. The trick there is to get a sponsor. The ideal sponsor is Saudi Arabia; that is where the money is—either that or Kuwait. Then make your case, but very effectively in one group, not fifteen. Before the next meeting prepare the ground. Decisions are not made in a meeting or conference. Decisions are made before the conference, or afterwards sometimes, but not in the meeting. If you come with all your case to make your presentation at the conference, you have already lost. You have to do your homework beforehand.

Finally, two more points. If the State Department denies the help we are giving, that should not bother you. First of all, you have to bear in mind what you get out of admitting it. In diplomatic language, as my ambassadorial colleagues know and as King Hassan of Morocco once explained very clearly, denial does not mean it is not true; denial means "I do not take the responsibility." Ambassadors have been defined as honest men sent abroad to lie for their country. This was a comment from the seventeenth century; and King James I, who heard this remark from one of his ambassadors, was so incensed that he never gave him another post.

On a very different subject, with great respect to Mr. Kushkaki whom I really respect because of his heroic attitude not only after the communists but even before, I have not found too many Muslim women, nor my wife who had better access, who really want to be quite so protected. On the other hand, I think they know better how to operate their societies and they ought not to be pushed, least of all by foreigners. But there is a practical aspect. The modernization process requires a sizable work force in all levels of the society and the industrialization process. A country which remains in a fundamentalist mode deprives itself of an enormous resource and is handicapped in its development. Development and fundamentalism are incompatible on a practical level. You can say what you want about the theory—that we want to accept only the good features of modernization and keep our traditional values—but that is not the way it is. This fine distinction and separation is not practical. If you want to modernize you go one way, if you do not want to you go another.

Thomas E. Gouttierre: Today we have had some concrete recommendations, which I think are interesting and offer some thoughts for the future, such as Louis's statement relating to the public relations organization. Ambassador Neumann has mentioned the question of the groupings and the unity of the Afghan *mujahidin*. It is a very important thing and one I have been discussing for four years. I was intrigued by your statement about the urgency of the war. You raised the question of how to make the war more salient. That is a good question for all of us to ponder. I was particularly pleased with Dr. Hamzah's remarks and suggestions regarding an Islamic fund and Third World participation. I feel that the costs we keep talking about concerning the war in Afghanistan for the Soviet Union have to come very much into the realm of the Third World impact and the Muslim world impact. I think there has been little impact there. Those who deserve the most criticism for what they have not done have been those from Islamic countries. I do not mean in any way to include Pakistan here; the Pakistanis have contributed greatly. I am talking about the world of Islam and its organizations in particular. They have not done what they might be expected to do in the face of the fact that a fellow Muslim country has been occupied.

Finally, I would like to mention one thing that is always interesting when we talk about the war in Afghanistan. We always talk about percentages of the country occupied by the Soviet Union or being maintained in the hands of the resistance and the freedom of movement within the areas under the control of the resistance. Professor Hamzah mentioned that we need to put this in perspective. One of the perspectives, of course, is positive. Dr. Malhuret was able to point out the freedom of movement and obvious resistance control in these areas. But the other thing we need to keep in mind is where the Soviets are concentrating their efforts in terms of maintaining control. Maybe 15 percent of the country is what they feel they need at this time; they can strike out at the other 85 percent as they want for their war of intimidation. Those of us who have lived in Afghanistan, particularly those of us who have had experience as Peace Corps volunteers, were always told that Kabul was not Afghanistan—the rest of the country was also Afghanistan. That is true, but Kabul *is* also Afghanistan, especially in considerations relating to power. When you say Kabul, you are talking about the urban part of Afghanistan, not just the city of Kabul. And until the resistance makes the Soviets uncomfortable in those pockets of security they have established for themselves, the costs of that nature are in some ways not as significant as these statistics.

Seyed Qassem Reshtia: My remarks are regarding the important comments made by Ambassador Neumann. I want to clarify that I do not belong to any party or group in the resistance. I am only a concerned Afghan. And as such, yesterday, I distributed a paper in which I mentioned a new initiative in the direction of the integration and unification of the different elements of the resistance. I would like to add now that this was intended to fill the gap Ambassador Neumann mentioned—the representation of the resistance. The war in Afghanistan is going on, and it will go on we hope, *inshallah*. What is more important is the question of the organization of the Afghan resistance. We have heard this from many countries. I am in Europe and close to the EEC countries. They have passed resolutions in the European Parliament and individually in the different European countries. They are always saying, "We want to see who are the real representatives of Afghanistan. When we have this, then we are prepared to provide material help including arms." This initiative was taken to fill this gap, and we hope that the Western countries in general, including the United States, will give their support to this initiative to encourage the integration of the different elements of resistance and the formation of the United Front, which is in the process of formation to enable the Afghans to speak with one voice. It envisages the gathering of representatives coming from inside Afghanistan, from among the *mujahidin,* from the refugees, and from Afghans all over the world. This gathering will decide about the formation of a body which could represent the Afghan resistance as a whole. But we know, and you understand very well, that it is almost impossible to bring all these different factions and sections under one umbrella. But still, we hope that the majority of

Afghans inside Afghanistan and outside will join in this initiative, which is not made for any other purpose or personal gain. This was initiated by the former king of Afghanistan, as a simple citizen of Afghanistan and not as a national leader or king. He was clear when he made some firm commitments about this. And this is why he will be available only to help the creation of certain organizations, especially for the purpose of coordinating the jehad and representing the resistance of Afghanistan abroad.

Peers Carter: Robert Neumann and I were colleagues in Afghanistan at one time and I am happy to say that I agree with practically everything he said—in many cases I agree by a factor of two. I have been greatly enlightened by this meeting, but I have had an increasing sense of frustration. A lot has seemed to me, to use Ambassador Neumann's words, somewhat academic. But it was like a breath of fresh air to hear practical suggestions, first from Dr. Steibel and later from Dr. Hamzah, concerned with the importance of raising the profile of this war.

Wars are now media events. I wonder whether their two approaches could not be forced together. The idea of hiring a public relations firm is very attractive theoretically, but when one beings to think of who would do the hiring and what the firm's terms of reference would be, one is confronted with what we called, when I was in our embassy in Washington, a bag of worms.

But if wars are now media events, as news is a business, the material consideration is that sending TV teams into Afghanistan is, in the first place, expensive; unless you get your ratings afterwards, you are going to loose money. Second, Afghanistan is rather dangerous, but TV reporters seem to be prepared to put up with that. So I wonder: if there is financing from strongly Islamic sources or elsewhere—could it not be used to finance the sending of strong reporting teams into Afghanistan? This, we know from experience, is not in practice a difficult matter; the resistance is perfectly capable of guiding such teams in Afghanistan, showing them some very interesting footage, looking after them and making sure they do not get shot—not too much, anyway. I wonder whether this is not a more practical way of using funds than just trying to project an image which would inevitably be biased and run into the problems Robert Neumann was talking about, such as the ideological as well as theoretical divisions between different parts of the resistance.

Eden Naby: I would like to just address very briefly the question of Central Asia that was raised by Louis Dupree and by Brigadier Husain.

For Louis, my only comment is that the question of the reason for the withdrawal of the Central Asians in those initial few months of the invasion is not one that has been settled to my satisfaction. I would not conclude with you that they were withdrawn because they were not reliable. But I certainly agree with you that there were sympathies expressed and that Soviet Muslims appeared eager to buy the *Holy Qur'ans* at the Kabul market. I think the Central Asian element is far more complex than we have had time to tackle here. There are not only questions of bureaucratically entrenched identities over a period of sixty years of Sovietization, but there are other factors as well that must be brought in. I am glad we referred to it so that we are aware that it is a problem that needs to be discussed.

Marvin J. Weinbaum: I wonder if the time has not come for those who support Afghanistan and its resistance to begin to consider whether they have a role to play, perhaps in determining along with the Afghans what kind of Afghanistan there would be in the future. We spent so much of our time here on the question of winning the struggle—whether winning through an armed victory, which seems so remote, or winning in the negotiations. There has to be some concern in this last session on what kind of Afghanistan will emerge. We certainly would not want to see the Afghanistan suffering today exchanged for an Afghanistan under the cloud of a civil war. And this is not impossible. We must be concerned that the Afghans get to choose their future, and that that future be realistic for them. You just do not remove the enemy, you have to replace it with something. It has to be something the Afghans consider legitimate. We know that some of the pillars of legitimacy are gone, such as the monarchy. We know that whatever kind of Afghanistan is going to emerge is going to have to be progressive. I would not use this term exactly as you have, but it is going to have to be an Afghanistan concerned with social questions as perhaps the Afghanistan of the past was not. I wonder whether the time has come, perhaps, for those who take Afghanistan seriously to decide who among those fighting should be supported. What values should be given reinforcement? Is this interference? I know it can be read as such. History will show, on one hand, that there is some danger of splitting things even more. On the other hand, we also recognize the fact that the help that is going to certain resistance groups does make a difference in their relative power and influence. At the moment we are spread very thinly. There is this problem that Mr. Reshtia points out very rightly: "Who is Afghanistan?" A definition of Afghanistan is important as an incentive for the Afghans to continue to fight over time, rather than among themselves. And it is also to be necessary for those who are on the outside to determine whether they are going to maintain this kind of support over the long run.

Sabahuddin Kushkaki: I just wanted to comment on what Professor Weinbaum was saying concerning what kind of Afghanistan we are going to have. Professor Naby was also referring to this in her paper on the first day, when she was speaking about a new generation of Afghans that emerged as a result of this jehad. Who forms the bulwark and the majority of the resistance throughout Afghanistan? They are the people who are trying to reconcile Western moral and spiritual values with their own ideological background. And they are the people that are going to have the reins of the future of Afghanistan in their hands. They are an emerging force of young people looking for a leadership that is not forthcoming, even among the ranks of the present jehad in Peshawar and Quetta. They are finding a gap between themselves and the leadership, and they think that their ideals and aspirations are not reflected in that leadership. This was also the case when Afghanistan was still free and not under the occupation of the Soviet Union, or under Communist rule. They want something which will give them the opportunity to put into practice their dynamism and aspirations. These are the people that we should be talking about.

Thomas E. Gouttierre: I would just like to comment a little further on the point Sabahuddin made. We got ourselves into a situation during these three days where we have been exchanging labels concerning the things we want to discuss. Perhaps this trivializes the topic and issues we are discussing. We have talked about fundamentalists, progressives, and Islamic revolutionary movements. It is important for all of us to understand, first and foremost, that these people are Afghans and that the movement we are talking about—whichever title or name we use—is reflective of the people themselves, and that they may have very different concepts of the way they are "progressive Islamicists," Muslims, "fundamentalists," or "revolutionaries." As Mr. Steibel remarked, these labels can be sources of misunderstanding about these people's objectives. It is important to remember, too, that many of these people who now are very strong Muslims have been searching a bit. Some of them used to search on the other side of the political spectrum when they were in the opposition, at a time when the Afghan establishment was different from what it is now. Many of us have gone through that experience. I was much more particularistic in terms of my political outlook before I was thirty, I suppose, than I am now at forty-three. We have to recognize that many of the Afghans that we are talking about, who are now moving into the very beginning stage of their middle age, and who are indeed the leaders of the thinking and fighting, have gone through some changes themselves. The changes have been forced by very dramatic conditions. I have always found the Afghan, more than anything else, to be a practical person in his religion as well as many other issues. We had a discussion earlier about the separation of church and state. Even though true, these institutions may be combined in the manner that Dr. Rabbani discussed in his well-written papers, and Louis Dupree has written about as well. In Afghanistan the state and the mullah have had a working relationship—rarely have they been combined. I am not disputing the terms that have been used, but I think we must remember that the Afghanistan of the future is not likely to be anything like what we may have seen in other countries, whether in Pakistan or in Iran, and particularly not like Iran.

Eden Naby: I would like to add a footnote to what ambassador Neumann and Carter said with regard to information. Another thing we have to watch out for as we leave this conference and continue to study Afghanistan is that disinformation is going to become far more widespread than it has been in the past. We have seen two examples of it. First, the statement attributed to people in the National Security Council under Carter that Americans want to see the Afghans fight to the last man. It is a very good example of this disinformation that is widespread. The other is the example that Mr. Ansari gave with a quotation about Mr. Newsome. There is going to be far more of that, and we are going to have to look out for it.

Robert G. Neumann: If I have learned anything, it is that when foreigners use their assistance to engage in social engineering it ends in either failure or disaster. We may have our preferences. I personally would not like to see a fundamentalist Afghanistan. But that is for the Afghans to decide. If we start that game, it is going to end badly.

Laurent Carrel: Ambassador Neumann noted that "the lack of a centralized organization, the lack of unity, contributes to the American difficulties in dealing with the resistance." I just wanted to say that this same factor contributes very much to Soviet difficulties in dealing with the resistance.

Zia-ul-Islam Ansari: There is a lot of talk about unity and leaders among the ranks of the *mujahidin*. All those things are a requirement of the state and of armies. And we know well that in Afghan society they deal with many matters in their own tribe, and they have a method of dealing with the issues which must be taken up at a higher level. So we heard about the commanders taking actions as they like in accordance with the situation. Much is said about Pakistan's role in bringing about unity, or of creating difficulties about the unity. I think this is unfair to these people. They are living there as guests, and we cannot have the Pakistani government or a Pakistani organization trying to impose any kind of unity upon them. They are doing as much as necessary in accordance with their needs and requirements. As Mr. Carrel just pointed out, this is also an obstacle to the Soviets in dealing with them. I would like to make it clear here that in Pakistan neither the government nor any group can be benefited by disunity among the ranks of the *mujahidin*. We wish for any kind of state or situation among the refugees and *mujahidin* which can be useful and practicable to achieve the goal—the freedom of Afghanistan. Pakistani society, private organizations, and the government are willing to extend any help to any group engaged in achieving that goal. These things that have been pointed out by Ambassador Neumann are small human weaknesses. If a group feels Ambassador Neumann is going to dole out some money, and there are two, three groups sitting here in Peshawar, they each would like to represent a larger number of people. I think it is a human weakness and it should be ignored. Unity is not a requirement to concern us very much. We should pay attention to two things. We need to give proper information to the rest of the world about the situation in Afghanistan, but it would be risky to send in TV teams. Another alternative is that when the TV teams are going into that area they may leave their cameras behind and give some sort of training to the *mujahidin* to handle those cameras. It would be very easy for them to send out films instead of you taking in cameras and then having to bring out the camera and the film.

Louis Dupree: I would like to look at what Noor Husain said about the short and the long term. I think they can be combined. We are going to see evolution occur at a much faster rate than we anticipate. I would like to say just a few words about attitudes and options. Few Afghans, unlike some of our outside specialists, expect the Soviets to leave Afghanistan unless forced. This will come through military pressure brought by the Afghans themselves inside Afghanistan, with considerable amounts of weaponry furnished by a sympathetic outside world. But, of course, much of the weaponry and ammunition comes from inside Afghanistan today. Still, the military pressure must be through the *mujahidin's* efforts during the jehad. These weapons should include sufficient quantity and quality to make an appreciable impact on Soviet men, material, and morale. That is a harsh thing for me to say and I hate to say it. This would have to take place over an unspecified period of time; I do not want it to happen next week. I want it to evolve logically the way it is going now. The friendly nations of the outside world should support all the groups which, as their own research indicates, are fighting inside Afghanistan. I have no real faith in the pronouncements of many of the outside groups as to what they are doing. I would like to have this done by some sort of practical means. French doctors will not bring weapons, I assure you, but they have been able to go in with large-scale amounts of medical equipment. I still think that this can be done inside Afghanistan while the fighting is taking place. If the Soviets and Afghans can be patient at what is happening now inside Afghanistan, the outside world can afford to be patient too. Things do not have to be rushed. Let them evolve logically. We do not want to pour our arms into Afghanistan, mix them up with Afghan blood, and then, voilà, you have an instant free Afghanistan. No, we want to do this calmly just as the Afghans themselves in many ways are doing this calmly.

The same is true on the diplomatic front. The choreography of diplomacy in Geneva should continue as long as all sides are willing to dance with one another. And somewhere along the way, I would not wager when, but somewhere along about Geneva XV, say, the Afghan *mujahidin* will have evolved into several significant, reasonably oriented national liberation movements. That would be the practical time for them to move into the diplomacy. While this evolution is taking place, we are going to see evolve the ideology for a new Afghanistan among the Afghan groups actively engaged in this liberation. The significance of these Geneva talks is the institutionalization of a diplomatic door which is there and can always be opened, if and when the Soviets are ever ready for some sort of political solution. The Afghan *mujahidin* must be a part of these Geneva conferences, ultimately, in order to satisfy the options for peace. However, at this stage of the military and diplomatic options, to deny or even to consider to deny the Afghans the weapons they need to continue their fight (and our fight as well) must be ruled out. They will continue to fight whether they get assistance or not, and that should be considered in the calculations. At this point it is unnecessarily emotional, immature, and even a bit naive to deny them these arms which they so desperately need.

Noor A. Husain: There is absolutely no element of truth about the Pakistani government or the people not wanting unity among the various groups. There are many misconceptions floating around and this is probably one of them. Certain parallels were drawn between Austria and Afghanistan, between Finland and Afghanistan, between Poland and Afghanistan, and also between Iran in the 1941-46 period and Afghanistan. But in each of these cases there is a totally different geopolitical factor involved. In the case of Austria it took them eleven years of negotiations to get neutral status. In the case of Finland they lost some of their territory before they were "Finlandized." In the case of Iran, the Soviets were there from 1941 to 1946, and it was not only the threat by President Truman but also the vote of the Iranian Majlis that caused them to leave. The attitude of the people of Azerbaijan was another compelling factor for the Soviets to leave. So we should not make a broad generalization.

I would like to comment on Louis Dupree's point about an Indian-Pakistani rapproachement. On our part, we have done our best. We have offered a nonaggresion pact to India; we have gone more than half way to mend fences. But I think you are aware of how things have gone, and I think the present situation with India is not entirely of our making. The policy of the government of Pakistan, as we know it, is to mend fences with India, because we know fully well that we cannot face a 2-front war. We are making every diplomatic effort to try to bring India around to see that the loss of Afghanistan to the Soviets is a loss of the security zone of South Asia, and that it is as much in their interest as in ours to have the Soviets out of the Hindu Kush.

Mr. Carrel raised two points. One was about costs and the other about the strategic goals of the Soviet Union. In assessing costs of a closed society it is always very hazardous, whether it is casualties or the costs of the conflict. The figure we found is probably the closest and pertains to the daily cost of not only sustaining the war effort but also of underwriting the Afghan economy. In return, they are getting all the natural gas and they fixed the meter on the gas on their side of the border. They are paying the Afghans far below what the normal rates for this gas should be. So these are the figures which one cannot really swear by, but I think they give an estimate of what it is costing the Soviets. It is the same with the casualties. There are conflicting figures emanating from the *mujahidin* and from other sources. We tried to get positive indicators and we got three indicators of their casualties. One was a factory in Kabul which was turning out twenty coffins per day. And you know Muslim soldiers are not buried in coffins. These were being used for Soviet soldiers. Then we got an indicator that there was a Russian transport plane equipped with about seventy-odd litters which used to fly once a week to all the air bases to collect their casualties and fly them to Central Asia. The third indicator we got was that the Lithuanians had about 300 casualties until last year. The Lithuanians are about 1 percent of the Soviet armed forces. They had a heavier representation in Afghanistan, and one could probably set the casualty rate for the killed, disabled, and wounded for the total Soviet army during that period of the last three and a half years at around 15,000-20,000, if not 30,000. Since there is no formal intelligence set up in an insurgency of this nature, just as there is neither a formal command and control nor communications set up, it is always hazardous trying to figure out the costs and casulaties, especially when they pertain to a closed society. Regarding Central Asian troops, the point has been well made by Dr. Naby already—there were the third-grade divisions available across the Amu Darya. They were pushed in with the first move of occupation, and when the second- and first-grade divisions became available these were changed around. But there is an element of truth in reports that there was some fraternization between Central Asian troops and the locals. Also, they had been buying copies of the *Holy Qur'an* from the bazaars of Kabul and Kandahar. But I would not read too much into that.

We recently had a scholar go to Moscow and when he returned he gave a talk. He brought back two main impressions. One was that the Soviets feel that neither the costs nor the casualties are of any significance so far, especially if you consider the various wars they have had and the casualties they suffered. Their total deaths in World War II were on the order of 20 million. The other point he brought back was that time was on their side. This is something we must sit down and figure—whether time is on their side or on the side of the free world. I frankly do not have an answer, but I am inclined to agree that time is on their side—especially when you look back and see that it took them sixty years to subdue the Trans-Caucasian region. They had been operating in that area for over 350 years.

Jiri Valenta: What was your estimate of Soviets killed, missing, and wounded? You gave us three figures.

Noor Husain: Those, I think, come to about 30,000. But they do not match up with other sources. They include dead, wounded, and prisoners of war.

Eden Naby: I believe there was a question about the Soviet theater command.

Noor A. Husain: Mr. Carrel asked about the creation of the new central command and what their long-term strategic aims might be. I alluded to this in my paper. Afghanistan certainly offers them many strategic options, including an open frontier with Iran, approximately 350-400 miles from the Straits of Hormuz. There are 3,100 kilometers of frontier with Pakistan. They have depopulated the Wakhan corridor and they are now located about 30 miles from the Karakorum highway in the Wakhan area. There are many strategic options open to them, and I feel that they are trying to bring the whole area under one central command which can work under various hypotheses that could arise both in the short and long term.

Jiri Valenta: Do you agree with the information, which is in open Swiss sources, that the new command includes three Soviet military districts—the Central Asian, Trans-Caucasian, and Turkmen?

Noor A. Husain: The Trans-Caucasian, I feel, is a bit far-fetched; the Pamir is more likely. Because the northern parts of Afghanistan and the Wakhan area, certainly the Pamir area, are being controlled by the headquarters at Murghab, which is the Pamir military district.

Ralph H. Magnus: This conference has demonstrated, as its title indicated, that there are alternatives in Afghanistan. Unfortunately, most of these seem not to be the ones that we would wish to see come about. But I do not think the ones we would wish are impossible, given what we have seen free men, especially free Afghans, can do. This is provided we make the right kinds of decisions and the Afghans, certainly, continue the course they have taken. With a bit more effectiveness and organization, and if they get the support they so richly deserve, things can change.

I keep getting the question, since I was over in Peshawar and the frontier areas this spring and summer, regarding the Afghans' prospects. When you return, the educated, interested layman or media person always asks you: "Well, are they winning or losing?" I have a hard time answering honestly. On the one hand, viewed from the dispassionate analyst's purely intellectual perspective you can say that we cannot see how the Russians can lose. On the other hand, when you go to the area and see the heroism of the Afghans and the heroism of our colleague Dr. Malhuret and his colleagues of Médecins sans Frontières and other organizations, such as journalists—some journalists have gone in very bravely, more Europeans than Americans, to report on this struggle—you come to a different conclusion. When you see all of this, and especially when you see the total unanimity of the Afghan people, you say that the Soviets cannot possibly win.

We have seen here over the past three days certain practical measures suggested. Ambassador Neumann's very cogent remarks and the initiative of our friend Dr. Hamzah gave us examples of practical things that can be done. It would be an even greater tragedy than that now happening in Afghanistan if we sat back and let the Afghan people—men, women, and childen—fight not only their war but our war as well by themselves.

About the Contributors

Thomas E. Gouttierre is dean of International Studies and Programs at the University of Nebraska, Omaha, and director of that institution's Center for Afghanistan Studies, the only center exclusively focusing on that country in the Western Hemisphere. He spent nearly ten years in Afghanistan as director of the Fulbright Foundation, as a Fulbright scholar, and as a Peace Corps volunteer.

Noor A. Husain is director of the Institute of Strategic Studies, Islamabad, and is also in charge of the Crisis and Conflict Analysis Team of the institute. He is the editor of the quarterly *Strategic Studies* and has presented papers on Afghanistan in a number of international conferences during the last four years.

Harmon E. Kirby, a native of Ohio, was educated at Harvard University and served in the U.S Army before entering the Department of State in 1961. He is a graduate of the Department's Executive Seminar and has served at foreign service posts in a number of countries, including India and the Sudan. He was director of Pakistan, Afghanistan, and Bangladesh Affairs in the Near Eastern/South Asian Bureau from 1982 to 1984, when he was appointed as deputy chief of mission in Rabat, Morocco.

Ralph H. Magnus is associate professor and coordinator of Middle Eastern Studies in the Department of National Security Affairs of the U.S. Naval Postgraduate School in Monterey, California. From 1963 to 1965 he served as an assistant cultural attaché with the U.S. Information Agency in Kabul. Magnus is the editor of *Documents on the Middle East* (1969), coeditor of and contributor to *Gulf Security into the 1980s: Perceptual and Strategic Dimensions* (1984), and is the author of a number of articles and contributed chapters dealing principally with Afghanistan, Gulf studies, U.S. security interests and policies in the Middle East, and Middle East oil. He is the executive director of Americares for Afghans, a division of the Americares Foundation, which is providing humanitarian medical relief to the victims of the war in Afghanistan.

Eden Naby is a faculty associate at the Center for Middle Eastern Studies at Harvard University. Naby began her professional interest in

Central Asia as a Peace Corps volunteer to Afghanistan. Since completing her Ph.D. in Central Asian Studies at Columbia University in 1975, she has taught at Pahlavi University (Shiraz, Iran) and at Harvard University. Her publications include articles on contemporary Afghanistan as well as on ethnic minorities and cultures of the region.

Jiri Valenta is associate professor and coordinator of Soviet and East European Studies in the Department of National Security Affairs, the U.S. Naval Postgraduate School, Monterey, California. While writing the present chapter he was a Woodrow Wilson Center Fellow. Valenta is the author of *Soviet Intervention in Czechoslovakia, 1968: Anatomy of a Decision,* coauthor of the monograph *The Soviet Invasion of Afghanistan: Three Perspectives,* and coeditor of and contributor to two books, *Eurocommunism between East and West* and *Soviet Decision Making for National Security.*

Marvin G. Weinbaum is professor of political science and director of the Program in South and West Asian Studies at the University of Illinois, Urbana-Champaign. He has conducted research and written about Afghanistan since 1970. Articles of his dealing with Afghanistan and its neighbors have appeared in *The International Journal of Middle East Studies, The Middle East Journal, Asian Survey,* and *Orbis,* among others.

Conference Participants

Charles J. Adams
Professor
Institute of Islamic Studies
McGill University
Montreal, Quebec
Canada

Zia-ul-Islam Ansari
Editor
Daily *Mashriq*
Lahore, Pakistan

Laurent F. Carrel
Major
Swiss General Staff
Bern, Switzerland

Peers Carter, C.M.G.
Director
Afghanistan Support Committee
London, England
(U.K. ambassador to Afghanistan, 1968-72)

Louis Dupree
Visiting Professor
Woodrow Wilson School of Public & International Affairs
Princeton University
Princeton, New Jersey

Katarina Engberg
Editor
The Swedish Institute of International Affairs
Stockholm, Sweden

Stephen A. Garrett
Chairman
Department of International Policy Studies
Monterey Institute of International Studies
Monterey, California
(Cochairman, International Conference on Afghan Alternatives)

Thomas E. Gouttierre
Dean of International Policy Studies and Director
Center for Afghanistan Studies
University of Nebraska at Omaha
Omaha, Nebraska

B. A. Hamzah
Head
Strategic Studies and International Relations
Armed Forces Defense College
Kuala Lumpur, Malaysia

Selig S. Harrison
Senior Associate
The Carnegie Endowment for International Peace
Washington, D.C.

Noor A. Husain
Brig. (Retd.)
Director General
The Institute for Strategic Studies
Islamabad, Pakistan

Sajjad Hyder
Ambassador (Retd.)
Islamabad, Pakistan
(Pakistan ambassador to the USSR, 1975-79)

Harmon E. Kirby
Director
Pakistan, Afghanistan, and Bangladesh Affairs
Department of State
Washington, D.C.

Gregory M. Kortanek
Major, USAF
Assistant Political Advisor
Headquarters, U.S. Central Command
MacDill AFB, Florida

Sabahuddin Kushkaki
Fellow
The Woodrow Wilson Center for International Scholars
The Smithsonian Institution
Washington, D.C.
(Former minister, Royal Government of Afghanistan)

Marian K. Leighton
Senior Research Scholar
The National Strategy Information Center
New York, New York

Ralph H. Magnus
Associate Professor
Department of National Security Affairs
Naval Postgraduate School
Monterey, California
(Coordinator, International Conference on Afghan Alternatives)

Seyed Bahauddin Majrooh
Director
Afghan Information Centre
Peshawar, Pakistan

Claude Malhuret
Director
Médecins sans Frontières
Paris, France

Eden Naby
Faculty Associate
Center for Middle Eastern Studies
Harvard University
Cambridge, Massachusetts

Robert G. Neumann
Senior Advisor
Center for Strategic & International Studies
Georgetown University
Washington, D.C.
(United States ambassador to Afghanistan, 1966-73)

Seyed Qassem Reshtia
Meyrin, Geneva
Switzerland
(Former minister and ambassador, Royal Government of Afghanistan)

Reinhardt Rummel
Senior Research Scholar
Research Institute for International Affairs
Ebenhuasen, Bavaria
Federal Republic of Germany

Gerald C. Steibel
Vice-President and Director of Studies
The National Strategy Information Center
New York, New York

Frank N. Trager
Distinguished Professor
Department of National Security Affairs
Naval Postgraduate School
Monterey, California
(Cochairman, International Conference on Afghan Alternatives)

Jiri Valenta
Associate Professor
Department of National Security Affairs
Naval Postgraduate School
Monterey, California

Marvin G. Weinbaum
Professor
Department of Political Science
University of Illinois at Urbana-Champaign
Urbana, Illinois

Glynn Wood
Academic Dean
Monterey Institute of International Studies
Monterey, California